GAME CHANGERS

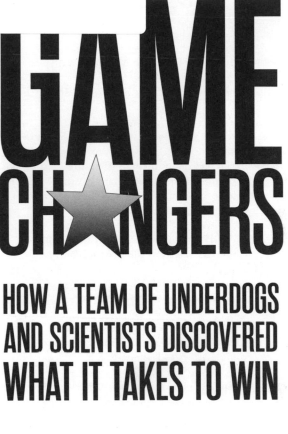

GAME CH★NGERS

HOW A TEAM OF UNDERDOGS AND SCIENTISTS DISCOVERED WHAT IT TAKES TO WIN

João Medeiros

Little, Brown

LITTLE, BROWN

First published in Great Britain in 2018 by Little, Brown

1 3 5 7 9 10 8 6 4 2

A CIP catalogue record for this book
is available from the British Library.

Hardback ISBN 978-1-4087-0846-0
C-format ISBN 978-1-4087-0845-3

Typeset in Bembo by M Rules
Printed and bound in Great Britain by
Clays Ltd, Elcograf S.p.A.

Papers used by Little, Brown are from well-managed forests
and other responsible sources.

MIX
Paper from
responsible sources
FSC www.fsc.org FSC® C104740

Little, Brown
An imprint of
Little, Brown Book Group
Carmelite House
50 Victoria Embankment
London EC4Y 0DZ

An Hachette UK Company
www.hachette.co.uk

www.littlebrown.co.uk

TO MY PARENTS

CONTENTS

Introduction ix

1. The demands of the game 1
2. Know your enemy 18
3. Professional zone 34
4. Winners and errors 55
5. Worst-case scenarios 68
6. The River Ignorance 86
7. The last shot 102
8. The former rower turned cyclist 109
9. The science of Formula One pit stops 120
10. How to make a champion 136
11. Skeletons on ice 150
12. The winner effect 170
13. A bittersweet victory 182
14. Women on the verge of gold 195
15. Home advantage 212

16. What it Takes to Win   228
17. Tickling the dragon's tail   242
18. Under constraints   259
19. Thinking Thursdays   281
20. Sixty-seven medals   294
21. The flying boat   305
22. The complex game   324

   Conclusion   346
   Acknowledgements   357
   Bibliography   361
   Index   381

INTRODUCTION

In 2012, I became obsessed with a story that mixed science and sport, about a community of researchers, coaches and analysts who, for the past twenty years or so, have pioneered new ways of addressing the most fundamental question in sport: what does it take to win?

It all began with a casual observation. At the London Olympics, I found myself wondering how on earth the British Olympic Team had come to be so good. After all, at the 1996 Games in Atlanta, Great Britain had ranked only thirty-sixth in the medal table, finishing below countries like Algeria, Belgium and Kazakhstan. That was their worst-ever result, a dismal performance labelled a national scandal by the British press.

The government was compelled to intervene. Money was promised; a dedicated agency, UK Sport, was set up to distribute the funds, a vast proportion of which were sourced from National Lottery revenue. The criteria for the allocation of funds were strict. The money could not be used to increase grassroots participation or even to simply improve the performance of athletes. Instead, it had to be used to target a specific number of world titles and Olympic gold medals. This policy became known as the no-compromise system, with targeted investment in the sports with the best chances of winning medals.

In other words, UK Sport invested in success. And at the following three Olympics – Sydney, Athens and Beijing – Team GB steadily rose through the ranks.

For the London Games, approximately half a billion pounds was spent over the four-year Olympic cycle. This was still significantly less than the amounts spent by countries like South Korea and Japan, and only a blip when compared to the billions invested by the sporting superpowers of Russia, China and the USA.

With the National Lottery money, national sporting centres were built and athletes were able to train full time. This funding also supported, in 2002, the launch of UK Sport's technology, science and medicine arm, the English Institute of Sport. At the core of the EIS's mission was the provision of sports scientists to all of the national sports teams. The EIS was modelled on the Australian Institute of Sport, which, at the turn of the millennium, had been seen as the best in the world for sports science. By 2012, it was clear that the EIS was now the model to emulate.

So how did a sporting nation reinvent itself so completely in less than a generation?

That was the question I asked Peter Keen, the performance director of UK Sport.

'I'm surprised very few people have asked that question before,' he answered. 'When I have spoken about this, I come across as clinical and cold and that clashes with people's view of sport as something poetic, but I will give you a blunt and conclusive answer.' He stood in silence for a few moments. 'What has happened in the past twenty years is that we've engaged with performance in a rational, scientific way. To apply the scientific method, you need data and you need the ability to set hypotheses and examine them in the simplest terms. Part of this formula of success is the ability to be objective. That level of objectivity, when harnessed, is very powerful.'

After London 2012, UK Sport made two major announcements. The first, made publicly in December 2013, was Britain's goal to take home sixty-six medals at the 2016 Rio Olympic Games, which would make them the first host nation to deliver more medals at the following Games.

The second was made internally, to all coaches, directors and sports scientists. A performance-planning process, 'What it Takes to Win', was to be rolled out across the British high-performance system.

As I immersed myself in the world of elite performance and met some of the sports scientists behind the scenes – the 'team behind the team' – I became invested in their four-year journey leading up to Rio.

During those four years, the phrase 'What it Takes to Win' gradually gained traction among coaches and scientists, an expression of a common philosophy. The concepts that underpinned this approach, however, were far from new.

It all started, in a sense, as a grand experiment: to rethink how sport is played, how it is performed, how people train and how people coach. This experiment had its origins at Liverpool Polytechnic (now Liverpool John Moores University), home to the world's first sports science faculty. It was there, in the late eighties, that a motley group – a mathematician, a physiologist, a psychologist and a former basketball player – pioneered the means to analyse performance. To do so, they hung around at courts and in changing rooms, made a nuisance of themselves in clubhouses, and hauled computers to football pitches. They closely studied elite coaches, proving that even the very best among them could not accurately recollect the most crucial events in a match; they conducted studies which for the first time quantified the physiological effort made by football players; and they wrote software that could predict the winners of squash tournaments.

This novel approach to performance underwent its first mutation in the early days of the English Institute of Sport, when many of the same sports scientists who had pioneered these methods in an academic environment were embedded directly within national teams. Now, their primary job was not to further science, but to help to win gold medals. At various locations, under similar circumstances, the first successful iterations of this model emerged: in squash, in rugby, in cycling and in Formula One.

As the UK high-performance system geared up for London 2012, these methods of achieving success became widespread, and the results were soon made clear to the world. Then, in 2016, at the Rio Games, Britain made history by not only winning two more medals than the sixty-five that they had at London 2012, but also clinching second place in the medal table, above China.

The real success was, of course, down to talented and dedicated individuals. Behind each medal was a closely bound triumvirate: a talented athlete, an astute coach and a methodical sports scientist. And theirs was invariably a story of struggle, guesswork, dedication and conflict.

It is true of any story about competition and sports. But this book leans towards the least well-known element in that equation: the sports scientist.

Sports scientists are the people behind many successful teams – winners of European football championships, rugby world champions, and Olympic gold medallists. They have helped teams disrupt their way out of an endless loop of defeat and ensure that winners retain their competitive edge. These are the people who, through a trial-and-error approach to the scientific method, have sought to address the most fundamental question in sport: what does it take to win?

1

THE DEMANDS OF THE GAME

The story begins on the evening of 5 January 1972, when fifty-two-year-old Harry Catterick suffered a heart attack while driving home from a football match.

At the time, he was the coach of Everton Football Club, a team competing in the First Division, at the time the top flight of English football. He had been hired in the sixties by the club chairman, John Moores.

Moores had founded the Littlewoods retail empire, which started in the early twenties as a betting business, and later transformed into a conglomerate of shops as well as a mail-order arm. But Moores's affiliation with football preceded his business success. As a child, he was passionately devoted to the game, and he continued playing amateur football until the age of forty.

Moores was first linked to Everton during the Second World War, when he became a club shareholder. Over time he invested deeply in the club, initially lending the money for installing floodlights at Goodison Park, and later financing the purchase of players. In 1960, 'Mr John', as Moores was known at Everton, became chairman of a club that hadn't won the national title in twenty-one years.

A year later, he sacked the existing manager and brought in Catterick, a former Everton player. In the previous season, Catterick had taken Sheffield Wednesday, a Second Division club only two years before, to second place in the First Division. 'Everton are my old team,' he said to the press, 'I am doubly keen on putting them at the top.'

And so he did. The new manager combined an aptitude for clever player acquisition with a stealthy modus operandi and an intense dislike of the press. He was strongly opposed to television broadcasts of Everton's matches, for fear that his team's tactics would become too well known to the opposition, and signed most of his players on the sly, during scouting missions that he disguised as golf holidays.

Bankrolled by Moores's millions, Catterick assembled a talented squad and soon transformed Everton into a high-flying team known for an exciting brand of football. 'He just let us get on with playing,' wrote Everton midfielder Colin Harvey, in his autobiography, adding that he couldn't recall Catterick ever sitting them down for a tactical talk.

Catterick's results were undeniable. Everton won the FA Cup in 1966, a trophy they hadn't won since 1933, and the First Division championship in both 1962–63 and 1969–70, and were poised to dominate English football in the seventies.

By 1972, however, they were a spent force. Their performances, once thrilling, had become lacklustre and erratic. On that cold, snowy evening in January 1972, when Catterick had gone to Sheffield to scope out the local team in a match against West Ham, Everton's next opponent, he was a manager under pressure. His team were a ragtag bunch, bereft of the élan that had once defined them as champions. Some surmised afterwards that this had weighed heavily on Catterick, and caused his heart attack.

When Catterick returned to his managerial duties in

March, he was a much-weakened man. His knack for finding the best new talent seemed to have deserted him. Everton's performance continued to decline, aggravated by a string of inept signings. The team won just one of the remaining thirteen games that season and finished fifteenth in the league.

By the end of the season, despite the loyalty Mr John felt towards his manager, it was clear that something needed to be done. It was around this time that he received a letter from Vaughan Lancaster-Thomas, a physiologist at Liverpool Polytechnic, who claimed he could help Everton.

At forty, Lancaster-Thomas was still a superior athletic specimen: muscular and sinewy, the product of years of physical cultivation. He was a former British national champion in both athletics and cycling; a record-breaking marathon race-walker; and the captain-coach of the British national basketball team. As his sporting career wound down, he decided to commit himself with equal vigour to more academic pursuits. 'I was a well-muscled cabbage,' Lancaster-Thomas says of himself. 'I hadn't developed my brain at all.'

After a degree in physical education from Loughborough University, he became the first physical educator in the country to earn a PhD in sports science. He then established one of the first physiology laboratories, at St Mary's College, Twickenham. There he subjected the very best athletes in Britain to extensive examinations, from weightlifter Louis Martin to cyclist Tom Simpson, who later collapsed and died during his ascent of Mont Ventoux in the 1967 Tour de France. 'He came for advice, I gave him some tests, then he went off to the Tour,' Lancaster-Thomas recalls. 'What he did not tell me was that he was also taking amphetamines, which were illegal, and a very hefty swig of brandy, which was not.'

During his stint at St Mary's, Lancaster-Thomas produced one of the seminal monographs in the field of exercise physiology. *Science and Sport: The Measurement and Improvement of Performance* covered the topics of athletic strength, speed, stamina, skill and 'soul'. His thesis was that if this nascent science was to make progress and gain credibility, an interdisciplinary approach was required.

Furthermore, the new field needed bona fide accreditation. At the time, the only way to become a qualified sports scientist was to earn a degree in PE. Lancaster-Thomas's ambition was to establish the first sports science honours degree, and cement the subject's academic standing.

This led him, in 1971, to apply for a position at Liverpool Polytechnic. The head of the Faculty of Science believed that Liverpool, being one of the country's great sporting cities, needed a sports science department. So he appointed Lancaster-Thomas to start one. 'We have no idea what you should do, but we'll help you as much as we can,' Lancaster-Thomas was told. He promptly replied, 'I have to have a sports science lab – how am I going to get it?'

John Moores had heard of Lancaster-Thomas's reputation and, upon receiving his letter, invited him to dine at Goodison Park's luxurious hospitality suite. The Everton chairman asked Lancaster-Thomas what he could do for the club. Moores could establish a sports science laboratory at the polytechnic, the physiologist answered. Such a lab would be placed at Everton's service, and as part of this Lancaster-Thomas would provide consultancy on fitness training. They would also launch a secret research project to help Catterick turn the team around. By the time they had finished eating, Moores had agreed to finance the most advanced sports science laboratory in the United Kingdom.

*

Lancaster-Thomas never planned to undertake the Everton project himself. In fact, he loathed football: 'I only went once to an Everton match and I wish I had stayed away. The referees kept a reasonable check on the players, but it was savagery. I imagined being at the Roman Colosseum. The behaviour of the fans was dreadful, with an atmosphere of threat and denigration of opponents. The whole thing was uncivilised, Neanderthal.'

Instead, he hired a research assistant to do the job for him, a twenty-five-year old Irishman named Thomas Reilly, who had a master's in ergonomics from the Royal Free Hospital in London.

Reilly's interest in sports had begun early in life. Growing up in County Mayo, he had played Gaelic football and hurling, but favoured long-distance running. As a child, he often ran the four miles between home and school, while as an adult he ran marathons, charmingly encouraging his competitors mid-race. He later ran a marathon in 2 hours and 37 minutes, a remarkable time for an amateur.

Reilly was the first of the group of scientists that Lancaster-Thomas recruited to help him achieve his ambition of converting the Physical Education Group at Liverpool Polytechnic into a fully fledged Department of Sports Studies. Following his appointment, a number of lecturers were brought on board to help research and design the core syllabus for the new sports science degree. One of these was a psychologist by the name of Frank Sanderson.

Sanderson vividly remembers his first day at work, which consisted of a jaunt down to the Mersey for a water-skiing lesson. Flush with Moores's funding, Lancaster-Thomas had acquired a speedboat, expensed to the university, and was keeping it in his garage. 'Tom struggled badly, and he couldn't swim,' Sanderson recalls. 'After about an hour, he was like a drowned rat. We had to pull him out for his own safety.' When the rector heard about the shenanigans, he told Lancaster-Thomas to return the speedboat immediately to university premises. Vaughan was reportedly quite affronted. In his opinion, he should have been charging the university for the boat's safekeeping.

Sanderson and Reilly soon became close friends. They shared a long, narrow office with two other colleagues, also recent hires. In one corner of the room was a sink, usually overflowing with unwashed coffee mugs; sweaty running clothes hung from the radiator. The office was often noisy and chaotic, with phones constantly ringing and students dropping in, but Reilly was often to be found working in solemn concentration at his desk. He had, according to Sanderson, staggering powers of focus, and would frequently call Sanderson late at night to discuss research and other work matters. 'He wasn't one to demonstrate his emotions,' Sanderson recalls. 'He was always understated. He would never roar with laughter, but he had this twinkle in his eyes.'

This equitable temperament not only made him a pro-lific researcher but also an exemplary assistant. One day, Lancaster-Thomas asked Reilly if he was willing to volunteer as a subject for a research project to investigate how a male athlete would respond to one hundred hours of continuous moderate exercise. 'This wasn't just the bullying supervisor making him do something he didn't want to do,' Lancaster-Thomas hastens to explain. 'He jumped at the opportunity.'

For four days, Reilly cycled on a stationary bike, ran on a treadmill or rowed on a machine. His only sustenance was Dynamo, a thick glucose syrup with added salts manufactured by the Beecham Group, for whom Lancaster-Thomas was a consultant. Reilly was allowed to go to the toilet every hour, and apply a modicum of Vaseline to relieve saddle-soreness.

During these short breaks, Lancaster-Thomas would weigh him, take his temperature and measure his heart rate and blood glucose levels. 'I believed that a steady physiological state could be achieved under the right conditions,' Lancaster-Thomas explains. 'People thought that circadian rhythms prevented this, but I disagreed. All you needed was the right fuel.' Reilly's heart rate increased at first, as expected, and then gradually declined over time as he continued at a steady pace. After forty-four hours, his physiological values stabilised. At the end of the hundred hours, Lancaster-Thomas shook his hand and thanked him for being a terrific subject and for a job well done.

Later, Lancaster-Thomas himself attempted to replicate Reilly's hundred-hour feat as a publicity stunt for the Dynamo brand. With the assistance of Frank Sanderson, a treadmill was installed inside a marquee at Wavertree Playground in Liverpool. Unfortunately, the Dynamo was diluted with contaminated water from a park standpipe and Lancaster-Thomas contracted severe diarrhoea. He stoically attempted to continue on the treadmill, holding a chamber pot between his legs, while Sanderson was in charge of emptying it. They never made it past the first day.

Lancaster-Thomas was, according to Sanderson, an egotistical and arrogant character, with a talent for making enemies. 'There's an expression in basketball called "give and go",' he says. 'In [his] team, they called it "Vaughan Thomas give and go". They would just give him the ball and go back on defence.' But Sanderson also admits that his employer was a charismatic polymath and a natural leader. 'Many people had warned me not to work with Vaughan,' he recalls. 'It was the best thing I ever did.' In those early years, Lancaster-Thomas had already mounted an ambitious public relations campaign to seek official recognition for Liverpool's new sports science degree. He played the political game well, and got himself appointed to the Council for National Academic Awards, the body responsible for awarding degrees. 'Other faculties resented us,' Sanderson says. 'I lost count of the times I was asked, "How many press-ups do you need to get a sports science degree?"'

Lancaster-Thomas seemed to positively rejoice in attracting adversity, and went about his work in boisterous fashion. 'I'm not particularly likeable. I'm blunt. I didn't have many friends. The students respected me. A couple of female students fell in love with me, but nothing happened,' he says. When ITV's *News at Ten* arrived to do a piece on the new sports science laboratory, Lancaster-Thomas asked one of his students to perform a 'test to destruction' live on television, in which he had to cycle faster and faster until he literally collapsed from exhaustion. 'They received a lot of complaints about the cruelty, but boy did we get some applications.'

At the time, much of the accepted scientific understanding of athletic performance was underpinned by the research of a Hungarian-born endocrinologist.

In the thirties, Hans Selye, a researcher in the biochemistry department at McGill University in Montreal, had conducted a series of experiments on mice to test their physiological reactions to a variety of mistreatments. He exposed them to extreme temperatures, intoxication, prolonged physical exercise and physical trauma, by cutting the animals' spinal cords.

Selye observed that their reactions seemed to follow a similar pattern, regardless of the form of punishment they had received. Within forty-eight hours of being subjected to trauma, the mice developed a spectrum of symptoms. These included bleeding ulcers, enlarged adrenal glands and atrophy of the thymus. Selye considered this first stage as a reaction of alarm, induced by the damage sustained. After that period, the mice would eventually start recovering, their affected organs slowly reverting to their original shape and regaining normal function. Selye called this the stage of adaptation.

However, when Selye continued to traumatise the mice, they entered what he called the stage of exhaustion: the animals would ultimately lose their resistance and succumb to injury, even death.

Selye detailed this three-stage process in a short letter, 'A Syndrome Produced by Diverse Nocuous Agents', published in *Nature* in July 1936. Here Selye argued that these responses appeared to occur independently of the nature of the damage inflicted, and represented the normal response of the organism to stimuli such as temperature changes, drugs and muscular exercise. 'Since the syndrome as a whole seems to represent a generalized effort of the organism to adapt itself to new conditions,' he wrote, 'it might be termed the "general adaptation syndrome".'

In describing the mice's physiological reaction to trauma, Selye used the word 'stress'. This was a term borrowed from engineering, where it is used to quantify the resiliency of materials. In his own words, stress was the 'response of the body to any demand made upon it'. To Selye, stress was synonymous with the body's response to life, 'the rate of all the wear and tear on the body'. 'Crossing a busy intersection, exposure to a draft, or even sheer joy are enough to activate the body's stress mechanism,' he wrote in his 1956 book, *Stress of Life*. 'Stress is not necessarily bad for you; it is also the spice of life.'

Later in life, Selye would express regret at having failed to identify the underlying biochemistry of his 'adaptation energy'. Nevertheless, his general adaptation syndrome offered a descriptive framework for the ways in which the human body was affected by stressors like injury, infection, frustration, even exercise.

Although his research had focused on rodents, Selye's theory of stress soon found an application in the world of athletics and exercise physiology. In September 1961, in a series of articles for the magazine *Track Technique*, Forbes Carlile, a highly regarded Australian swimming coach and physiology lecturer at the University of Sydney, suggested that coaches should adopt the general adaptation syndrome as their guiding hypothesis for athletic training. They could do this, he proposed, by learning what stresses affect the athlete, from dietary insufficiency right through to lack of sleep, and what symptoms signal a failure to adapt, 'from general muscular tension to psychic unrest, irritability, intestinal upsets, colds'.

According to Carlile, although astute coaches should detect the warning signs displayed by a fatigued athlete, the line between training and straining was very thin indeed. He wrote: 'Training him may be likened to bending a green twig. The body may eventually mould itself to the force of continuously imposed physical exercise, but a little too much and the body, like the twig, may show signs of strain. More stress and the breaking point may be reached.'

As exercise physiologists adopted Selye's theory, they began to refine it in the context of athletic training. Take, for example, the principle of overload, which states that in order to improve athletes must work at an intensity higher than normal. This notion posits the existence of a threshold at which stress becomes a stimulant to physiological adaptation, creating stronger muscles, more powerful hearts and higher-capacity lungs. The strengthening of a bicep provides a simple and illustrative example. Lifting a weight – a stressor – tears muscle tissue at the microscopic level, triggering a stress response. During recovery, the body transitions to an anabolic state, in which extra muscular tissue is created. The body adapts by building more muscle, which in turn is able to tolerate higher loads.

The challenge for physiologists was to measure specific adaptations to stress, and to find reliable tests to measure an athlete's capacity to withstand them. Specificity is a crucial element of physical training. 'When you know what the demands of an activity are, then you can adapt your training to that,' Lancaster-Thomas says. 'You had to analyse a sport to what its constituents are and tailor our training to that.'

That was Tom Reilly's challenge at Everton. Prior research on the specific physiological and psychological stressors of football was scant, and often tarnished by poor methodology and limited statistics. Football might well be the world's most popular sport, but when it came to understanding its demands, it was fair to say that no one knew anything of worth.

The experiment that would cement Reilly's position as one of the pioneers of sports science began on 10 July 1972. The Everton players had just reported back from their summer holidays, ready for the start of the pre-season. At the time, Everton's Bellefield training ground was recognised as one of the most modern in existence. It consisted of a two-storey main complex, a sports hall with an artificial pitch and two full-sized outdoor pitches.

On the first day, the club's medical officer carried out a standard examination. The following day, the players were asked to report to the new sports science laboratory at Liverpool Polytechnic, where they were met by Tom Reilly. Reilly meticulously submitted thirty-one professional

football players to a battery of tests, following a protocol
devised by Lancaster-Thomas. Players stripped to their socks
and shorts, before being weighed and their height measured.
Ankle mobility was measured, along with grip strength with
a dynamometer. To test their reaction times, the players were
asked to respond to a visual stimulus by pressing a button
with their index finger. Reilly made the players perform the
Harvard step test, where they had to step up onto a bench
twenty inches high thirty times a minute for five minutes.
Their personality was assessed using the Cattell's Sixteen
Personality Factors test, a lengthy questionnaire containing
a continuum of options ranging from 'strong agreement' to
'strong disagreement' for statements such as 'My daydreams
are always very elaborate' or 'Honesty is not always necessary'. The players' maximum heart rates were measured by a
shuttle-run test to exhaustion. 'The slightly elevated systolic
blood pressures require some explanation,' Reilly would
write later in his report. 'The subjects with no previous experience of the test protocol may have felt apprehensive at their
first visit to the laboratory.'

This testing protocol was subsequently repeated at the end
of the pre-season, at mid-season and at the end of the season.
Throughout, Reilly enjoyed unrestricted access to the squad.
He was invited to join the team during their pre-season tour
in Sweden, and given carte blanche to go into players' bed-
rooms between three and four in the morning to measure
resting heart rates. He was given access to medical records and
specially designed personal diaries, where players were asked
to record their daily activities in detail – apart from sexual
activity, which was considered an unwarranted invasion of
privacy. Before each game, he would measure players' heart
rates in the dressing room as they laced their boots and prepared to go out onto the pitch.

During the weekly training sessions at Bellefield, he would record one player's heart rate at a time. The heart-rate monitor consisted of two electrodes, fixed to the player's chest with adhesive tape and an elastic belt, and connected to a transmitter box on a rubber belt worn round the player's waist. The heartbeats were transmitted via a whip antenna and the signal captured by a boxy receiver that Reilly operated on the sidelines.

Harry Catterick himself seldom appeared on the training grounds. 'Managers sat in offices and talked on the phone to each other, buying and selling players,' Lancaster-Thomas explains. There was a laissez-faire approach to training, which was usually conducted by a freelance ex-army instructor and consisted of little more than long runs and games. 'Team training was ridiculous,' Lancaster-Thomas says. 'They were decades behind where physical education was at that stage, let alone sports science.'

To calculate the distances covered by the players during matches, Reilly and Lancaster-Thomas had to devise a hand notation system. They drew a map of the pitch and superimposed a grid, using the line markings on the pitch as a reference, along with gradations in the colour of the grass due to mowing and the advertising hoardings along the sidelines. Reilly, having memorised the chart, attended every Everton game. He would sit in the directors' box as a guest, and pick a player and follow his every move throughout the match. Using a cassette recorder, he would comment on the player's movements: 'He's walking backwards, now he's standing still, now he's sprinting diagonally towards the last third of the pitch . . .' A stopwatch was used to time the different movements, which he divided into walking, backing, jogging, cruising and sprinting. He also filmed every game, and by again superimposing a grid over the screen he was able to compute the distances covered by the players and their speeds over those distances. Measuring the work rate of the different players in this way allowed them, for the first time, to quantify with precision the physiological demands of the different playing positions in football.

The 1972–73 season had been disastrous for Everton. Following a promising start, during which they were unbeaten for seven consecutive games, the club won only ten of the remaining thirty-five matches. They managed just one win in October. In November and December, they endured a miserable run of six straight defeats, the worst sequence in the club's history.

Catterick blamed the supporters, claiming that the players were frightened of the crowd's hostility. The reality was that the team was undermined by a partying culture and a chronic lack of discipline. Just before Christmas, Bernie 'The Bolt' Wright, a giant centre forward whom Catterick had scouted, bought and then subsequently demoted to the reserve team, was caught drinking whisky from a broken bottle at Bellefield. On being admonished, Wright smacked one of the coaches and charged after Catterick, who managed to escape via a back entrance and drive away. On 3 February 1973, when Everton lost to Third Division Millwall at Goodison Park in the fourth round of the FA Cup, eleven Millwall supporters were stabbed and the team showered with seat cushions hurled from the stands.

It was no surprise when, in April, John Moores finally removed Catterick.

His replacement, Billy Bingham, immediately terminated Reilly and Lancaster-Thomas's research project. 'Mostly because it hadn't been his idea and he didn't want anything to do with outsiders telling him how to do his business, which is fairly typical of poor management,' Lancaster-Thomas says.

When Bingham requested that the players' data be returned to the club, Lancaster–Thomas printed out the reams of data and sent it, packed in boxes, in a taxi to Goodison Park.

Despite Bingham's intervention the project had, for Lancaster–Thomas, already proved a success. They had helped to rescue Everton from relegation. Perhaps even more importantly, they had documented the physical demands of professional football. For instance, they found that players covered, on average, a distance of 8680 metres every game. Nearly 37 per cent of that distance was covered by jogging, 25 per cent by walking, and 11 per cent when sprinting. Of course, these mean values disguised the specific demands of the different positions. Midfielders covered more distance than any other group of players, typically around ten kilometres per game. Central defenders, on the other hand, covered the least distance but spent more time running backwards, whereas strikers were the ones frequently involved in heading balls.

Reilly also concluded that less than one-third of a typical training session actually produced the stress intensities that players would encounter in a match. Furthermore, he classified the players' daily activities as 'moderate work' and 'considerably less than the numbers found for other top-class athletes'. 'A striking feature of the habitual activity of the group studied was the high proportion of time spent in sedentary and recumbent postures,' he wrote, concluding that time spent lying and sitting amounted to nearly twenty hours per day. 'It seems that the professional footballer can be described . . . as "Homo sedentarius".'

Reilly equated the work of a professional footballer to that of an actor, someone made to perform and entertain a large audience after a long period of training and rehearsal. According to their psychological profile, Everton was a team of extroverted, neurotic, unconscientious, highly apprehensive, self-sufficient and driven individuals. 'He also found a correlation between the flexibility of the ankle joint and intelligence,' Sanderson laughs. 'The data would often throw out anomalous correlations.'

By mid-season, the players' dominance and adventurous-ness – traits generally linked with success – had registered a marked decline. 'This coincided with poor results,' Reilly noted.

These results were later published in Tom Reilly's thesis, 'An ergonomic evaluation of occupational stress in profes-sional football'. He concluded by recommending that the training regime could be made more extensive without imposing 'resultant duress' on the players, suggesting that a combination of aerobic and anaerobic training – intermit-tent short periods of high-intensity sprinting, interspersed with jogging – would better prepare them for the demands of football. Throughout that season the Everton players had gained much respect for Reilly. 'They thought he was magic because he was pointing out things to them that they'd never realised before,' Lancaster-Thomas says. 'I think the players would have spotted a bullshitter a mile off, and he wasn't one. He was such a gentle soul that no one ever took offence at him, and when he made suggestions, they listened.'

Following publication, Reilly and Lancaster-Thomas's work attracted much attention in the academic world, and their studies were replicated across many other sports. It was the pioneer work that launched a new field of the study of sport, which would later become known as performance analysis.

The footballing world, however, would remain ignorant of the findings for many years to come. Reilly wrote of the game's scepticism, even hostility, towards scientific enquiry, as a consequence of its 'multifaceted and enigmatic nature' in his 1979 book, *What Research Tells the Coach About Soccer*:

'Match play frequently defies successful forecasting, and confidently predicted outcomes are reversed, and where unexpected defeats are rapidly dismissed by players and managers as accidents tantamount to acts of God. In short, myth still very much pervades the soccer world . . . outsiders purporting to represent an objective and detached perspective are either shunned or frostily welcomed.'

It would take several advances in squash, and the development of a new technology start-up, before football began to really take note of what science could offer.

2

KNOW YOUR ENEMY

Every time Stafford Murray played in a junior squash tour-nament, his father would watch from the balcony, while his mother locked herself in a toilet. Lynda Murray would become so nervous that she would only emerge during breaks to ask about the score, before returning to the safety of her cubicle. But she was always supportive of her son, no matter what the outcome.

His father's support, on the other hand, was conditional. If Murray lost a match, Malcolm Murray would inevitably lose his temper. Murray remembers a particular moment at the England Open, when he came off court to hear his father arguing with his mother: 'Staff is playing crap,' he said and his mother replied, 'Why, it doesn't matter, he's tired.' 'I just sat there crying,' Murray recalls. 'If I wasn't winning, it wasn't good enough. If you're not first, you're last. Simple as that. He was probably driving an eleven-year-old kid a bit too hard.'

It had been his father who introduced Murray to squash at the age of six. The sport was massively popular in in the eighties, and Malcolm, a pipe-fitter, played recreationally. The Murrays lived in Tarrington, a village in Herefordshire.

The village hall was a corrugated iron building with an undersized squash court. The court had a low ceiling ('If you hit a lob, you would hit the lights') and an entrance door right in the middle of the front wall ('You would always get smacked in the head by a ball if you entered when someone was playing'). It was here that Murray would train every night, for hours on end, all year round. In winter, melting ice trickled down the wooden walls. Malcolm would always end each session by ordering his son to sprint up and down the court. He would then fetch a bucket from the cleaning cupboard and place it in the left-hand back corner. Murray would have to serve the ball against the front wall and slot it into the bucket ten times. Only then was he allowed to go home.

The young Stafford Murray thrived within this punishing training regime. Three times a week before school and at the weekends he would go running for two hours, emulating his idol, the six-time British Open winner Jonah Barrington, a physical and aggressive player. 'I thought it was good fitness training at the time, but it probably just damaged my back,' Murray says. 'But it made me mentally stronger. An hour of squash wasn't too bad compared to two hours running in the snow.'

At twelve, Murray was competing almost every evening and at the weekends, and was selected for the national under-10s team. Later, he became the country's number one player in the under-12s. He won Herefordshire County's regional senior championship at the age of thirteen, which he claims is a world record for the youngest-ever senior regional champion in the sport.

At school, however, his academic performance was lacklustre, and the experience was occasionally traumatising. 'Mathematics scared the life out of me,' Murray remembers. 'I still have a recurring dream that I'll have to go back to school and resit my maths exam. With no clothes on.' He was twice suspended for minor misdemeanours: once for shaving his head, in strict violation of school regulations, and again for placing a stinkbomb under the headmaster's chair. 'ADHD wasn't recognised then. If it were, I would have it,' Murray says.

He began dabbling in music, travelling around the country as a roadie for his older brother Warwick's band. He discovered a talent for the guitar, and was soon playing covers of Stevie Ray Vaughan, Chuck Berry, Jimi Hendrix and the Rolling Stones. He and Warwick later formed their own band, the Murray Brothers. Their first gig took place in a local pub, the Glass Pig at Tarrington. Murray could barely see anything from the stage because the room was choked with tobacco smoke. At some point, a fight broke out. The Murray Brothers left owing twelve pounds because their mates had drunk their entire night's wages at the bar.

At this point in his life, if it didn't involve running around a squash court or riffing on a guitar, Murray wasn't interested. In 1990, he was the country's number one junior player. He was winning prestigious tournaments such as the British Junior Grand Prix, and was beating players like Thierry Lincou, the Frenchman who ten years later would become the best squash player in the world. A year later, aged sixteen, he became a professional squash player. His first sponsor was Avenue Cars, a Gloucester second-hand car dealership, who gave him a blue Ford Escort, emblazoned with STAFFORD MURRAY INTERNATIONAL SQUASH PLAYER.

'My mother would drive me in that car to school,' Murray says. It was embarrassing, but he didn't care all that much.

Murray was certain that one day he would be the world's best squash player. But this never came to pass. A few months into his professional career, Murray succumbed to a mysterious illness. He had felt extreme exhaustion, which he at first attributed to overtraining. 'The mentality then was that if you're tired, you need to train through it, then you need to work harder,' Murray says.

And so he did. Soon he was losing against opponents who in other circumstances he would have beaten. He struggled along for months. It was only later that he was diagnosed with glandular fever. But by then, crippled by fatigue and increasingly riddled with self-doubt, he had already started wondering if there might be more to life than travelling the world to play in a small square room.

His father, to his surprise, was philosophical about his predicament and gave him three options: he could train harder, he could apply to university or he could get a proper job and start pipe-fitting with him.

At first, Murray chose the proper job. It took him six months – working twelve-hour shifts on freezing building sites, digging out toilets at six in the morning, carrying twelve-inch pipes in the freezing cold – to realise that a university degree didn't sound too bad after all.

He had heard about a new programme for sports and human movement studies at the University of Wales Institute, Cardiff. He applied, and on the strength of his squash background was admitted. On his first day, in September 1994, he was told by the Admissions Department to go and meet one of the tutors, a lecturer called Mike Hughes.

Mike Hughes had never planned to become a sports scientist. He had a comfortable senior position in local government, and a PhD in aeronautical engineering. He had been a keen athlete in his youth, playing football and rugby until a cycling accident left him with a damaged left arm. He then took up squash, competing one-armed.

Hughes also coached the Merseyside under-19s girls' team. They trained at a Victorian villa that boasted its own squash court, after a friend had introduced Hughes to the owner. 'He was very gracious about it,' Hughes remembers. 'He said I could help myself to anything in the fridge, which was behind the court.' Hughes never actually met the owner, instead dealing with him exclusively over the phone.

One day, the same friend told Hughes that there was an opening for a position as a lecturer in statistics at the polytechnic, in the School of Sport and Exercise Science. Hughes expressed polite interest. Later that day, he received a call from the head of the department. To his surprise, it was the very man who was letting him use his private squash court, and that was how Hughes came to meet Vaughan Lancaster-Thomas.

By the time Mike Hughes joined the School of Sport and Exercise Science at Liverpool Polytechnic in 1981, the staff included a biomechanist, a nutritionist, a physiologist and a sociologist. Lancaster-Thomas told him to hang around for six months, attend some lectures and give some thought to how he could contribute to the School's work.

Hughes soon became friends with Frank Sanderson, when the two discovered they shared a common passion for squash. Hughes, just like Lancaster-Thomas, was a larger-than-life character, competitive on the squash court, and full of bravado off it. As Sanderson recalls, 'He once told me to fuck off in front of the students, which was somewhat shocking since I was his boss.'

One day, Sanderson asked Hughes if a research student might follow him around for a year to observe his squash games. Sanderson had created a hand-notation system that could be used to describe the movements of the players and the events of a game of squash. It consisted of a set of symbols

for the seventeen different shots: drive (|), drop (.), boast (,),
volley (V), lob (L), serve (S) and so on. These codes were
annotated on an A4-sized representation of a squash court.
The notational analyst would stand on the balcony at the back
of the squash court and note down everything that happened
on court on an acetate overlay: every action made by each
player, along with the position. In a match containing about
a thousand shots, an analyst would typically use more than
fifty sheets, and processing that data afterwards would take
nearly forty hours.

Sanderson's notational system provided the first insights
into the patterns of play in squash. It showed that the backhand drive was the preferred stroke, the drop shot the most
erratic, and that every player had a distinctive pattern of play
from which they would rarely deviate, regardless of whether
they were winning or losing. 'He concluded that players can't
change their patterns of play,' Hughes says. 'As a coach I know
it's very difficult to get players to change the way they play.
In fact, with most players I wouldn't even try.'

One night, after a squash match and a few bottles of wine,
Hughes turned to Sanderson's student and remarked that he
should computerise the analysis. As a mathematician whose
PhD had involved using sophisticated mainframe computers,
he was vexed by the pen-and-paper methods. The next
morning, when a hungover Hughes tottered into his office,
he found Frank Sanderson and his student waiting outside his
door. As it turned out, Hughes was the only member of staff
who could 'computerise' anything.

This was in 1982, when the single computer at Liverpool
Polytechnic was a mainframe IBM, for which data had to
be typed line by line on punch cards. The first program that
Hughes wrote automated Sanderson's data analysis. 'The
computer was so slow that we'd only have the printout of the

data a day later,' Hughes recalls. When the first personal computers came onto the market, and the department acquired a Commodore PET with a 16k memory, Hughes wrote a program to input and output data courtside, as the match was happening in real time.

By then, Sanderson, saddled with administrative and management duties, was only too happy that Hughes, with all his energy and drive, had taken over his project. And so for two years, Hughes lugged his Commodore around the country. He would set it up behind the squash courts, plug it in and type away. 'Inevitably people kept coming up to me and asking me what I was doing, while I was trying to work,' Hughes says. 'It was really stressful, trying to get all the data and not miss anything. I used to be sweating more than the players.' Eventually, Hughes decided to put up a sign next to him, which read *I'm entering data. Piss off and don't bother me.*

As saving data during a match slowed the computer too much, Hughes stored it in the random-access memory, which would be irretrievably lost if the computer was turned off. On top of this, the Commodore's floppy disks were unreliable. This meant that after every match, Hughes would spend twenty minutes downloading the new data onto a cassette tape.

Hughes remembers notating one particular match between two very highly ranked England players. 'The rallies were very long and very quick,' Hughes says. 'I was soaked through. After an hour and a half of typing away, a guy walked past and kicked the plug out of the wall. The screen went green, then black. There were no batteries in those days, so I lost the whole match. I was only three rallies from the end.'

In 1983, Hughes signed up to present this work at the Micro-computers in Sport conference in Liverpool. He was initially reluctant, recalling that 'Tom Reilly twisted my arm into presenting.' Then it occurred to him that he could well be the first person to ever present a computerised notational analysis in real time. 'I thought, well, nobody else is using computers. I'm the man! I'll show these scientists! I'm going to absolutely smoke this conference!' On the day, however, the agenda showed that his talk was to be preceded by one by Ian Franks, a lecturer at the University of British Columbia. Hughes was dismayed to read the title of Franks' talk: 'Computer assisted sport evaluation'.

'Bastard,' Hughes murmured to himself. He had been scooped.

Ian Franks, a Mancunian, had emigrated to Canada in 1970. There, he researched skill acquisition at the University of British Columbia and coached at the Olympic Soccer Training Centre in Vancouver. He monitored players' heart rates during matches, analysed biomechanical motion using high-speed cameras, tested real-time radio communication with players on the pitch and put microphones on coaches to study their communication patterns with athletes. 'A high-ranking Canadian coach described it as "academia gone mad",' Frank says.

At around the time that Hughes was developing the first computerised analysis of squash in Liverpool, Franks was developing something very similar for football in Vancouver. He programmed the keyboard of an Apple IIe computer to record the events of a match: the top row of keys represented discrete game 'events', from passes to shots, and the rest of the keyboard covered the physical location of the event on the football field.

Doing sophisticated performance analyses in football stadiums proved a complicated task. When Franks took the computer to an under-23s tournament in Mexico for a first trial, the border authorities confiscated the material, only releasing it when bribed; at the tournament, they installed the computer in the top row of the stadium, the only location where an electric socket was available. Even then, they soon ran into more trouble. Street urchins loose in the stadium started pinching the floppy disks, leaving the analyst to run after them while the game was in play. 'It was chaos,' Franks remembers. 'We had to get a bodyguard so nobody could get in his way.'

At the Liverpool conference, he presented a computational analysis of all the games in the 1982 World Cup. At the end of the talk, Hughes introduced himself and the two academics soon found common ground. After all, they had simultaneously developed the first real-time computational notational analysis.

In 1988, Hughes took a sabbatical and went to Vancouver for a year. There, he and Franks set out to produce the seminal compendium on performance analysis. Owing to the constant turnover of editors at their publishing house, it took more than five years for the book – *Notational Analysis of Sport: Systems for Better Coaching and Performance in Sport* – to be published.

It was a slim volume, with a deep blue cover dominated by a diagram of a tennis court, over which was superimposed a sequence of dashed lines depicting the trajectory of a tennis ball. Inside was a quote from Sun Tzu: 'Know your enemy as you know yourself and you need not fear one hundred battles; know yourself but not the enemy, for every victory gained you will also suffer a defeat; know neither the enemy nor yourself and you will succumb in every battle.'

In the short introduction, Hughes and Franks assured the reader that although notational analysis found its direct application in sport, its methods could be applied to 'nursing, surgical operations, skilled manufacturing processes, unskilled manufacturing processes, haute cuisine, etc'. The two hundred-odd pages that followed elaborated the basics of notational analysis in a typically academic fashion – how to use video in sport; the identification of effective verbal coaching strategies; how to develop a computerised notation system – but the topic that underpinned the birth of this new science was tackled in chapter one: feedback.

'Traditionally, coaching intervention has been based on subjective observations of athletes,' they wrote. 'However, several studies have shown that such observations are not only unreliable but also inaccurate.' They cited a study done by Franks which showed that during a match, international football coaches could recollect only 30 per cent of the key factors that determined a successful performance. Worse, 45 per cent of what they *could* recall was simply wrong. They were wrong even when they were told in advance which questions they were going to be asked after the game. Other studies found that when both experienced and novice gymnastics coaches were asked to detect technical differences between two routines, the expert coaches identified more false positives.

Together, those studies shattered the belief that coaches had special expertise in accurately recalling and judging the critical elements of sports performance. In fact, it emerged that their decisions were being corrupted by the very same cognitive biases that affected any person with a brain. As further evidence, Hughes and Franks referenced the considerable body of applied research that quantitatively measured the accuracy of observers, albeit in slightly different circumstances: criminal eyewitness situations. 'There are a number of similarities between the situation of the coach observing an athletic performance and that of the eyewitness to [a] criminal event,' they argued. Both were prone to errors induced by arousal, cognitive bias and lack of focus.

That, in a nutshell, was the case for a new sports profession:

that of performance analyst, whose expertise lay in collecting objective data that would eliminate guesswork, opinion and bias. The job of a performance analyst was to find out what *really* happened, as opposed to what coaches *thought* had happened. Their job was to find the truth of sport.

That morning in September 1994, when Stafford Murray arrived to see Mike Hughes he could hear shouting in a strong Scouse accent. Something about it sounded familiar. Hughes was in his office with another student, at whom the shouting was directed. Murray waited until this meeting concluded, and then entered to find Hughes sitting with his back towards him, facing his desktop computer. When the professor turned around, Murray immediately recognised him.

Murray was tall and skinny, with a stud earring and a shaved head, apart from a tuft of hair at the front. His fashion sense was similarly idiosyncratic, with his penchant for cowboy boots, waistcoats, bootlace tie and Stetson. He had a deep husky voice, punctuated with constant expletives and an occasional stammer.

'All right, ace?' Hughes boomed. 'I heard you were fucking coming! Come in!'

Hughes had first met Murray at a national squash camp in 1988. Hughes had been there as a volunteer assistant, helping out with the physical testing of the players. Given his proficiency with computational analysis and statistics, he had been asked to conduct the fitness testing for their junior camp.

Armed with a BBC Micro and a bulky printer, Hughes set his computer up courtside and had the players perform a series of twelve tests, including sprint runs, Harvard step tests, standing jumps and press-ups. He would then print out a fitness report and hand them to each athlete. 'He was doing this thing called sports science, which at the time nobody had heard about,' Murray remembers. Despite his dread of mathematics, Murray became fascinated by the quantification of what he had always seen as subjective and intangible into something objective: hard numbers. 'A lot of players, even some of the coaches, pooh-poohed what Hughes was doing. To me, that's when shit made perfect sense.'

Hughes had joined UWIC in 1991, at the invitation of an analyst called Keith Lyons. Lyons was an authority in the field of video analysis and the author of the first book on the subject, *Using Video in Sport*. In Cardiff, Hughes became a founding member of the new Centre for Performance Analysis.

The Centre was soon thriving, as a variety of sports teams, ranging from the Lawn Tennis Association to the Welsh football team, began approaching Hughes and Lyons to sign up their students as analysts – compiling statistical reports and videos of players' strengths and weaknesses, from which a selection of positive clips were set to each individual's favourite music track – in exchange for cheap pay and work experience. 'The course was very popular. Students would be working at the coalface, rather than in a lab, where you stick a mask on the face of athletes and ask them to run to exhaustion with a thermometer up their arse,' Hughes says. 'Here you would actually measure athletes in world championships and Olympic Games.'

The Centre had a library of more than five thousand VHS tapes, including ten years of recordings of every rugby match in the world, ordered chronologically, alongside two large video-editing machines. On the wall outside, a noticeboard was covered with posters which read: *In Wimbledon, the percentage of the ball in play time is five per cent. Not many people know that!* Or *In rugby, average ball in play time is twenty-eight minutes. Not many people know that!* Across the corridor was the performance analysis laboratory, with a VHS deck recorder and monitor in one corner and twenty desktop computers.

At that first meeting, Hughes made Murray sign a piece of paper that stated: *I hereby agree to try as hard as I can. I hereby agree to buy toast for my supervisor. I hereby agree to bring biscuits to each meeting.* In return, Hughes made three promises: he was going to get Murray fit again, he was going to make him captain of the squash team and he was going to turn him into the best analyst in the country. 'He was so excited he was almost shouting,' Murray remembers.

Murray accompanied Hughes to the university cafeteria, where his new professor ordered eight rounds of buttered toast. Hughes then pulled out a piece of paper on which he sketched out a hand notation system, drew a squash court, divided it into sixteen cells and tutored Murray in the basics of performance analysis. 'I had never seen anything like that,' Murray recalls. 'It just captured my attention because it made complete sense. I still have that piece of paper.'

Murray also remembers his first lecture, the following day. Hughes, wearing a dicky bow and a pair of squash shoes, stood in front of two slide projectors, which he was using simultaneously. 'He was projecting the most random photos – it could be a football player, it could be a gorilla – and he would always have a story for each. It was wacky,' Murray says. 'If the students weren't paying attention he would admonish them, shouting right in their faces: "Are you listening? This is fucking interesting, you bastard!"'

Murray listened. Throughout his studies, he spent most of his spare time in the performance analysis lab. All the computers were configured with a programmable touch-sensitive pad that Hughes had brought in from Liverpool John Moores University. Called concept keyboards, they consisted of 128 touch-sensitive cells on which the analyst could superimpose a chart depicting a squash court or a football pitch. In the case of football, the keyboard also had keys with the numbers of the eleven players of the team plus two substitutes, along with specific keys for events, from DRIB for 'dribble' to LOST POSS for 'lost possession'. The final analysis could output myriad statistics, depicting for example where players dribbled, the distribution of passing, how possession was lost and how free kicks were conceded.

It was a slow process. If player A passed the ball to player B, Murray would pause the video to press the right key for player A, then press the 'PITCH' key for the point at which the pass had been made, then press the 'PASS' key, then press the key for player B, then the key for the point on the pitch where he had received the pass. Analysing a football match could take a day. An hour of squash would typically take four to process. Each day, Murray would buy a pack of beer, sit at a computer and practise annotating video footage of matches. He would do this for hours, rarely leaving before midnight.

Murray wrote his undergraduate dissertation on the effect of data feedback on player performance in squash – 'terrible work, but it got published', and by the time he finished his degree in 1998, he had become the first analyst able to notate a match in real time. 'He would just sit there and chat away with the coach, while his fingers worked magic,' Hughes says. 'It was impressive to witness.'

In the months following his graduation, however, Murray struggled to find a full-time job. He spent three months working as a match analyst for the South African cricket team's Test series in England. As he was paid only fifty pounds a day, which had to cover all his food and accommodation expenses, Murray slept in a van that he had bought for £120 from his father. The job consisted of filming and analysing the Test matches, using a video camera connected to a large portable workstation which he called the lunchbox. At Lord's, Murray wasn't allowed anywhere but the roof of the commentary box, where he would sit with the lunchbox on a plastic table, covered by an umbrella and his beloved Stetson, to which he added a shirt and tie in order to abide by the ground's dress code.

At the end of each match, Murray would edit the tape to include all the statistics that the coach required – from batsmen's dismissals to specific types of deliveries – using the Crickstat software that had been developed by the South African Council for Scientific and Industrial Research. 'The coach would play it to the team, on the bus on the way back to the hotel,' Murray recalls. 'A lot of players would just sit at the back of the coach, playing cards, messing about. They didn't trust me because I was English.'

Murray also lectured on research methods at UWIC, and moonlighted as a doorman-slash-bouncer at a city-centre nightclub called Winstones, along with his best friend, a corpulent Irishman nicknamed Wank. 'He was hard as nails,' Murray says. 'Whenever there was a fight, I would just stand behind him.' Murray remembers once accompanying his friend to Caroline Street, informally known as Chip Alley, to find a doorman who owed him money. 'He made the mistake of saying he wasn't paying,' Murray says. 'We were in the car – he pulled him through the window, headbutted him, and shoved him into the street.' As Murray drove off, in a state of shock, he thought, 'I need to stop doing this.'

Family drama compounded Stafford's hardships. His parents were going through a lengthy divorce and his mother had taken out a restraining order against his father. She then moved to Fiji, where his brother Warwick was then living. This caused Murray such distress that his hair started to fall out.

Murray's problems didn't stop there. He then got engaged to a woman who happened to be his boss at Winstones, and bought a house with the help of her parents. However, he ended the engagement after three months because she began insisting that Murray was having an affair (an accusation that Murray denies).

Amid the turmoil, his tutor Mike Hughes was a pillar of strength. 'He was like a father to me,' Murray says. 'He knew I was skint so he would ask me to come round to coach his son, which he paid in advance. I knew Mike Junior wasn't going to be there. I would drive there and they would invite me for dinner and give me food to take home in containers.' Murray would ask if there were any jobs going, and Hughes would tell him to hold on tight. 'But I couldn't hold on for much longer. I was living hand to mouth.' He was about to give up on a career as a performance analyst when Hughes told him he had a very interesting job offer to discuss. The performance manager of the Squash Rackets Association was expecting his call.

3

PROFESSIONAL ZONE

At 3.50 p.m. on 18 March 1950, a Royal Air Force account-ant by the name of Charles Reep was watching a Third Division football match between Swindon Town and Bristol Rovers. He took out a pencil and a notepad, and started writing down his observations, using a system of symbols he had invented.

Seventeen years earlier, Reep had attended a talk by Charlie Jones, a winger who played for the legendary Arsenal team that dominated English football in the thirties. When he spoke about Arsenal's game strategy, and particularly about the ground-breaking tactical formation known as the WM system (because of the shapes described by the position of the players), Reep began to wonder if the principles of accountancy could ever be used to gain a better statistical insight into the sport.

'The continuous action of a game is broken down into a series of discrete on-the-ball events such as pass, centre or shot,' Reep later wrote in a paper he co-authored in 1968 with the Chief Statistician at the General Register Office, Bernard Benjamin, published in the *Journal of the Royal*

Statistical Society. 'A detailed categorization is made for each event, for each shorthand codes have been developed. For example, each pass in a game is classified and recorded by its length, direction, height, outcome, as well as the positions of the field at which the pass originated and ended.' Such a system was, according to Reep, 'a counter to reliance upon memory, tradition, and personal impressions that led to speculation and football ideologies'.

Over the years, Reep annotated more than 2200 matches, often attending evening matches wearing a miner's helmet complete with lamp. The data analysis was slow work, with each game typically taking eighty hours. The 1958 World Cup final alone took him three months to analyse.

What Reep showed was that football, supposedly a dynamic and unpredictable game, had constant and predictable patterns. He discovered, for instance, that the odds of completing a first pass successfully were only 50 per cent, and that these odds diminished with every additional pass completed. He also found that nine out of ten times a team would lose the ball after completing no more than three passes. But what really surprised Reep were the numbers behind goal scoring. Teams, on average, scored once out of every nine shots at goal; 80 per cent of goals were scored from plays of fewer than four passes; and half of all goals came from balls recovered within thirty metres of the goal line, in the last third of the pitch.

These statistical insights led Reep to suggest that teams would be more efficient if they spent less time trying to string together passes and more time lobbing the ball into their opponents' half. He believed that three passes – a long ball, knockdown and strike – was the path to success.

Reep's long-ball theory soon found followers in the domestic league. Stan Cullis, who managed Wolverhampton Wanderers during their glory days in the fifties, was one of its early adopters. In the seventies, Reep was advising Graham Taylor, the manager who in five years took Watford from the Fourth Division to the First, and who later managed England.

The man who was perhaps most instrumental in promoting the long-ball strategy was Charles Hughes. In 1983, Hughes became the coaching director for the Football Association and part of his remit was to write the official coaching manuals for football managers and youth academies across the country. He wrote thirty-one books, but none so popular as *The Winning Formula* (1990), which extolled the virtues of the long ball, presenting it as an evidence-based theory of the game. He derided possession football, the game played by Brazil and Argentina, replete with artistry and complex patterns of consecutive passes that he claimed weren't conducive to scoring goals. Although Hughes acknowledged Reep's work, he claimed he had derived his conclusions from his own match analysis. (Reep would later accuse him of something akin to plagiarism.)

This philosophy would have a profound impact on the patterns of play of British football, finding many supporters in the domestic league and on the national team.

But one notational analyst at Liverpool Polytechnic had a very different view of the long-ball theory. 'I hated it,' Mike Hughes (no relation) says. 'It was stupid.'

Football, in the general sense of the word, is a category of team sports that involve kicking a ball to score a goal. Many variations – or codes – exist: Association football (or soccer), American football, Australian Rules football, rugby football and Gaelic football. On 13 April 1987, under the auspices of the Department of Sport and Recreational Studies at Liverpool Polytechnic, they came together at the first World Congress of Science and Football, organised by Tom Reilly.

Hundreds of football players, coaches, managers and scientists attended. The event included Gaelic football teams demonstrating their skills at Anfield, professional coaches conducting workshops and a vigorous debate on the merits of the long ball. Dick Bate, the coach of Notts County, gave a presentation based on unpublished research by Charles Hughes, which consisted of a litany of long-ball mantras: play the ball forward as often as possible; increase the number of long forward passes; and play the ball into space behind the opposition defence as early as possible. In the audience, Mike Hughes fumed. 'He was saying that actually the more times you gave the ball away, the more times you have possession,' he says. 'Of course, your possessions are short but you'll get the ball back again quicker. And the more possessions you have, the more chance you have for scoring. Just statistics gone crazy.'

Hughes presented his first football analysis at that same event, using his recently developed concept keyboard. His study consisted of a statistical comparison of successful and unsuccessful teams in the 1986 World Cup in Mexico, and his conclusions were antithetical to the long-ball dogma: on average, successful teams maintained possession for longer and had more touches of the ball per possession than unsuccessful ones. 'This would therefore imply that this long-ball game was a load of twaddle,' Hughes says. The World Cup had, of course, been won by Argentina, a team driven by possession football and led by one of the most compelling artists of the ball the game had ever seen, Diego Maradona. 'Of course, you need skilled players to sustain long-passing moves,' says Hughes. 'But up until then, everybody was ignoring the blatant fact that teams who weren't using a long-ball strategy, like Brazil and Argentina, were winning the World Cup.'

Hughes and Ian Franks later decided to re-evaluate Reep's

research, using their data from the two most recent World
Cup tournaments. At first, they found their data compatible
with Reep's analysis; after closer scrutiny, however, they
discovered that most goals happened after fewer than four
pass movements simply because most movements in football
contain fewer than four passes, not because the odds were
better. In other words, the frequency of goals scored was not
the same as the odds of a goal being scored. Indeed, Hughes
and Franks found that teams which completed more passes
had a better chance of scoring. Unsuccessful teams, meanwhile, lost possession of the ball significantly more frequently
in the outermost sixths of the playing area, closer to the
goals, both during attack and defence. And whereas successful teams approached the final sixth of the pitch by playing
predominantly through the centre, unsuccessful teams played
significantly more to the wings.

At first, their paper was rejected for publication. 'One of
the reviewers was a Reep devotee,' Hughes claims. He was
inclined to give up, but Franks encouraged him to persist
and work together to address the criticisms. They eventually
published their paper, in the *Journal of Sport Science*. 'I believe
that the idea of direct play – of few consecutive passes leading
to a goal – wasn't so much about the long ball but about pen-
etration, of passing the ball accurately between and behind
defenders,' Franks says. 'Whether that's a long or short ball,
it doesn't matter – but some coaches abused these ideas and
thought that all it meant was to pump lots of balls into the
front of the field and have people chase them down.'

What Franks and Hughes demonstrated was that Charles
Reep wasn't wrong, but his interpretation of the data was.
'Collecting data is always the first step and Reep was a great
accountant,' says Chris Anderson, a political economist at
Cornell University, who has been studying football statistics

since 2011. 'But he wasn't a great analyst and had a limited understanding of what the numbers were telling him.' Reep, according to Anderson, had very strong preconceived notions and when he found what he was looking for – a chance to play the game with minimum input for maximum output – he didn't investigate other hypotheses. 'He was welcomed into football by people who wanted to play a long-ball game, and just wanted to know how do it without considering how wrong this approach could be,' Anderson explains. In *The Numbers Game: Why Everything You Know About Football Is Wrong*, Anderson and David Sally write, 'Reep's quest to use the numbers to inform strategy fell short because he was an absolutist, determined to use his data to prove his beliefs. He needed to abandon his idea that he was looking for the one general rule, a winning formula, and learn to seek the multiple truths and falsehoods in the numbers themselves.' But Reep's core assertion that statistics offer a chance to see things which would otherwise be missed was absolutely correct.

In 1998, two Frenchmen arrived unannounced at Liverpool John Moores University to meet with Tom Reilly. By then, Reilly was the director of the department, now a thriving school known for producing the best sports scientists in the world. He called his team the Liverpool mafia. A prolific researcher, whose interests now encompassed chronobiology and ergonomics, Reilly had mentored most of them at some point.

At the time, Reilly would regularly meet with outsiders – freelance analysts, technologists and foreign academics – who liked to pitch the latest idea for how the patterns of football should be analysed. But the two academics from Nice simply showed up without an appointment. They asked to see Reilly, but he was not at the department that day, so some of his colleagues agreed to a meeting. Among them were two students named Danny Northey and Ben Dickinson.

The Football Association had recently commissioned the department to produce a series of detailed match analyses from international tournaments. Charles Hughes had left the FA in 1994, after England failed to win a single match at the 1992 European Cup or to even qualify for the 1994 World Cup. His successor, Howard Wilkinson, who thought Charles Reep a zealot, was eager to modernise the game. Northey and Dickinson had been assigned to the FA project, as they had both written their dissertations on performance analysis and were familiar with the concept keyboards. 'We got paid game by game,' Dickinson says. 'We were cheap student labour.' They worked on the project throughout the summer and published their findings in a series of articles for the FA Coaches Association journal, *Insight*.

Most of their findings represented a further refutation of the long-ball approach, and highlighted a stark contrast between English football and the rest of the world. When goals were scored in domestic football, they found, the ball was typically regained in the attacking third; in international football, most goals were scored after regaining possession in the midfield and defensive thirds. Also, in English domestic football most goals were scored from moves lasting approximately five seconds and involving two or fewer passes, whereas in international football most goals involved between three and five passes and the moves leading to them were approximately ten seconds long. Finally, in international football more goals were scored from moves involving more than ten passes and lasting for more than fifteen seconds than in the domestic game.

One of their most interesting findings related to the so-called zone 14. The researchers divided the pitch into eighteen areas within a six-by-three grid, and discovered that controlling the area on the edge of the box – zone 14 or, in coaching parlance, 'the hole' – was one of the performance indicators for success. The four nations that reached the semi-finals of the 1998 World Cup – Brazil, the Netherlands, Croatia and the host country, France – made an average of twenty-five passes from zone 14 and directed 70 per cent of those passes forward, towards the penalty area. Other teams, in contrast, had made just fifteen passes from the hole.

Neither Northey nor Dickinson had any idea what to expect from the two Frenchmen, but they were curious to find out. The visitors introduced themselves as Jean-Marc Giorgi and Antoine David, the CTO and CEO of Sport Universal.

Their presentation was simple, and devastatingly effective. First, they played a short clip from a recent Champions League match, Manchester United versus Juventus. Then they played the same match in overhead viewpoint animation mode, which visualised the entire pitch in two dimensions, from a bird's-eye perspective, with the players rendered as moving dots, similar to the classic computer game *Championship Manager*. The software worked by converting video images into animation using its pixel-tracking algorithm, named Amisco, which could identify the player positions from match footage. Amisco allowed each player's movement to be tracked to a tenth of a second.

'We were absolutely blown away by seeing the live movement of the players,' Northey says. 'As soon as we saw it, we knew it was going to be revolutionary.' Amisco also allowed the user to play, replay, draw offside lines and select specific movements. The software tracked everything in such detail – registering an average of three thousand touches of the ball per game and easily calculating distances – that it could answer a range of statistical questions, ranging from the total number of passes to the distance covered by a given player when sprinting.

On the car journey home, Dickinson and Northey, still giddy from what they had witnessed, knew that they absolutely had to get involved with Sport Universal. They quickly negotiated a three-month work experience contract at the start-up, and packed their bags for Nice.

Jean-Marc Giorgi had originally developed the program as part of an ambitious university research project to build an artificial intelligence system that could provide real-time tactical solutions for rugby coaches. The initial phase of the project consisted of designing a pixel-tracking algorithm, capable of automatically tracking both the ball and all the players, based on match footage alone. Giorgi and David patented Amisco in 1995. But when they struggled to raise any funding, the project stalled.

In 1997, one of their contacts, impressed by the technology, arranged a meeting for them. It was with Aimé Jacquet, the French national football manager, and the team's technical director, Gérard Houllier. Before the meeting, Sport Universal was permitted to film a friendly match with the French national team, at the Stade Vélodrome in Marseille.

When Jacquet saw the results, he was ecstatic. 'He started running around the table and saying "This is it! I've been waiting for this for years!"' Giorgi recalls. The meeting started at 2 p.m. and ended shortly after midnight. Jacquet grilled Giorgi and David on every single aspect of the software. He asked questions such as: could they create a graphic that continuously displayed the distance between the defence, midfield and attack positions? Could they automatically replay all the goal kicks and show how the team was spread out when the ball landed?

Giorgi and David said they could, but added that it would not be ready in time for the following year's World Cup. Still, encouraged by the feedback, they left the University of Nice and spun out a company.

In the summer of 1999, Northey and Dickinson arrived in a quiet village called Plan-du-Var, thirty kilometres north of Nice. They stayed in a hostel across the street from the Sport Universal offices, which had been set up in a converted school.

Amisco required the installation of several cameras to cover the whole pitch, so that every player would always be visible on video. One analyst was needed to tag match events such as red cards, offsides and tackles. At the beginning of every match, each player had to be identified individually. In theory, the software could then automatically track the movements of all players, the referee and the ball between ten and twenty-five times per second throughout the whole ninety minutes of play, resulting in a database of 4.5 million positions and 2500 ball touches.

'When they first claimed that the tracking was fully auto-mated, we were astonished,' Dickinson says, 'but when we asked how, they never gave us a clear answer. It was something along the lines of, "we program the computer and it follows the players". It's not that they were cagey, but they were being a bit reluctant to elucidate us.' Shortly after their arrival in France, Northey and Dickinson realised that this claim to be fully automated was not exactly accurate. The truth was that although the software could easily track players across open spaces, when they overlapped in the camera's field of vision the tracking became erratic and the players were often misidentified. The only way to troubleshoot the issue was to recalibrate the software manually. And to do that, every Saturday night after a match Sport Universal required the services of a small army of part-timers and students willing to pull an all-nighter manually cleaning the football data to ensure that it would be quality controlled in time for presentation to the clubs on Monday morning. 'It was drudge work,' Dickinson recalls. 'You had eight cameras around the pitch, each with its own coordinates. You would press play and manually track the player all the way through a whole match, one player at the time.'

Sport Universal was looking to break into the English market, as the Premier League was the world's wealthiest competition. But it quickly became apparent that Giorgi and David didn't really know much about football.

'What they were doing was very much raw data extraction,' Northey says. 'We had to tell them the sort of information that coaches would want: where are the passes going, and were they successful? Who's in the right position and who isn't? How do you score goals and how do you stop them?' The two students suggested the implementation of new software features, such as a heat map of player positions and a full-pitch view of all the passes that a player had made in the game, with failed passes coloured in red and successful passes in green.

Towards the end of Northey and Dickinson's stint of work experience, two businessmen from Leeds turned up at the Sport Universal offices. They introduced themselves as Ram Mylvaganam and Neil Ramsay, the directors of a company called Prozone. They were curious as to what two British lads were doing in Nice, and so invited Northey and Dickinson out to lunch. There, they explained that they were bringing the technology to the English Premier League and were closing a deal to do so with Giorgi and David. Would Northey and Dickinson be interested in working at Prozone?

*

Ram Mylvaganam is a Leeds-born businessman from a Sri Lankan immigrant family, who had trained as an engineer before embarking on a high-flying career as a marketing director for Mars Chocolate in Japan, South-East Asia and Latin America. When he returned home to Leeds, Mylvaganam met Neil Ramsay, a former football agent, at his local golf club. The two men began developing business ideas together. Their first enterprise was a franchise for a brand of massage chairs developed by a music professor in Finland. The chair emitted electrical pulses that supposedly relaxed the muscles and increased flexibility and blood flow.

That business was quickly going nowhere when Ramsay, who knew Derby County's manager Jim Smith, arranged for them to meet at the club. Derby had just been promoted to the Premiership. When Mylvaganam first visited the Baseball Ground, he was dismayed by the club's run-down facilities. 'The coaches were basically using a glorified garden shed as the team's meeting and changing room,' he says. As a Premier League club, they would require a war room, where they could prepare for the next game.

With the help of his architect wife, Mylvaganam designed the blueprint for a dedicated space where the coaches could meet and instruct their players. He called it the Prozone', a contraction of 'professional zone'. ('Simply because what they had before was very unprofessional,' Mylvaganam says wryly.) When he presented the project to Derby County's manager, Smith was enthusiastic about the prospect, but said they couldn't afford it. Mylvaganam suggested to Ramsay that they finance the project themselves, but his business partner revealed that he was newly bankrupt. Mylvaganam had no option but to raise the funds himself and start a company that could develop the project.

The first version of Prozone consisted of three linked

Portakabins, equipped with twenty-two of the Finnish massage chairs. These proved very popular with the players. A routine soon developed: at 10.30 every morning Derby's players reported to the Prozone, where they sat on the chairs for fifteen minutes listening to the assistant manager, a young coach called Steve McClaren, talk them through presentations on a video screen. McClaren would discuss their previous performances and their game plan for the following Saturday's match, along with an analysis of the opposition. Feedback, McClaren used to say, was the breakfast of champions.

One day, Mylvaganam and Ramsay found McClaren working in his office, where he would stay on long after the players had gone home, using two video recorders and a single screen to edit footage from *Match of the Day*. 'What a waste of time. Why don't you get one of your monkeys to do it?' Mylvaganam asked. 'How do they know what's a good move and what's bad?' McClaren replied. 'I want to show them how you win matches.'

Believing they could do better, Mylvaganam contacted a London-based company called Showtime. Showtime was able to convert McClaren's video reports into sophisticated PowerPoint presentations and animations. 'The problem with using *Match of the Day* highlights was that the focus is on what happened with the ball,' Ramsay says. 'Coaches were not only interested in the ball, they were also interested in where their team is relative to the ball.'

At that point, the vision for Prozone became to design what Ramsay described as a 'moving magnet board', a form of visual display that would enable the coach to have a bird's-eye view of the whole game. The two businessmen began searching for patents. That's how, in 1997, they came across Sport Universal.

Mylvaganam and Ramsay approached the start-up and

suggested a partnership, in which they would be Sport Universal's commercial arm in the UK. As part of this deal, Prozone bought 25 per cent of Sport Universal. 'I emailed Derby and Chelsea, telling them about the system and asking if they would be willing to trial it,' Ramsay recalls. 'Jim Smith immediately returned my call, so we went with Derby.'

Prozone installed a system of eight cameras around the Baseball Ground, guaranteeing absolute coverage of every square metre of the pitch. Sport Universal were responsible for the data processing and quality control. 'We still had problems,' Mylvaganam says. 'For instance, the camera technology was so bad, sometimes we'd get the analysis back and there'd be players missing. We had to keep redesigning the software. Still, it was revolutionary. We were defining the statistical variables that defined the game of football.' Every Monday, Neil and Ram would travel to Derby County's training ground to present the Prozone data to McClaren and Smith. McClaren introduced a top-ten notice board, listing the players with the most tackles, shots, sprints and largest distance covered. Ramsay says, 'Suddenly the players were competing amongst themselves to be on that board.'

Given that Derby didn't have the wherewithal to pay Prozone, as part of their agreement Ramsay and Mylvaganam were allowed to approach teams visiting Derby's ground and pitch their services to rival managers. They would arrange a meeting for the week after the game, and then travel to the club to demonstrate the software using that game's data. Ramsay, a former football agent, was comfortable around football people, while Mylvaganam felt more at home speaking to executives, so Ramsay would usually make these trips. Once, after West Ham played at Derby, Ramsay was away on holiday so opted to send a CD-ROM with the Prozone video files. A few days later, Harry Redknapp, West Ham's manager, rang him.

'There's nothing on the CD,' he shouted.

'Where are you?' Ramsay asked.

'There's nothing coming out of it!'

'Are you in front of a computer?'

'No, I'm not in front of a fucking computer! I'm in the car. The CD is in the stereo – Neil, this isn't working!'

At that moment Ramsay realised that, no matter how sophisticated their software, Prozone could fail simply because coaches didn't know how to use a CD-ROM. They were going to analysts to teach coaches at elite football clubs both about performance analysis, and how to use a computer.

Derby County finished in a comfortable twelfth place in their first year in the Premier League, outperforming all expectations. In the following season, they opened a new stadium, Pride Park, and reached ninth place, narrowly missing out on a standing that would have qualified them for the European competitions.

By the 1998–99 season, many of their players were starting to be noticed by other clubs. Steve McClaren, meanwhile, had developed a reputation as one of the country's most tactically sophisticated coaches and a pioneer in the use of video analysis. In February 1999, he was headhunted by one of the best managers in the Premier League, Alex Ferguson at Manchester United.

When McClaren joined Manchester United, he asked Ferguson if they could sign up for the match analysis software he had been using at Derby County. Ferguson acceded, and invited Ram Mylvaganam to Old Trafford to demonstrate the system. Impressed, Ferguson arranged that same day for Mylvaganam to meet David Gill, the club's financial director.

At the meeting, Gill told Mylvaganam that he was only there because Ferguson had asked him to be. And, he continued, if Mylvaganam was asking for money, he could leave immediately. Prozone had been working pro bono for Derby, and still had no paying customers. So he pleaded: they were a small company and needed the money. Gill asked him how much. A hundred thousand pounds a year, Mylvaganam replied. 'You must be joking,' Gill told him. 'I'll tell you what: if we win one competition, I'll pay you half of that fee the following year.' Mylvaganam made a counter offer: if Manchester United won any silverware that season, they would pay fifty thousand pounds and then sign a full contract for the following season. Gill eventually agreed.

That season, United won the treble – the Champions League, the Premier League and the FA Cup – and so, just as the big dot-com crash was about to happen, Prozone finally earned its first pay cheque. 'I remember Steve McClaren talking about how Prozone had helped them win the Champions League,' says Marvyn Dickinson, another Liverpool John Moores alumnus who was later hired by Prozone says. 'But he would spend twenty minutes in a week with the analyst over a cup of tea and that was it. I can't imagine that Prozone helped Ole Gunnar Solskjær stick his foot out in the last minute against Bayern Munich. I'm not having that.'

Still, whenever people asked Mylvaganam if Prozone had helped Manchester United win the treble, he would confidently reply 'Of course.' By August 2000, Derby County, Manchester United and Aston Villa had become paying customers. Prozone's business model in these early days was subscription-based: they covered the camera installation at the venues, and charged five thousand pounds per game, which amounted to approximately a hundred thousand pounds a season for each club.

They were the only technology start-up in the cutthroat world of the Premier League, home to world champions and the best players around, and populated by Luddites and old-fashioned coaches averse to innovation.

Danny Northey and Ben Dickinson became the first two employees of the company. Northey was responsible for finding new clients, while Dickinson was asked to liaise with Derby. Marvyn Dickinson was hired to work with Manchester United. Mylvaganam told them Arsenal had signed up for next season and they needed the system ready by August. Soon they were run ragged on twelve-hour shifts. They went to the local employment agency and asked for anyone who could use a computer, just to do quality control of the files.

They still needed consultants to liaise with their new clients, so they went on a hiring spree for sports science graduates straight out of university. At sports science hubs like Liverpool John Moores and UWIC they distributed flyers that advertised a vacancy for a consultant at the 'world's leading football analysis company', based in Leeds, starting salary between 14 and 16K. They added a couple of screengrabs of the animation mode, a few stats and the Prozone logo.

Picking the right consultants was crucial. During the first part of the interview process, Northey and the two Dickinsons took time to get acquainted with the candidates. They would ask a few football-related questions, to see if each candidate could hold their own. The Prozone team also paid attention to the candidates' appearance. They were aiming for a very particular aesthetic: late nineties footballer – spiky hair, athletic, smart suits, swagger. 'It was going to be hard enough making people use the software, never mind getting used to someone who didn't look like they belonged in a football club,' Marvyn Dickinson says. They would then introduce the candidates to the software and instruct them to pick six clips that would be of importance to a coach and present them to the interviewers. They would then pose hypothetical scenarios and evaluate how they responded. They would say, for instance, 'Imagine there's twelve people stuck down a mine shaft and you can only rescue eight because by the time you reach the last four, oxygen has run out.' The twelve were all different characters – one could be a ninety-year-old veteran who had fought in the Second World War, another could be a refugee from a war-torn country, and so on. By how the candidates responded, they could judge who the leaders were, who the organisers were, what they were like under pressure, what they were like as negotiators, what their biases were. Finally, the candidates were asked to deliver a ten-minute presentation on why they should be employed by Prozone.

The first cohort of Prozone consultants was a diverse bunch: Simon Wilson, a semi-professional player with a science and football degree from John Moores; Barry McNeill, a psychology graduate who had previously worked as a research project manager in the NHS; and Gavin Fleig, a brilliant UWIC graduate who had studied under Mike Hughes.

These consultants split their time between the football clubs and Prozone's offices in a warehouse in Leeds's red-light district. The warehouse had the feel of a manufacturing plant, with a bank of two hundred computers arranged on long workbenches in parallel rows across the floor. The windows were barred, and Prozone shared a kitchen with the hosiery company that occupied the ground floor. 'It was a shambles,' Marvyn Dickinson recalls. 'On the top floor, we had the most sophisticated match analysis in the world. On the ground floor we had a place that sold vests and socks.' When executives from UEFA, FIFA, Sky, BBC came to their offices they would immediately realise that Prozone didn't spend any money on their premises. 'We spent it on developing the product,' Ramsay says. Apart from the equipment, Mylvaganam had hung a picture of a *trompe l'œil* drawing by the pavement artist Julian Beever, an artwork that, if viewed from the right angle, created a three-dimensional illusion. To Mylvaganam, the data they were collecting was like that Beever chalk drawing: everything they needed to make sense of it was hiding in full view, right in front of them. 'But if you stand in the wrong place, the data looks like shit. We need to convert data into wisdom. If you don't, we are dead.'

The consultants worked together, lived together and went out together. On match days the Prozone consultants would typically capture the data from their respective stadiums, return to Leeds at 2 a.m. in the company fleet of silver VW Golfs, process the data overnight and then return to their clubs to deliver the analysis. The warehouse would be thronged by part-timers working through the night. 'It was like a conveyor belt. You had to finish a game fast because the next game was about to arrive,' Ramsay says.

Twenty-seven computers were assigned to each game: one per player, plus the two linesmen and the referee. Each corrector followed one player and sorted out any problems with the pixel-tracking algorithm, then all the data was stitched together at the end. 'Once we had this game that would get to twenty-five minutes and the animation would crash,' says Ben Dickinson. For hours they combed through the code, line by line by line, until they found the error. 'Turned out that this was an outdated version of the program and the programmer had written in "red car", instead of "red card". So a player got sent off and the actual code didn't match what was the expected command. It was four in the morning and this game had to be with the coaches the next day. Red card! For God's sake! It was madness.'

'Every now and again these little bugs would bite us on

the bottom whilst we were in front of coaches at Premier League football clubs,' Marvyn Dickinson says. 'Sometimes we would see, from the overhead view, a player suddenly jump from one side of the pitch to another, which meant he covered, like, 250 metres within a second. The players would basically turn into Iron Man.'

On Thursday evenings they would convene at one of Leeds's nightspots to share war stories. Marvyn Dickinson's favourite anecdote was about a goalkeeping coach who had once asked him to teach him how to use the software. Dickinson immediately obliged, and told him to start by moving the mouse cursor to the top of the screen. When the coach grabbed the mouse and literally moved it in the air, Dickinson nervously asked what he was doing. The coach replied, exasperated, 'I don't fucking know!'

Not all coaches were Luddites, of course. Carlos Queiroz, the Portuguese coach and one of Alex Ferguson's assistant managers, avidly embraced the technology and deftly manipulated it to fit the distinct sensibilities of both players and coaches. Queiroz used to tell Marvyn Dickinson that they were no longer dealing with footballers, they were dealing with multi-millionaires who played football. 'Beckham, for instance, was suspicious of Prozone,' Dickinson says. 'Queiroz just said to him, "David, this is where we turn you from a thirty-five million player into a fifty million player."' Once, when analysing a Champions League match against Maccabi Haifa, Dickinson noticed how dismal the performance of France's central defender and World Cup-winner, Laurent Blanc, had been. 'I couldn't believe what I was seeing,' Dickinson says. 'He was leaving players unmarked, being outpaced by attackers, handing over players for other defenders to mark. He was clearly a player past his prime and getting away with it.' When Dickinson showed his footage to Queiroz, the Portuguese coach shook his head. 'There's a problem,' Queiroz told the analyst. 'Ferguson loves Blanc.' It was a textbook halo effect. Queiroz suggested holding a session with Blanc and another defender, Gary Neville. 'We showed about eight clips of Laurent basically committing criminal offences. Gary Neville, being so Mancunian, stood up animated and started shouting, "Laurent, what the fuck is going through your mind there?" Laurent just sat in his chair, arms folded, a jumper tied around his shoulders, just shrugging it off. It was a privilege to be there, watching two top athletes using this sports science tool to crucify each other.'

Managers like Queiroz were the exception, not the rule. Although the Prozone consultants were tireless and committed to showing what the software could do for a team, most managers couldn't make the intellectual leap from the game they saw first-hand on the sidelines to the multiple extra dimensions offered by Prozone's data. The truth was that most coaches liked the idea of being associated with Prozone, but they didn't really know what to do with it. 'We were guilty sometimes of just thinking that all we had to do was deliver the golden egg to the coaches and they would instantly know,' Dickinson says. 'The software was able to answer millions of questions. I couldn't believe how few questions they were asked after a game.'

4

WINNERS AND ERRORS

Stafford Murray's first tournament as an accredited analyst took place in January 1999 at the prestigious Tournament of Champions in New York. The early rounds had been held simultaneously at various squash clubs across the city. To film them, Murray had to set up his camera at one venue, press record, then jump in a cab to the next venue, set up another camera there, and repeat. 'The first few days I was literally running across New York, filming as much as possible,' Murray says. A few players were suspicious and protested the legality of it, as the England squash governing body had only bought the rights to film their own players' matches. When this happened, Murray would simply turn off the camera's red light and film the matches anyway.

England had sent nine players to the tournament. Paul Johnson – England's top player, and ranked fourth in the world – made it to the semi-finals. Murray planted himself in the stands, video camera in hand, and filmed Johnson's defeat in a drawn-out, hundred-minute affair against the Egyptian Ahmed Barada. Following Johnson's loss, Murray was led to the VIP bar. The next thing he remembered was waking up in his hotel room at 4 a.m. in a panic. He ran back to Grand Central Station, where the final rounds of the event were being held in an all-glass court in the middle of the concourse. There he was met by a large NYPD officer holding a Sony DV camcorder. 'This yours?' the officer asked.

Just as he was on the verge of giving up on performance analysis altogether, the SRA job had come Murray's way as the result of the launch of new high-performance sports agency UK Sport, whose role was to distribute National Lottery funds to national sporting associations.

Sports that previously had to make do with a budget of a few hundred thousand pounds were now being funded in the millions. Each governing body had to submit a World Class Performance Programme, requesting financing in support of specific targets. This usually entailed allowing athletes to train full time, with dedicated coaches and support staff.

Up to this point, the England men's coach, David Pearson, had been employed only part time. He had enjoyed a respectable career as an international squash player, but retired in 1988 to become a coach, a decision taken out of necessity rather than choice. His second daughter, Emma, had been born with cerebral palsy and needed constant care. 'I wouldn't have been able to manage as a player. I had to start making a living,' Pearson says.

When Lottery funding was allocated to the England squash team, Pearson was promoted to a full-time position. 'Suddenly I was working with physios and psychologists,' Pearson says. 'I was like a child in a chocolate store.'

Shortly after, Matt Hammond, the performance director of the Squash Rackets Association, told Pearson to expect a call from an analyst called Stafford Murray, who had come recommended by Mike Hughes at UWIC.

'Hello, Mr Pearson,' came the voice down the line. 'This is Stafford Murray in Wales. I don't know if you remember me.'

Pearson did. The two had met when he was still a national junior coach and Murray a promising player with a cocky attitude and bad fashion sense. 'Looked like someone you wouldn't want to cross in a dark alley,' Pearson recalls. He asked Murray if he wanted to play a game with him. In less than twenty minutes, Pearson had demolished his younger opponent 9–1, 9–2, 9–1. 'I thought I knew everything,' Murray says of the match. 'He took me on court and I didn't know where the ball was going.'

Pearson, for his part, thought Murray a formidable player with a crisp touch of the ball. Murray remembers differently: 'He told me I had no finesse, no feel for the game, no touch.'

It was little wonder, then, that Murray was deferential during the call. 'He started getting nervous and began to stammer: "Ye-yes, Mr Pearson, I-I remember,"' Pearson recalls. 'He must have called me Mr Pearson about twenty times, and I was killing myself laughing. I told him to stop calling me that.'

In the end, Pearson agreed to a one-year contract. Murray never called him Mr Pearson again. 'He called me other things, though,' Pearson adds, laughing.

For six months, Murray travelled the world with Pearson and his players as they competed on the international squash circuit. His job consisted of collecting match video, tagging matches and, most importantly, compiling a dossier of detailed analytical profiles of the twenty top players in the world, across both genders. After the Tournament of Champions he went to the Hong Kong Open and the World Championships in Giza. In his luggage he carried six cameras and two laptops.

During the matches, Murray would sit next to David Pearson, laptop perched on his lap, and notate the match as it happened. At first, Murray was shy with his new employer, afraid to say boo to a goose. He remained strictly a yes-man. Mike Hughes had drilled into him that to be a good analyst he had to have a good relationship with the coach. So Murray sat quietly as he tagged the match, using notation software developed by Hughes. It was called SWEAT, short for simple winner-error analysis technology.

In the parlance of performance analysis, a performance indicator is a game statistic that is correlated with a successful outcome. There are many such indicators – shot execution, shot selection, rally length – but the one which proved the best predictor of success was the ratio of winners to errors. Winner-to-error ratios described technical proficiency on the court. Frank Sanderson had been the first to demonstrate that if a player had a winner-to-error ratio higher than one for a given match, that player was likely to win the encounter. While Murray was notating the match, Pearson would some-times ask him to plot statistics as simple as the overall ratio for each player, or as complex as the frequencies of winners and errors for each position on court.

The evening before a match, Murray and Pearson would sit down to debate tactics with the players. Murray would talk them through a video of the opponent, highlighting just three of their strengths and three of their weaknesses. 'David was adamant that we had to keep it simple,' Murray explains. 'Not because the players were stupid, but because when you go on court, you can't have too much information in your head.'

Making these motivational videos was a blend of art and science, intended to galvanise the players. Murray could spend as much as a quarter of his working hours just com-piling these bespoke videos. 'It was very detailed,' he recalls.

'I'd make sure that the drumbeat of the song would coincide with the racket hitting the ball. Athletes spent their life either training or watching TV, so if it wasn't Sky Sports quality, they would switch off.'

Murray's first montage was for someone who was about to face the world number one at the Pyramids Tournament in Giza. 'I was feeling quite proud of my work, but he went and lost in twenty minutes. I got back on the bus and asked him if he wanted to keep it. He told me to shove it up my arse. Which was fair enough.'

According to Murray, three key factors made the perfect motivational video. First, they had to use the player's favourite songs, and in particular those that would get the player pumped up. Second, players had to be shown the video at exactly the right time for them – some players liked to see it thirty seconds before the match, others the night before. And finally, of course, they had to have appropriate content.

'I once made a great tape for a squash player, including an amazing shot that she had made,' Murray says. This was for Cassie Jackman, who won the World Open in 1999. When she watched it, she yelled at Murray, 'Bloody hell! Why did you put that on there?' – 'What I hadn't realised was that that shot was from a match that she had actually lost.'

After he'd been on tour for a few months, word started getting around about the British analyst turning up to competitions with a camera and a laptop, a novel sight on the squash circuit. 'I was the secret squirrel with a shitty laptop and camera, tapping away,' Murray says. 'You either loved me or you bloody hated me.'

After six months on tour with England, Murray was asked to present his technical profiles at a national squad camp in Nottingham. He drove up from Cardiff in a battered old

Rover SD1 that he had borrowed from Mike Hughes, wearing a pair of cream chinos and a red shirt. 'That was my idea of dressing up smart,' Murray says. 'I wanted to pretend to be clever and appear like a professional scientific guru.'

On the way, self-doubt and insecurity began to assail him. Who was he to tell these players how to play? They were some of the best players in the world! Murray began to perspire profusely. By the time he arrived at the Park Squash Club, he was a mess, with wet patches at his armpits, his buttocks and his groin. 'Fucking hell!' Paul Johnson said when he saw Murray. 'You bloody pissed yourself!'

'I'm just a bit nervous,' Murray replied meekly. In the meeting room, David Pearson, the support staff and players awaited. The projector wouldn't work and the temperature was stifling.

To compile the technical profiles, Murray had used a different program, called a lapsed-time analysis system. For this, he re-watched all the footage from the tour and tagged every single shot, where it was played and its outcome. The SWEAT system could output about twenty pages of data per match, whereas the lapsed-time system churned out closer to eight hundred, complete with graphics and extra information on players' body language, their weaknesses and their strengths, and the shots preceding the rally's ending stroke. To complete a player profile, Murray had to analyse at least six matches per player. This was the minimum number of matches for the performance indicators that defined a player's style to be statistically relevant.

As he was about to launch into his presentation, a loud voice interrupted him. It was Simon Parke, England's top-ranked player. 'I'm not going to tell these guys my secrets,' he shouted, pointing at the other players. 'I might be playing them next week!' David Pearson tried to appease him, arguing that they were doing this as a team, and that it was for everyone's benefit, but Parke was adamant. 'That's my intellectual property!' he shouted. An awkward silence filled the room. 'He had a point,' Murray concedes. He moved on, and began presenting the opponents' profiles he had compiled, starting with the then world number one, a Scotsman named Peter Nicol.

David Pearson had been Peter Nicol's first coach. Nicol was only sixteen when someone cold-called Pearson and asked him to travel to Scotland to take a look at the young player. 'I was going to hang up on him, but there was something in his voice that made me decide not to,' Pearson recalls. 'I don't know what it was, but it made me want to see what this kid was all about.' In Aberdeen, Pearson met Nicol for the first time. The boy was frail-looking and polite, and seemed to pay close attention to everything Pearson told him. When they played a game together, the first thing Pearson noticed was how well he volleyed. 'He didn't let the ball come off that floor. He was a natural,' Pearson says. 'I knew then that, with the right guidance, he was going to be shit-hot.' Pearson told Nicol that he was willing to train the boy, on the condition that he moved down to Yorkshire.

All of Pearson's players were trained in Harrogate, where Pearson lived with his wife Jo. Players would regularly come to stay at their house and train at the somewhat dilapidated Harrogate Squash and Fitness Centre, with its leaking roof and creaky floorboards. Evenings were usually spent around the dinner table, where family and players talked shop. 'I coach the person first and squash after,' Pearson says. 'I've never fallen out with any of them. In my career as a coach, I've always looked at the longer view. It's about life. It's not about squash coaching.' To Pearson, the game of squash was akin to a form of physical chess, or, as he also put it, 'boxing without brain damage'. He emphasised its technical and tactical ingredients, sculpting his players' skill with patience and deliberation. Winning meant driving an opponent to defeat through tactical superiority.

For eighteen months Nicol trained and lived with Pearson in Harrogate, until he moved to London in 1992 to become a professional squash player. His mother would die that same year, the victim of a rare autoimmune disease called scleroderma. Despite the personal tragedy, Nicol persevered. It was Nicol who, in 1998, finally brought to an end the dominance of Jansher Khan, a legendary player who had been ranked number one in the world for over a decade, and who is still considered one of the best players of all time. Nicol went on to spend sixteen months as the new world number one.

Thin and supple, the left-handed Nicol displayed supreme control and an elegant technique. He was known on the squash circuit as 'The Boss'. Murray was impressed by the ease with which he moved around the court, his movements both graceful and full of intent. Nicol's style of play was methodical and patient. 'He floated around the court like a bumblebee. It was beautiful,' Murray says.

On reviewing the match footage, Murray noticed how Nicol was consistently hitting the ball early, barely letting it bounce off the floor. Doing this meant sacrificing some accuracy, but increased the pressure on his opponent. 'Everyone was saying that he read the game so well', Murray says. 'Actually, what was happening was that he was putting his opponents under so much pressure that he really only left them with a couple of shot options, so they became easy to read.' That year, Nicol had played all the members of the England team on many different occasions and had only lost once.

At the Nottingham meeting, Murray provided Parke with a comprehensive technical profile of Nicol: 'very strong on the front of court ... creates most of his winners from the backhand front corner ... will hit errors from the service box when put under pressure ... gives away 50 per cent of his strongest from the front forehand corner ... average ratio of winners to errors of 33:14.'

The next tournament in the calendar was the British Open in Aberdeen. The two players were expected to face each other in the final, and it was hoped that Parke could beat him again.

Instead, they met in the semi-final and Nicol won in three sets. 'It was a brutal match,' Murray says. 'Afterwards, some of the players were still saying we would eventually learn how to beat him regularly. I was thinking, no fucking chance.'

Pearson had always kept in touch with his old pupil. He was aware that Nicol, now twenty-six and approaching the pinnacle of his career, was increasingly struggling to find sources of funding. Sport Scotland, arguing that Nicol was already earning well because of his success, refused to grant him any funding. Nicol, as the world number one, was earning well, but he had to pay his coach and for accommodation himself. 'If I took everyone I needed to a squash event, I had to make the semi-finals just to break even,' Nicol says. 'I didn't need money, I needed support and professionalism around me.'

Pearson tried to entice him to play for England instead, and was always rebuffed. But Nicol was aware of the support that was now available to the England squad, from physiotherapists and psychologists. He was also aware of the new performance analyst who the SRA had just hired. Murray was now on a contract in Manchester, where the team was based, making him the first analyst to be embedded full time in a team, and he still sat next to Pearson at every match. In January 2001, at that year's New York Tournament of Champions, Pearson begged Nicol, once again: 'Come on, Pete, come play for England.' 'He went quiet for five seconds,' Pearson recalls. 'I knew I had him.'

Finally, that March, after an England Squash meeting, Pearson came out to meet Murray in the car park. 'Peter Nicol is coming to play for us,' Pearson told him. 'You're one of the reasons. He wants your analysis.'

At first, a few of the English players were unwelcoming, so Pearson asked Murray to bring Nicol to the European Championships, even though he wasn't playing at that event.

They met en route, in a bar at the airport. 'Bloody hell!' Nicol said when he saw Murray. 'I remember you now. You were the bloke in the bloody leopard-skin shorts.' The pair immediately hit it off, chatting for hours, a conversation fuelled by beer. 'I guess officially he wasn't supposed to be drinking,' Murray reflects, 'but in my defence, David did tell me to make him feel welcome.'

Nicol recounted the tribulations of his transition to England, and explained how his father, a staunchly patriotic Scotsman, had given his blessing to do whatever it took to become the world's best once more. He told Murray about the insults, the anonymous calls and the death threats. He shared his pain over the loss of his mother. In return, Murray shared his own hurt over his parents' divorce. 'We talked about everything but squash. There was a lot of raw emotion at that time in our lives,' Murray remembers.

At his first tournament for England, the PSA Masters in Hurghada, Egypt, apart from Murray and Pearson, Nicol's entourage included a physiotherapist, a psychologist and three other coaches. In Egypt, Nicol made it to the quarter-finals, where he lost 3–0 against the number seven seed, the Australian David Palmer. 'This is bullshit, it's overkill,' Pearson complained. 'Too many people giving the player too much advice.'

After that, they reverted to a simpler configuration, working as a self-sufficient triad of player, coach and analyst. Murray devoted himself to further scrutinising Nicol's play, watching hundreds of hours of video and producing a detailed report that dissected his game, his movement, his style. After every match, Pearson and Murray would forensically analyse the source of each error. Was it a lack of concentration? Was it poor movement? Was it fatigue? Pearson, who had learned from Murray the importance of a positive winner-to-error ratio, was adamant about keeping errors to a minimum. 'It was a revelation to me that a player's strong points become their weaknesses when they are tired,' Nicol says. 'Shots that are guaranteed winners when I'm fresh become errors when I'm struggling.'

Around that time, Murray, Mike Hughes and one of his students, Julia Wells, had just completed the first comprehensive assessment of how elite players played – what they called the elite template. It included everything from the average number of shots – both winners and errors, categorised by winning and losing players – to the distribution of shots in the court, a breakdown of shot types, and how winning players responded successfully to short and long shots. The elite template was effectively the first blueprint of what it took to win a squash game. Even to a player of Nicol's calibre, this sort of analysis was a revelation.

By January 2002, Nicol had regained his number one spot in the world rankings. One of his priorities then was to find a way to consistently defeat his arch-rival, a Canadian player called Jonathon Power. 'Power was the John McEnroe of squash,' Murray says. Flamboyance aside, the Canadian was also a very deceptive, very fast player. Nicol held a 15–14 record against Power, but had lost their last four encounters. To win, Murray realised that Nicol was going to have to change the smooth, patient way he moved around the court. Power was so aggressive in his offensive play that in order to counteract him Nicol would have to become more explosive and powerful.

Nicol, Murray and Pearson would sit and look at video for hours, the coach pinpointing where an alternative movement across the court could have created a better outcome. They would then go onto the court and try to replicate the new movement. Murray would film the session using a high-speed camera set to two hundred and fifty frames a second, and break down the movement using new software called Quintic. This could track any part of the body and extract real-time measurements for acceleration and velocity, and even measure the angles of joints. The program also allowed them to split the screen and compare movements before and after the coaching intervention, in slow motion. 'When the coaches first saw it, they realised that their job had just changed. They could show to the athlete what they could only perceive in their heads,' Murray says.

Given that squash is not an Olympic sport, the Commonwealth Games are considered its equivalent, the highest level possible in the game. Nicol had won the men's singles in 1988, while still playing for Scotland. That final, against Jonathon Power, had been a theatrical affair, with the Canadian repeatedly swearing at the referee, colliding with Nicol and displaying a creative array of antics, from throwing his racket out of the court to rolling dramatically on the floor. On 31 July 2002, Nicol again faced Jonathon Power in the Commonwealth Games final. Unexpectedly, he lost.

'He was too aggressive,' Murray recalls. 'You could see every sinew in his body.' At the press conference following the match, a dejected Nicol vowed to win the men's doubles with his partner, the British champion Lee Beachill.

The lead-up to the final was just as fractious as might be expected. The semi-final, against Australia, was a highly antagonistic match, with constant altercations erupting between the players. At one point, according to Murray, one of the Australian players thought that Nicol had offended his girlfriend, and the two started shouting at each other. The next thing anyone knew, Murray was about to whack an elite Australian squash player over the head with his laptop, while Nicol was trying to pull him aside, shouting, 'Calm the fuck down!' 'I was embarrassed afterwards,' Murray says. 'When you're an analyst, you're supposed to be objective and you're supposed to be scientific, and I was just swollen with emotion.'

Nicol and Beachill went on to win the final and the coveted gold medal. The ensuing festivities carried on until the early hours. Sharing a breakfast of pepperoni pizza and a bottle of Peroni the following morning, Murray finally asked Nicol what had happened in the final against Power. 'I was over-fired. It was so bad that I wasn't really thinking about the game,' Nicol replied. He had been so eager to prove himself to his new team, the country he now represented. 'I just wanted it too much.'

5

WORST-CASE SCENARIOS

When Dave Reddin was first hired as the strength and con-ditioning coach for the England rugby team, he was given a simple brief: to turn them into the fastest, most powerful team in the game. Their coach, Clive Woodward, wanted England to adopt a style of play that he described as 'total rugby', an open, fluent approach that focused on scoring tries and involved all players at all times. Total rugby was more about playing by ear than playing by the numbers. It avoided pre-set strategies and rigid positions in favour of the players' abilities to adapt to what they saw in front of them: their opponents, the crowd, the weather, the ever-changing state of play. And to achieve total rugby, Woodward needed a team that could play at speed, maintain territorial dominance and physically intimidate the opposition.

In his previous life, Woodward had been a salesman and the owner of a computer-rental business. When he became England's first-ever professional coach in 1997, he managed his team like a CEO, focusing on aspects such as culture and preparation. *Winning!* (exclamation mark included) was Woodward's leitmotif. Everything, from PowerPoint presentations to the screen that divided the showers from the changing rooms, displayed the legend: *WINNING!*

To Woodward, this wasn't just about victory in the field, it was the trait that should define the actions and thoughts of both coaches and players. He had adopted as his personal mantra something that Humphrey Walters, a businessman who in 1997 completed an eleven-month round-the-world yacht race, had said: 'Success comes not because of one thing done a hundred per cent better, but because of a hundred things done one per cent better.'

From another mentor, a dentist turned business consultant, Woodward had borrowed the idea of 'critical non-essentials'. Hundreds of critical non-essentials underpinned Woodward's *Winning!* philosophy: all players had to arrive ten minutes early for meetings; players not selected must always congratulate teammates who were; shirts were changed at half-time to foster a change of mindset; the morning before a match, the BBC Weather Centre would update them on the forecast, wherever in the world they were. These steps were a prerequisite, under Woodward's regime, for being prepared to compete.

Woodward considered Dave Reddin to be one of the best fitness experts in the world. Reddin had previously worked with Woodward on the England under-21 team in 1994, and he would often berate him for his focus on critical non-essentials. 'Why are you wasting your time on all this stuff,' he would ask, 'when we're miles away from where we need to be to compete physically with South Africa, New Zealand and Australia?'

Reddin had a point. In December 1997, after England held the All Blacks to a 26–26 draw in an extremely tense game, players could be found sprawled on the changing room floor, heaving, while others retched into bins. At that stage, the

English team were simply not fit enough to cope with the demands of Woodward's game plan.

When Reddin arrived at Twickenham, he obtained the fitness reports of both New Zealand and Australia. These contained physical results based on tests such as 3km runs, phosphate decrement tests and dynamometric assessments of player contact. When he presented the numbers to the England players, there was a stunned silence. 'I used that to show the gap in performance between where we were and where we needed to be,' Reddin says.

Reddin didn't subscribe to the prevailing wisdom around physical training, particularly periodisation. Periodisation partitioned training programmes into four-year cycles, designed specifically so that athletes could peak when it mattered: at the World Cup or the Olympic Games. The different cycles emphasised different training elements, from aerobic conditioning through to skills acquisition.

Periodisation had been first established in the late fifties and sixties in the Soviet Union. The treatise that laid down its principles was published in 1965 by the Soviet sports scientist Lev Pavlovich Matveyev. As a doctrine, it was very much a product of Soviet political philosophy, which emphasised top-down, centralised planning. Its central pillar, however, was none other than Hans Selye's general adaptation syndrome and the idea that training could be optimised by a cycle of overload, recovery and adaptation.

Although use of periodisation was widespread in the Eastern Bloc, its adoption by Western coaches had been slow. Coaches were initially reluctant to take on methodologies inspired by communism and were particularly sceptical of how much of the Soviet Olympic success in the seventies and eighties was actually due to training, as opposed to the abuse of illicit chemicals. Gradually, however, coaches became persuaded by the merits of the rigorous and meticulous Soviet training, which contrasted with the amateur spirit experienced in the West. By the late nineties, Matveyev's *Periodization of Sport Training* had been translated into English, and the adoption of its methods became widespread.

And yet there was surprisingly little evidence to back up its long-term outcomes. Besides, much of the periodisation approach was focused on endurance sports. The doctrine instructed athletes to start their seasons by building aerobic fitness and to only incorporate high-intensity and strength training later in the season. To Reddin, it made no sense to apply this to rugby. 'We would have to spend a lot of time investing in basic endurance,' he says. 'We didn't do that. We started working on very high intensities. This was certainly not universally accepted.'

When it came to nutrition, Reddin also railed against the common practice at the time: plenty of carbohydrates, little fat, a morsel of protein. 'I couldn't persuade anyone to look at bodybuilding and other ways of approaching nutrition,' he recalls. 'They just completely refuted the fact that the high protein intakes consumed by bodybuilders had anything to do with the results that they achieved.' Under Reddin, England's new regime involved the individualisation of energy intake, specifically timed meals, nocturnal supplements of arginine and amino acids, plus two and a half grams of protein per kilo of bodyweight a day. 'I admit we over-trained them and overdid it with their nutrition,' Reddin says. 'I would describe that approach as like throwing jelly at the wall and hoping some of it sticks.'

In 2001, Ram Mylvaganam got in touch with Woodward to pitch Prozone. The England coach was already very familiar with video analysis. Tony Biscombe, his performance analyst, would film training sessions from a 25-foot tower and record matches from a number of different angles. They would later replay footage to pinpoint how players had been injured. Ground staff planted flags alongside the pitch so that Biscombe could map out the wind direction and brief players who were about to go on. Woodward was focused on doing one hundred things one per cent better, and analysis was no exception.

'I was trying to take the team to a whole new level, and I knew if you have better software, you tend to win,' Woodward says. Prozone consultant Barry McNeill took Woodward to Arsenal Football Club, where Arsène Wenger had just installed their system. At Highbury, McNeill demonstrated the features of the software – how it tracked the players' movements every tenth of a second throughout a match, including how far they ran and at what speed – while Wenger spoke to Woodward about how he used it in his coaching. Woodward, whose first passion was football, and who claims to be a frustrated football player, was a Chelsea fan, so McNeill demonstrated the system using a recent match against Chelsea. 'When I saw how it worked, I just went "wow",' Woodward says. 'I'd never seen anything like it.'

After just five minutes, they no longer needed to pitch the Prozone system to him. He wanted it. Immediately after the meeting, Woodward rang Mylvaganam again and asked for Prozone to be set up at Twickenham.

Within three months, Prozone's programmers had adapted the system to the different geometry of the rugby pitch, and installed twenty cameras around the stadium. They assigned one of their original analysts, Danny Northey, to work closely with Tony Biscombe.

The first game captured by Prozone was against France, on

7 April 2001. 'I couldn't wait for that first game,' Woodward says. 'You saw so many things that we were not doing well, and the things we were.'

Soon, the England team were using the software not only at matches, but every day during training, to obtain data on how quickly the players were arranging themselves into the proper defensive and attack lines. From time to time, Woodward would suddenly stop training to ask what attack had been called, and to check whether the players were lined up correctly. 'They suddenly realised there was no hiding place,' he says. 'They started calling it Big Brother.' Woodward soon had the players using Prozone to analyse both their own performance and that of their opponents, and deliver group presentations on team tactics.

'It changed the real dynamic of how we coached, because historically most coaching is about telling the players what to do. That was very old-fashioned.' This new approach allowed Woodward to study in detail every single team that came to play England at home. 'Suddenly we could see all their data.'

But Reddin required still more information. So he asked Danny Northey whether the Prozone software could output a more detailed assessment of a player's physical data. 'He came to me and said I need to be able to do all these things with the fitness data,' Northey recalls. 'Reddin was really the instigator in changing the way the fitness data was analysed by Prozone, which we then migrated [back] into the football product. He took it to a different level.'

Before Prozone, there was no way of consistently measuring the distances and speeds rugby players ran during a game. The new version of the software included data on the number of sprints, the duration of high-intensity work and recovery periods and the frequency of interventions and player contact in the game. 'That gave us a lens on what we felt were the demands of the game,' Reddin says. 'There was no point in me saying that I wanted to make England the fittest team in the world otherwise.'

Prozone also allowed Reddin to zoom in on the most critical moments of the game, when typically the team was under extreme physical pressure. Reddin called these moments worst-case scenarios. He explains it this way: 'Let's say we're defending for two and a half minutes constantly, and then there is a turnover and we need to make a quick decision. He wanted an insight into the demands of the game not only from an *average* perspective, but most crucially from an *extreme* perspective. 'The extremes are really when good or bad things can happen,' he says. 'That's when the game is breaking up. If you can be competitive in those extreme situations, that's when you win.'

By understanding the demands of worst-case scenarios, Reddin realised that there was a disconnect between how players were being assessed and what it took to prevail during those moments. Players who, for instance, excelled at tests like the 3km run were not necessarily those who had the best work rate in the field. 'All these laboratory-based tests,' Reddin says, '[were] very scientific ... but didn't predict much.'

He introduced tests designed to mimic the physiological states that accompanied worst-case scenarios: highly anaerobic, explosive combinations of speed, muscular effort and body collisions; extreme lactate levels and ventilation rates. He would validate and refine these tests by asking the players if that was how they physically felt when under pressure in a game.

He installed a temporary gym at Pennyhill Park, the England team's training base in Surrey, so that the players could do all their training in one place. They soon nicknamed it the House of Pain. One of Reddin's tests involved racing in teams of three on the rowing machines. The goal was to cover the greatest distance over a period of, for example, thirty-five minutes, with each player only allowed to row for a minute at a time.

'I was not just training their physiology, but their psychology as well,' Reddin says. 'These were a series of maximal efforts in a very competitive environment. What happened was that they went really hard immediately, which is really what we want them to do. Then they have to learn to hang on throughout that period of time because the competitive nature of the drill forces them to do that. It certainly builds physical resilience – but maybe, more importantly, it's building mental resilience.' In short, Reddin wanted to make his players comfortable in very uncomfortable situations.

Sherylle Calder landed at Heathrow one cold morning in autumn 2003 and took a taxi to Pennyhill Park. When she arrived at 7 a.m., Woodward welcomed her, and informed her that they had a meeting in an hour. She assumed she would be seeing Woodward alone, but when she walked into England's War Room – a boardroom style meeting room complete with flip-charts, whiteboards, laptops and a U-shaped table – all staff, coaches and players were present. Calder, who is petite and speaks in a soft, barely audible voice, stood in the middle of the room, surrounded by rugby players, and introduced herself.

'I can make you better players,' Calder told them, 'if you're willing to train your eyes.' Woodward then took everyone outside to conduct the first session. With one finger raised, Calder approached each player, asking them to track her finger as she came towards them, and touched them on the bridge of their nose. This was how she determined their dominant eye, which she then instructed them to cover with an eye-patch. She asked Woodward to resume training as normal. The players floundered, fumbling passes and missing catches.

The next morning, Woodward told Calder that he wanted her in the team.

Calder had grown up in Bloemfontein, in South Africa. As a child, she would often be found playing outside, climbing trees or walking on walls. 'Before my parents went to work in the early morning I was already outside,' Calder says. To challenge herself, she would devise little games like throwing balls against uneven garage doors and walking on walls with her eyes closed. She could beat the boys at school at marbles because, she says, she actually practised playing marbles on her own.

At the age of seven she took up hockey. Later, at Stellenbosch University, male students would challenge her to play against them. 'It seems that all they wanted to do was to beat me,' Calder says. 'I could easily outmanoeuvre them. They only got the ball because they were stronger and shoved me aside.' After finishing her degree, Calder became a player-coach for Stellenbosch.

South Africa under apartheid was banned from taking part in any international competitions. 'I yearned to measure myself against other players in the world,' Calder says. 'I wasn't happy just playing against the same people. They would be doing exactly the same thing year after year. It got boring.'

In 1988, she decided to travel to Europe in the off-season, on her own. 'My parents told me it was my decision,' Calder says. 'They didn't try to stop me. If they had, I probably wouldn't have done it. I was very respectful.'

A couple of days before Calder was due to fly to England, she received a letter from her host telling her that she was no longer welcome because she was South African. Unable to cancel her flight, Calder flew to Luxembourg, where she was supposed to be making the connection to London. Instead, she left the airport and took a five-hour bus trip to Amsterdam, cursing herself the whole way. She had no idea where she was going. She had no money and no credit card. All the twenty-year-old was carrying was a change of clothes in a red rucksack, and a hockey stick.

In Amsterdam, she found a job working in a kitchen and accommodation at the local sports institute. She worked during the day and played in the evenings and at weekends.

The next year, she returned to Europe again, in the off-season. This time she made it to Cologne, where they didn't allow her to play because of her nationality. It was the first time she saw artificial turf, and she stepped onto the pitch just to feel its texture. 'Someone asked me what I was doing,' Calder recalls. 'When I said I was South African, they told me to get my feet off the turf. I wasn't allowed in there.'

Undaunted, she kept flying to Europe year after year, during the winter months, playing hockey in Spain and England, and taking part-time jobs in shops or waiting tables in cafés.

When the international ban was lifted, Calder was selected to play for South Africa at the Olympic qualification tournament in Cape Town in 1995. South Africa came last; a goal from Calder secured their only victory, against Canada. After their final game of the round robin, against Great Britain, Calder received a letter from a supporter who had watched her play: 'I just want to congratulate you. You're the only international hockey player I've ever seen that doesn't run on the field.'

'I did run a lot,' Calder explains, 'but what he was saying was that I always seemed to be in the right place when

something happened.' It wasn't the first time that someone
had noticed her quick reactions and perfect sense of timing.
Players and coaches used to ask her if she had eyes in the
back of her head. Calder had always presumed that everyone
else saw what she saw. It was that letter that finally made her
realise that she saw things differently. Her superior vision was
what gave her an extraordinary ability to anticipate challenges and the skill to tackle them. This realisation led her to
retire from international competition and apply for a PhD.
She wanted to study what made her unique.

She did her PhD at the University of Cape Town, under
the supervision of Tim Noakes, co-founder of the Sports
Science Institute of South Africa, the first of its kind in
Africa. Noakes, a well-respected sports scientist in the area of
endurance physiology, had published the popular book *Lore
of Running* in 1985, and had tested Roger Bannister. Around
the time Calder first contacted him, Noakes was working
on the idea that fatigue is induced by the brain, rather than a
result of physiological changes in the muscles. When Noakes
asked Calder what she wanted to do, she tried to explain to
him the special ability she had. She wanted to understand it.
'He told me he knew nothing about it, but he would teach
me how to do research,' Calder says.

Although it was widely assumed that athletes, in particular
those in sports involving hand–eye coordination, possessed
superior vision, when Calder began her research it was still
unclear how exactly elite athletes' visual skills varied across
different sports. Calder became the first scientist to address
that question, systematically testing more than a hundred elite
international athletes, from cricketers to rugby players. She
used a reaction board – a grid of squares with hidden touch-
sensitive LEDs – to test reaction times and peripheral vision.

Her results were surprising. Across the spectrum of sports,

she found no discernible differences between the different athletes. 'In fact, some of the best players were pretty bad and made crazy mistakes,' Calder says. 'They compensated for their weaknesses by doing the things they were good at all the time. They just did the same thing all the time. They didn't want to go out of that comfort zone.'

It was Calder's belief that forcing athletes out of their comfort zone would induce physiological adaptations that improved their eyes, and by that she meant the gamut of skills encompassed by the ocular system, from peripheral vision to reaction time, from balance to decision-making. Under the pressure of competition, an unfit visual system contracts, becoming unable to focus on new information and impaired by blind spots and tunnel vision. 'My belief was that athletes reach a point where they need all those skills, like in World Cup finals, and they don't have them,' Calder continues. 'I don't think it is necessarily the best team that wins games, but the team that can think correctly under pressure.' Train the eyes, Calder would say, and the hands get better, and so does decision-making. This idea, of course, stemmed from Calder's own experience, but the notion that visual skills could be trained was a novel, and unproven, concept.

To test it, Calder took twenty-nine elite female hockey players and divided them into three groups. One group underwent a specially designed visual awareness training programme. The athletes were instructed in how to keep a neutral head position, which gave them better awareness of their surroundings, and also how to use their dominant eye more effectively. They trained three times a week for four weeks, and were then tested on twenty-two basic hockey skills, from passing to penalty corners. The results validated Calder's idea. The special visual-awareness group showed improvements across twelve categories, whereas a group that had been trained in generic visual skills only improved in two. The control group saw no improvement.

After finishing her studies in 1999, Calder began working with the Pakistan cricket team and the New Zealand rugby team. With the help of a programmer, she designed her own vision-training program called EyeGym, which allowed her to monitor her clients' assiduity remotely.

Clive Woodward heard about Calder from a player who had read an article about how one can 'weight-train' the eyes. 'I literally imagined small dumbbells on your eyelids,' Woodward said. He contacted Calder and asked her to come to England, but she refused, due to her contractual obligations with the All Blacks. 'He was very insistent,' Calder says. 'He probably called me about thirty times.' After her contract expired in 2001, Calder, fed up with the long flights from South Africa to New Zealand, emailed the English coach to enquire if he was still interested in her services.

'Yes,' Woodward wrote back. 'Can you fly here tomorrow?'

Woodward's philosophy of total rugby demanded much more than peak physical conditioning from his players. It also required a complete understanding of the geometry of each move, a multidimensional assessment of positions, paces, angles, depth and distances. They needed to see, absorb and react to all the visual information available to them on the pitch at any given moment, as if Prozone had been downloaded into their brains.

One thing that Woodward realised, looking at Prozone's visualisations of the matches, was how his team was failing to exploit all the free space that was available. Woodward was trying to get the players to run towards that empty space, rather than towards the tackle. 'One of the myths at the time was that there wasn't any space to run on the pitch any more because most teams were playing an extensive game,' Woodward says. 'That, it turns out, wasn't true at all.'

Once, after his players kept insisting that there was no space on the field to attack, Woodward produced a printout of a Prozone freeze-frame taken twenty-four seconds into a match against France. It showed both teams huddled around the ball, the England players as white dots and the French as blue, in a small area of the pitch, with acres of unoccupied space around them. He stuck the picture on a board with the message 'The space is the green stuff. The good guys are wearing white.' The room fell silent. 'End of debate,' Woodward recalls.

When Woodward played Calder a Prozone match visualisation, she immediately said, 'I don't understand rugby, but why are we going that way when all the space is this way?' Woodward laughed. 'You do understand rugby,' he replied. 'That's the problem that we need to fix.'

The issue, Calder discovered, was that the players simply weren't taking in all that was happening around them on the pitch. They tended to look up only when they had the ball in their hands. At all other times, they watched the ball. If players could perceive the space on the rugby pitch correctly, they could create better opportunities in attack. For that, players needed to form a habit of continually looking around the pitch throughout the game. Her job was not just improving their vision, but making them see, understand and communicate about where the space was.

Woodward and Calder's answer was to invent a new exercise called CTC, which stood for 'crossbar, touchline, communicate'. During training, they would hang large banners emblazoned with the letters CTC off the posts. At every phase of play each player was instructed to look at the crossbar, then look at each touchline.

Calder would stand under the crossbar or in other parts of the field, holding up a coloured baton. When they were training, she would raise the baton to see how quickly the players noticed her, having asked them to shout out her name when they did, followed by the colour of the baton. 'When it got really intense, she'd be standing there maybe thirty seconds and no one had looked up,' Woodward says. 'As soon as someone shouted out "Sherylle black" or "Sherylle white" they all looked up and thought, Oh shit, we've been looking at the ball again.'

In November 2002, a year before the World Cup, Woodward gave a press conference in advance of a Test against Australia. During his presentation, he used Prozone to illustrate how New Zealand, a team they had recently beaten, was using what he deemed an illegal method of blocking.

In truth, this was just an excuse. What he wanted to do was unnerve the opposition by showing the world that his team was using a sophisticated analysis program no one else had. The press, who had never seen the software before, were intrigued. 'The Australian coach later told me that he was spooked by it,' Woodward says. 'I definitely would have been annoyed if I found out just before the World Cup that they were using something that innovative that I had no idea about.'

Woodward had by now been using Prozone for two years, employing it to spy on every team England had played at Twickenham in that time. The system had enabled Woodward to see their opponents in terms of the moving geometry of their defence strategies, picking up patterns and identifying individual player roles, allowing him to design potent attacks that were effective against any type of defence. 'The most important thing it did was to remove a lot of the preconceived thoughts about how other people played, especially New Zealand, South Africa and Australia,' Woodward says. 'We suddenly realised they were not different than us . . . It made a big difference, a psychological difference, when we realised that they weren't as good as we thought they were.'

In the final few months before the World Cup, Woodward prioritised fine-tuning his own team, by then considered the best in the world, rather than studying the opposition. In the Tests that preceded the World Cup, for instance, he would often name the team on the Monday before the match, when he didn't have to do so until the Thursday. 'Analysts from other countries would see the line-up and do a heck of a lot of analysis and worry more about us than themselves,' Tony Biscombe says. 'One analyst told me that England was one of the most infuriating teams to prepare analysis for because they didn't know which way we were going to play.' If the way England opened a game wasn't working, the players would just change their approach on the fly. 'We could play any way – we could play a kick and chase, we could play a complete field attack, we could play nine-man rugby, we could play wet-weather rugby, we could play dry-weather rugby, we could do anything,' Biscombe continues. England was a team prepared to deal with any contingency.

At the 2003 World Cup, England was in a pool with South Africa, Samoa, Georgia and Uruguay. When she saw the draw, Sherylle Calder told Woodward that England would beat South Africa at the pool stage, beat France in the semifinals and beat Australia in the final. Woodward was sceptical. But she knew. She had worked with the All Blacks and with South Africa, and she saw something special in England. 'I could predict games,' Calder says. 'I can't explain how. It's something I feel when I walk into a team.'

Calder began avoiding people, because everyone she

encountered would ask her for a prediction. They asked her during the quarter-finals, with England down at half-time against Wales in Brisbane. 'I said, don't worry, we'll win it,' says Calder. 'Everyone relaxed.'

England went on to beat Wales 28–17. Then they beat France in torrential rain and swirling wind. 'When it started to rain, I knew that the French were already beaten,' Biscombe says. 'The French would keep it tight and we would grind them into the ground.'

As Calder had foreseen, England faced Australia in the World Cup final at the Telstra Stadium in Sydney. As the team prepared to go out onto the pitch, Calder went to fetch something from the team room. Woodward was sitting there, pensive. 'I hope he doesn't ask me anything,' Calder thought.

'What do you think?' Woodward asked.

'We're okay. We'll win,' Calder replied.

'Okay. I can relax now!'

By the end of the second half, the score was 14–14. In extra time, with thirty seconds to go and the score at 17–17, England's Matt Dawson made a fifteen-metre dash into the Australians' 22-metre line. This started a routine that England had practised relentlessly. The play unfolded through the middle of the field, in a zig-zag pattern. Dawson was one of the players most adept at using Prozone and, from the analysis, he knew that the Australian defence would focus on marking fly half Jonny Wilkinson, giving him free space to exploit. It was a decoy tactic: as the Australians charged down on Dawson, he was able to pass the ball to a now-unmarked Wilkinson in the pocket for the drop goal.

The pass was poor, forcing Wilkinson, with only twenty-six seconds to play, to change his body angle and kick with his right foot instead of his dominant left – and score. Wilkinson was one of the most diligent students of Calder's science, logging many hours with EyeGym and practising his vision skills assiduously. He once told her that he used to just get the ball and kick, but now, when he received the ball, he had at least three decisions to make, and he made sure to make the right one.

6

THE RIVER IGNORANCE

At the end of 2003, Stafford Murray stood in front of an audience at the national strength and conditioning conference at the University of East Anglia in Norwich. Next to him was Michael Hughes, son of Mike Hughes. Just like his father, Michael was short and fit, with a sharp intellect and an engaging, relaxed manner. Both men were wearing dark polo shirts, with the slogan 'Making the Best Better' printed on their sleeves, and the acronym EIS emblazoned across the front.

A year earlier, Murray had been contacted by a manager at the new English Institute of Sport and asked if he would be interested in applying for a job there. He had no idea what this Institute was supposed to be. It had only just been launched, as a new initiative designed to provide sports scientists to any national sport teams that requested their support.

Murray was interviewed by Alex Newton, the EIS manager, and Scott Drawer, a researcher who had just been assigned to head the Institute's Research and Innovation programme. They asked him what his KPIs were going to be. Murray didn't know what that meant. Then they asked him about his operations strategy. Murray had no clue. 'At the time, I didn't understand the business talk at all,' Murray says. All he knew was how to get along with coaches and present the numbers in a way that those coaches could understand. He got the job as the EIS's first performance analyst.

When the EIS advertised for a second performance analyst a year later, Mike Hughes told his son to consider applying. When Michael was growing up in Cardiff, his father would give him simple analysis projects to do during the school holidays, and so Michael had been using squash systems and concept keyboards long before Murray ever had. Michael had just done an eight-week stint of work experience with Murray at the EIS, and had enrolled on the new performance analysis master's at UWIC. He hadn't even thought about applying for the EIS job, but his father encouraged him to do it just for the experience.

The evening before the interview, Murray and Michael went out to the local pub. Murray told Michael that many of his father's older and more experienced PhD students had also applied for the position. 'I don't think you're going to get the job,' Murray said, nicely, for Hughes was like a nephew to him. 'You don't have a chance.' They duly proceeded to get inebriated. 'I played good cop at the interview and tried to sway the panel to give my mate the job,' Murray says. 'But there was no need: he absolutely smashed it out of the park. I was so proud.'

Their original office at the EIS had been a Portakabin in Manchester city centre. Shortly after, they were moved to an office at the Sportcity complex in east Manchester, built to host the 2002 Commonwealth Games. Among other features, Sportcity boasted a new National Squash Centre, complete with a moveable glass-walled show court; the City of Manchester Stadium; and the National Cycling Centre.

'It was a melting pot. You would go to the gym and there would be Chris Hoy doing press-ups and Peter Nicol on the treadmill,' Murray says. 'Well, I didn't go to the gym much. I preferred the sauna. Some coaches found me there sleeping at 11 a.m., sweating out a hangover.'

Murray, who was about to get married, tried to keep in shape by cycling to work. His habitual attire was steel toe-capped work boots, large woolly socks, a big jumper, a woolly hat and shorts, even in winter. 'I found cycling in trousers really uncomfortable,' Murray says. 'I would sometimes over-take Chris Hoy on the red light. The cycling coaches used to joke, "There's Murray, the future of the cycling programme."'

Murray and Hughes occupied a small office with two desks, VHS decks and a video editing suite. Their office was always impeccable, apart from the distinct whiff of curry and beer, the staple diet of performance analysts. Murray would always tell Hughes or anyone else who came into the office to leave it spick and span. 'Some of the boys would take the piss by messing up the angles of the papers on the desk and hiding the analysis tapes, which was pretty annoying,' Murray says. 'It's not just about my OCD. It was about setting a good impression for the coaches.'

Apart from a favourable impression, what coaches also needed was an education. Few were familiar with perfor-mance analysis. And so, for a year, Murray and Hughes travelled the country meeting with different sports teams, selling their services. 'If you're already producing the best in the world – sorry, we'll go elsewhere,' Murray would tell them. 'We don't want any glory, we're simply here to help you make informed judgements rather than relying on mys-tical opinion and intuitive guesswork.'

They called it the EIS performance analysis roadshow. This involved demonstrating simple proofs of concept, such as film-ing a relay team with high-speed cameras and using tracking software to monitor weightlifters' technique. Along with this, they had a few concrete case studies: a before/after comparison of Peter Nicol's backhand using a split screen on Quintic after he had suffered an injury; injury prevention through gait analysis and tracking the angular asymmetries on the torso; and opponent profiling and elite templates for squash players.

All the detailed examples, at least at the outset, were based on squash, but the higher-level concepts of performance analysis could apply to any sport. One of the first slides in their presentation was a diamond-shaped diagram:

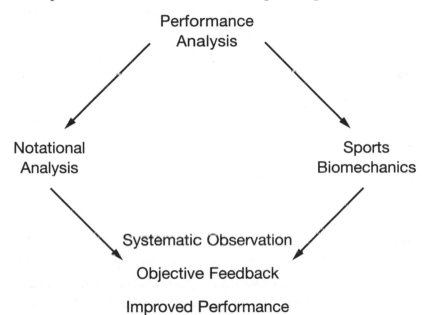

This was followed by the '6 Is' slide, a concept that had been concocted in a pub in Didsbury after a few too many drinks. 'At the time, it was like buzzword bingo and everyone had an acronym for everything,' Murray says. 'So we came up with the six Is.'

It went something like this: a slide depicted a river, called Ignorance, and its banks on either side. On one of the banks was a monkey, and the opposite bank was named 'Sport'.

'This is the Analysis Monkey,' the analysts would explain. 'He has to cross the River Ignorance to reach the other bank, where Sport is. To do that we have to build a bridge with the six building blocks.' These represented the methodology of performance analysis: Introduction, Irrefutability, Indicators, Implementation, Improvement and Impact.

'Some of those were a bit tenuous,' Hughes admits. 'Basically, we were saying if you don't use analysis, you won't cross the River Ignorance . . . It was absolutely ridiculous.'

Then, there were the quotes they used:

'If you always do what you've always done, you'll always get what you've always got.'

'Statistics are like a mini skirt . . . they give you an idea . . . but they hide the best bits.' – Ebbe Skovdahl, ex-manager of Aberdeen FC

'If it ain't broke, don't fix it.' – Murray's grandfather

'We weren't exactly popular,' Murray says. 'Sports didn't have much money and we at the Institute were being given Lottery money. We would turn up with our black T-shirts, telling them how to do things and they're like, "Fuck off. We've been doing this for twenty years."'

In the early days, one of the key goals of the roadshow was to break down the coaches' perceptions of their work. A lot of them saw performance analysis as questioning what they did, as opposed to complementing their coaching. It was an educational process, and the reception they received ranged from welcoming to hostile.

The strength and conditioning coaches, for instance, were impressed when Murray demonstrated how they could use video analysis to look at weightlifting technique and track the biomechanics of the movement. On the other hand, some athletics coaches thought that it was all mumbo-jumbo. 'Once they told me we had to sing for our supper,' Murray says. 'I don't sing for anyone's supper, mate.'

It was during their roadshow that one day Murray and Hughes walked into the National Cycling Centre, which adjoined the EIS centre. Although the British cycling team were based there, this was the first time they had ever been inside, and they were struck by the cavernous weirdness of the velodrome, with its steep banked turns and oval geometry, and were baffled by the esoteric rules of events like the keirin and the Madison. As they watched a training session, they realised they had no clue about what was going on. The whole sport seemed impervious to any sort of analysis. Murray and Hughes looked at each other, at a loss.

The performance director of British Cycling at the time was Peter Keen, a methodical sports scientist with a penchant for experimentation and an obsession with data. Having been in his role since 1997, Keen was taking steps to modernise an underfunded, understaffed team with no adequate training infrastructure. Moreover, no British cyclist had won a gold medal between the team pursuit in 1908 and Chris Boardman's individual pursuit in 1992.

In 1996, after Lottery funding was announced, Keen put together his own World Class Performance Programme, an ambitious and detailed plan. He stated his vision very clearly: to make Great Britain the world's top cycling nation by 2012. Few believed it was possible. When he gave presentations, people would tell him, 'You're quite good, but this is nonsense. You're talking out of your arse.'

Keen told the team's physiologist, a man called Simon Jones, that if the World Class Performance Programme was to work, they would need some sort of performance benchmark for their cyclists. A man with an intense manner and a piercing intellect, Jones had joined British Cycling in 1995, on the basis of a job interview where he mentioned a theoretical concept – critical power, the highest power average a cyclist could hold for a particular time period – which none of the cycling directors had heard of at the time. 'They couldn't ask me any questions about it – that's why I got the job,' Jones says.

When Jones joined, British Cycling had around ninety cyclists on its roster, and there was little clarity about how athletes were selected to compete. 'There wasn't anything that linked results to performance,' Jones recalls. 'Racers would win national competitions, go to international competitions and get their arses kicked.'

Keen was adamant that they needed to draw a line in the sand. So he devised a laboratory test that set a minimum performance standard that athletes needed to hit in order to be accepted into the programme and receive funding.

The test was a one-minute maximum power test on the ergometer, a stationary bike equipped to measure power output. The power result from the test allowed Keen to calculate a parameter they called the 'fitness index'.

Initially, the threshold for selection was based on estimates that accounted for different ages, weights and events. A top-ten endurance cyclist, for instance, would need to record a fitness index of between 25 and 30. To compete in the Tour de France, the fitness index was around 32. Anything below these standards and the cyclist was out.

'People would come in and shit themselves because they knew their livelihood and their selection for the national team depended on that bloody ergometer,' Jones says. They began culling a large number of cyclists from the programme.

Although the test was simplistic, and more than a little controversial, it provided athletes with a clear selection target. 'We had people sending letters to the Prime Minister, complaining about discrimination,' Jones continues. 'There was a lot of upset and to some I was the evil person.'

In 1998, with two years to go before the Sydney Games, Jones took over as coach of the men's team pursuit squad. Keen had promoted him because, according to Jones, he wanted to start employing a different type of coach, more knowledgeable about physical conditioning: 'Overnight I became the national coach, without any experience. Most of the athletes were older than me. I used to be the lab rat, making them suffer, now I was the track coach and they could clearly tell this guy knew fuck-all about a lot of the things that mattered to them.'

Then, riders used to train long hours on the road to develop endurance, and Jones noticed that, although they were fit, they didn't have the necessary speed and power to be competitive in team pursuit. He overhauled their training, prioritising developing power on the track instead of endurance on the road. 'We understood what it took to win and we trained specifically to the demands of the event,' Jones says. 'It seems obvious now but it was counterintuitive at the time.' He still remembers fondly the 2000 Olympics, when the British team took an unprecedented silver medal in the team sprint. 'The highlight of my coaching career,' he says. 'It sounds sad because how we approached the thing was, looking back, really simple.'

After the Sydney Games, Peter Keen hired a Canadian physiologist called Andrea Wooles to replace Jones as the team's lab technician. Wooles's fiancé was a soigneur at the cycling programme, but other than dating a cyclist, she had no knowledge of the sport.

Instead, she was hired based on her strengths as a researcher.

Wooles had a master's in exercise physiology, and had written her thesis on the effects of exercise on tissue swelling post-breast cancer surgery. She had been taught by Alan Martin, a scientist who validated body composition analysis by dissecting cadavers and separately weighing the fat, muscle and bone. 'Instead of assuming that the measurements people were doing were accurate, he went to Belgium and took people apart,' Wooles explains. 'He gave me an A+ in research methods.'

During her master's, Wooles had experimented with a new type of bicycle power meter called an SRM (Schoberer Rad Messtechnik, or 'Schoberer's bike measurement technology'). These were mobile devices, which could be installed in bikes to measure the power that cyclists produced when training or competing. Wooles's experience was useful to Peter Keen, as he had just acquired 130 SRMs.

On her first day at work, Keen took Wooles down to a room in the bowels of the velodrome. He showed her a broken SRM and asked her to fix it by the time he was back from the Sydney Olympics. 'He left the following day,' Wooles says. 'Here I was, with this busted piece of equipment. I turned on the computer, and the program was not only in DOS, but in German, so I had to figure out how to read German to get this stupid thing working.'

The power meter had been invented by Ulrich Schoberer, a German cyclist and engineer. The device measured power, cadence, heart rate and speed. The first version was the size of a cereal box. Once, while out racing himself, Schoberer's SRM box had dropped off his handlebars and so he stopped, mid-race, to pick up the pieces. That was when he realised that he was more interested in his invention than he was in the actual race. So he promptly retired as a cyclist, and dedicated his life to developing the device.

'The SRM was the most elegant and beautiful engineering

solution that you could come up with,' Wooles says. 'The perfect example of German engineering.'

The British team was one of the first, after the Germans, to use power meters on their bikes. For Keen, a logic-driven man, the ability to measure physiological effort and quantify performance on the track, rather than in a sterile laboratory, was paramount. Before this, cyclists had had to rely only on monitoring heart rate, speed and perceived exertion, all of which were easily influenced by environmental factors that had nothing to do with performance: warm or cold weather, caffeine, sleep quality, stress levels, hydration levels, allergies, nutrition and so on.

Power output, on the other hand, was truly objective. It was the perfect tool for performance-based training.

Soon, it became Andrea Wooles's job not only to calibrate the SRMs but also to run the laboratory tests, ensuring that testing protocols were consistent and results accurate. 'Before, there was no standardisation, no repository for the data, no historical records. It hadn't been calibrated in God knows how long, so there was no faith in the numbers,' Wooles says. 'Within a year, people went from asking, "What's wrong with the SRM today?" to "What's wrong with the athlete today?"'

Wooles quickly realised that her job was to understand what the coaches wanted to know, and what they had difficulty believing. 'For instance, for long road rides, the SRM allowed one to see how many beats of your heart it took to increase your power output by a watt,' she explains. 'How many watts can you produce if you're riding along at a hundred and fifty beats per minute? That relationship changed with your fitness. It also changed when you were dehydrated, because the heart rate would go up even though the power remained the same.'

At that point, the cycling programme only had between

forty and fifty athletes. 'I had some athletes come in four times to try and make this minimum standard, and they'd miss it by two watts,' Wooles says. 'If they've been training for this test and that was the best they could do, I guess they shouldn't be on the team.' By then, the tests had evolved into a regular method of evaluating performance. If something wasn't quite right with a rider, coaches could bring them in to the laboratory.

'I knew nothing about cycling, but I slowly started to understand the data-driven nature of it,' Wooles says. 'These guys weren't scared to look at what was really going on, and what you really needed to do was to win and work back from that, rather than the kind of traditional European approach of well-you-just-do-what-everybody-else-has-always-done.'

In addition to the SRMs the velodrome had a timing system called 'Timy' that could be wirelessly plugged into speed traps mounted on the track, and would print out little receipts with the riders' times and speeds during training sessions. The Timy didn't record the data digitally, however, so Wooles would sit beside the track, configure the timing system, write the rider's initials and their SRM power outputs on to the tiny printouts, and then glue them into a big red folder. When Murray and Michael Hughes visited British Cycling in 2003 to talk about how a performance analyst could assist them, they were met by Andrea Wooles. She listened to their spiel, and then gave them her red folder.

'Here are all the numbers from the past four years,' she said. 'Can you professionalise that?'

'Is she serious?' Hughes thought. 'What on earth are we supposed to do with this? It's just absolute gibberish.'

In August 2003, Murray assigned young Michael Hughes to be the first performance analyst to work full time at the

Manchester Velodrome. Peter Keen had left a few months before. His successor, Dave Brailsford, a former business manager who had been hired as operations director by Keen in 1997, was equally supportive of performance analysis.

'We had a lack of history in terms of cycling. There were no professional cycling coaches, so we hired smart sports science graduates,' Brailsford says. 'You might say that, with hindsight, was a great decision. We were lucky to have this group who came up with all kinds of weird and wonderful ideas. Nobody ever said that something was not going to work.'

When Michael Hughes joined British Cycling he started by setting up a system that could record every practice session with a video camera; they would then analyse the footage with specialised software. When the team competed abroad, Andrea Wooles would film their races covertly from the stands with a handheld camera. 'We used to be chased away by the stewards all the time,' Wooles says. 'If you looked official enough you had a chance of going unnoticed.' Back in Manchester, she would hand over the tapes to Murray and Hughes, whose job was to convert them into digital files and sort them into different categories, a process which could take days as the computers kept crashing.

Team pursuit was considered the blue-riband event of track cycling. Two teams of four riders race over sixteen laps, a distance of 4km. The teams start on opposite sides of the velodrome, and the riders follow each other in line. The leading rider works the hardest, as he absorbs most of the air resistance, while the others ride in his slipstream. About every other lap, as the team enters the banking, the first rider peels off the front, moves up the track and drops down to the rear of the line. The winning team is the first to get their third rider across the finishing line.

The longer he worked with British Cycling, the more Hughes became involved in helping Simon Jones, the team pursuit coach, analyse the demands of the event, using technology to break it down into fine-grained detail. 'It was the most coachable event,' Hughes says. 'There's a technical component in terms of the turns on the front, how you change, get on the back, stay in line, close to the wheel, and keep your body position aerodynamically. Then there's a tactical component in terms of turns on the front, who is doing a lap, who is doing a lap and a half, in what order, how to get the best out of the riders, who should follow who.' Hughes noticed that Simon Jones had been using the finish line, in the middle of the straight, as the reference point for lap times. Since the riders switched positions at the turns, this meant that he didn't know how much each rider was contributing individually.

Instead, during competitions, Hughes started sticking gaffer tape around the bends of the tracks, on the first and third corner, to give him a visual marker from which to record the timings as the riders passed that point. 'We weren't supposed to do that,' Hughes says. 'But other teams didn't complain, because eventually they started using our tape to get their own timings.'

With timings now being measured from banking to banking rather than from straight to straight, Hughes and his colleagues could align them with the power data from the SRMs and build individual profiles for each rider. Now, finally, they knew what the power was for each of the turns, whether a rider sped up or slowed down, and how consistent they were.

'That's when we realised how punchily they'd been riding and how much damage it was doing,' Hughes says. 'They always thought that the guy at the front needed to go as hard as possible, but we found that accelerating and decelerating were really damaging and really fatigued the athletes.'

This led to a change of tactics: riders were to keep to a schedule of even splits and constant speed. After each lap, Simon Jones would place himself on the finishing line, to signal to the riders whether they were keeping to the plan. Maintaining a steady pace with constant speed was crucial.

Andrea Wooles replaced Jones as the in-house laboratory expert, and assisted him on the track. 'He had this constant cynicism,' Wooles says. 'You couldn't come to him with half-baked ideas, you had to come with fully formed, strong ideas and be willing to fight for them, because he was going to say no anyway. But when you finally persuaded him, it was so rewarding because he was absolutely committed to it.'

By then, the simple laboratory testing that had caused so much upheaval in the early days had evolved into a more sophisticated evaluation of performance. The power meters, along with other technologies such as video analysis and aerodynamic testing, allowed coaches like Simon Jones and analysts like Mike Hughes to create a systematic analysis of the numbers – lap times, cadences, power outputs, drag factors – that their riders could produce. They would also do an in-depth analysis of the demands of the event. In other words, the numbers their riders needed to hit to win races. 'We would go to the nth degree in terms of truly understanding what winning looked like,' Brailsford says. 'We spent more time than any other team in the world doing that particular work.'

They studied competitors, scrutinising opponents' times by splits and understanding how they trained. Then they set target times not just for the whole race, but for each lap and for the transition of the lead rider from the front to the back. They then analysed how much power the riders would need and what sort of metabolism they would require. To reduce drag, tyres were benchmarked and riders tested in a wind tunnel. 'We set out with our goal time and then started breaking down the problem,' Jones says. 'We just kept asking questions like, how can we reduce drag? Or, what's the ideal way to go around the track? It's a tedious process but it changed the programme.'

Jones remembers modelling Bradley Wiggins's performance in the individual pursuit. He estimated that, to win the event, Wiggins would need to cover the 4km in 4 minutes and 15 seconds flat. To do that, Wiggins would have to be able to produce 575 watts on the ergometer.

'It was super simple – it's almost embarrassing to call it modelling,' Jones says. 'He was thirty watts off that mark and I convinced him that if he hit that number he would win the race.' Of course, Jones knew it wasn't that simple. So many factors could affect the outcome of the race. 'We did loads of ergos and one day he hits 575. It was just me and him in the lab. He was ecstatic, like he had won the gold medal. Because I had convinced him that he was going to! I was thinking, Fuck, what if he loses now?'

At the Athens Olympics in 2004, the effort paid off. There, Wiggins won the individual pursuit in a time of 4:16.304. This was one of two gold medals the cycling team earned at that Olympics, with the team pursuit riders winning silver.

In March 2005, Michael Hughes flew to Los Angeles with the team for the Track Cycling World Championships, his first time attending as an accredited performance analyst.

Two days before a major competition, Jones would become irascible. 'You could set your watch by his temper,' Wooles says. 'He would always be unmanageable because he cared so much about the result.' Once, Jones and Murray even got into fisticuffs in a corridor at the Velodrome. 'Your data is shit!' Jones reportedly shouted at Murray.

'He was accusing us of not doing our job and that we weren't committed,' Murray says. 'I said, bullshit. It didn't help that later my analysts got drunk and missed the bus to the airport on the final morning of the World Championships. Our saving grace was that two members of the leadership team missed the bus as well. And one even lost his passport.'

In Los Angeles, even with Bradley Wiggins absent, the team pursuit squad was riding faster than ever in practice sessions. Jones didn't trust the numbers, so he ordered Wooles to measure the track with a tape measure and double-check the input numbers on the timing system. 'It turned out there was nothing wrong,' Wooles says. 'They were just going that fast.'

Great Britain were top of the World Championships medal table that year, with four gold medals, a silver and a bronze. Peter Keen had predicted that they would be ranked number one by 2012, and people had called him crazy. As it turned out, his prediction, rather than delusional, had been too conservative.

7

THE LAST SHOT

In February 2004, Murray and Pearson flew to the Tournament of Champions in New York with a contingent of England players, including Peter Nicol. A few hours before the first round, Nicol asked Murray if Pearson would be attending his match.

'No, he's across town with another player,' Murray replied.

'Fuck. I need DP. I'm nervous,' Nicol said.

Nicol won his match comfortably, but swiftly retired to his hotel room afterwards. Murray called him and asked if he was coming out to dinner.

'I can't even get out of bed,' Nicol replied, so Murray and Pearson brought his dinner to his room. Nicol was feeling cold and shivery and looked feverish. He told Pearson that he couldn't play another game. The coach told him not to worry; he would feel better soon.

Nicol didn't leave his room for the next two days. It transpired that he had bronchitis. They considered forfeiting the tournament, but they were aware of the implications that would have for Nicol's world ranking. He would have to play.

It was obvious that Nicol was not going to be able to play

his typical relentless game of accumulated pressure, constantly moving his opponent around, tiring him out. He was too weak. So Pearson told him that he would have to play in a very different style. He had to keep rallies short and try to win matches in less than an hour – any longer and he would begin struggling to breathe. The plan was to attack the ball whenever possible, unpredictably. 'Instead of waiting, as soon as he had chance to go for a winning shot, he'd bloody go for it,' Murray says.

And so he did. In the second round, Nicol beat Shahier Razik of Canada in forty-seven minutes; in the quarter-final, he beat Nick Matthew of England in forty.

After each game, Nicol would meet Murray in the hotel bar, eat curry for dinner, drink White Russians until 3 a.m., sleep all day, wake up, sit down with Murray and Pearson to watch footage and analyse his opponent, and then play again. They dispensed with practice sessions entirely.

On a good day, Nicol could beat anyone in the world, bar the player he was going to face in the semi-final: his old nemesis, Jonathon Power. Murray, having profiled Power during the tournament, sat with Nicol and relayed the game plan to him: counter-drop Power in the front right-hand corner whenever possible. Nicol feared that such a simple plan would benefit Power. Instead, it took him by surprise. 'He had no idea what Peter was doing,' Murray says. 'He was slotting winners from everywhere.'

Nicol went on to win the final against his former compatriot John White. It was the only tournament in his career that he won without dropping a set.

'It confirmed to me that the stuff we had been doing worked, from a scientific point of view,' Nicol says. 'From a personal perspective, it justified all that I had been through.'

As soon as Nicol received the trophy and prize money, he
turned to Murray and Pearson and said, 'Right, we've been
going to the same bar, having the same meal for over a week.
Now, let's celebrate.'

By then, the three men had become inseparable. On tour,
they would share meals and hotel rooms. They would spend
hours together on the squash court and hours afterwards
talking over drinks – about politics, religion and truth.
To Murray and Nicol, Pearson was a father figure. And in
Murray, Nicol had found a brother at a time in his life when
he most needed one, still conflicted about the sacrifices he
had made to become a squash player, and still angry about
the death of his mother. At Murray's house in Wilmslow, he
would sometimes punch doors and throw objects. He would
get angry and he would cry. 'Once he rugby-tackled me into
a flower bed in Bermuda,' Murray recalls. 'David and I were
his punch bags, really.' But they were also his team and his
closest family.

A few months after the New York tournament, Murray
and Nicol had climbed to Everest Base Camp to raise money
for charity in memory of Nicol's mother. 'We took seven
days walking up and three days coming down,' Murray says.
'He was probably one of the fittest men on the planet. I was
smoking fifteen rollers a day. I was shitting myself, nervous I
couldn't keep up.' On the way up the mountain, they saw a
shack where a family lived with three kids. They stopped and
talked to them. A week later, walking down, they noticed
that the shack had burned down and the family were outside,
sitting on a log. 'We were like, "Bloody hell, aren't we lucky".
Just being up there and the bloody two of us sat in the fucking
freezing cold with a bowl of soup in a shed. It just made us
realise that, fuck, it's not all about being the best in the world,
is it? It's about survival. Pete cried a lot, I bloody cried a lot.

We bared our soul to each other about life and about people dying. It was highly emotional.'

September 2004 was the last time Nicol occupied the world number one ranking. At the age of thirty-one, he was beginning to struggle with the rigours of the international squash circuit, and so had been curtailing appearances at tournaments. He knew his career was coming to an end, and seemed at peace with that. 'He is finally happy in his own skin,' Pearson would say.

But Nicol still wanted to make a final push. He had decided he was going to put everything on the line to win one final match, an apt climax to one of the most extraordinary careers in the history of squash: a triumph at the 2006 Commonwealth Games in Melbourne.

By then, however, Peter Nicol was no longer able to cope with long, punishing training sessions, so he adopted a method invented by Murray called replication ghosting. Murray had come up with the idea in 2004, when the former world champion Cassie Jackman was trying to return to competition after back surgery. Although her coach believed that she had regained her fitness, she had lost her confidence. 'One day she said off the cuff that she would love to be able to perform like she had when she won the World Open,' Murray says. So Murray and Hughes came up with the idea they called 'replication ghosting'. This involved projecting the video of the match onto the front wall of the squash court from the balcony. The image covered the entire wall, immersing the player in a virtual reality.

'It was like shadow boxing, but exactly replicating the match play,' Murray says. 'There was no guesswork.' Players could play against any opponent, ghosting the movements in the match – the same movements they would be making, were they playing in the real match. Physically, they would cover the same distance. Their heart rate would be almost the same.

For two years, Nicol had been preparing to reach the Commonwealth Games in peak condition. However, when he arrived in Melbourne in March 2006, he was in dismal form, jet-lagged and cranky.

'He was slamming his racket on the floor and behaving like a prima donna,' Pearson says. On a few occasions, Nicol walked away from training. Once, during a practice game, Lee Beachill had deceived Nicol by feigning a straight drive and then changing his swing at the last moment to a 'boast', a shot where the ball is directed at the side wall. This threw Nicol the wrong way. He started shouting and then stormed off. On the bus back to the hotel Beachill pointed into the distance and said, 'Hey, Pete! There's the shot you missed!'

'Fuck off,' Nicol replied, and put his headphones on.

'What you usually find is that athletes struggle before an event – they're like two-year-olds with a rattle,' Pearson says. 'But when the event starts, there's a switch of mentality.'

When Nicol saw the draw, he visibly relaxed and regained his confidence. 'He would tell me every day he was going to win the tournament,' Pearson says.

In the semi-finals, a security guard stopped Murray as he entered the venue and informed him that laptops and cameras were no longer allowed inside. With half an hour to go until the match, Murray ran to the front desk, handed them a CD and asked them to print off two hundred copies of his squash court diagram. Instead of sophisticated computer analysis, Nicol would be looking at sheets of paper between games. He then went to fetch a camera that he had previously hidden under a plant pot as a contingency and shoved it down the front of his tracksuit. Michael Hughes, who was in Melbourne as an analyst for the England cycling team, sat next to Murray and placed the camera between his legs, covered with a towel, and turned it on. Murray put the red pen behind his left ear and the blue behind his right.

The final took place on 20 March 2006. Nicol had progressed easily through the earlier rounds. When he walked out to the court for the gold-medal match, he waved at his team, while a crowd of three thousand Australians booed him and screamed the name of his opponent – the world number one, David Palmer. Nicol spun his racket on his finger and smiled. He was about to play his last major final, and Murray had never seen him so at ease.

Palmer's profile indicated that he played most of his winning shots – nearly a third of them – in the front left-hand corner of the court. This also happened to be one of the weak points in Nicol's game. 'We came up with a very simple tactic,' Murray explains. 'Avoid all of Palmer's strengths. Just don't give him that front left corner.' In the days before the final, Nicol relentlessly trained his forehand counter drop shot, tailoring his game to neutralise Palmer's.

Nicol considers the following hour and fifty-five minutes to be the best performance of his career. Every time Palmer hit a winner, Murray marked a red cross on his piece of paper. If Nicol hit a winner he marked a blue cross. 'A pattern started emerging,' says Murray. 'It was just the same as all these amazing data visualisations and dashboards that we have now, but it was happening with pen and paper.'

In game 4, the score remained at 5–2 for a few minutes, during a furious exchange of winning shots from both sides. Then Nicol played a boast into the front right-hand corner and Palmer fell to his knees trying to reach it. The score was

6–2. Nicol let out a scream, fist clenched, as Palmer slowly regained his composure.

'That's when I knew the match was won,' Pearson recalls. 'There was no way he was going to lose now.'

Two stewards entered the court to mop up the sweat-drenched floor. Then Nicol played another winner to the front left-hand corner. 7–2. Another winner followed, a forehand counter drop shot into the same corner. 8–2.

After the final winner, Nicol sank to his knees, then came to the back of the court, banged on the glass, pointed to everyone in the England team and kissed the badge on his shirt. 'He wasn't kissing it because it was England,' Murray says. 'He was kissing it because of the people there, what they represented.' This was the culmination of all the work they had done together, and of all the times they had spent together. 'Fuck, this is amazing,' Murray thought, tears welling up. 'He's found himself. It's beautiful to see.'

That summer, his goals achieved, Peter Nicol retired.

8

THE FORMER ROWER TURNED CYCLIST

One day in 2006, shortly after the Commonwealth Games, a rower named Rebecca Romero came to see Dan Hunt. Hunt was the coach of the women's cycling endurance team. British track cyclists had had a successful Games, with the endurance and sprint teams claiming five gold medals. The medal tally of the women's endurance team, however, had been a mere bronze.

Even that medal surprised Hunt. When he had taken the job as coach in September 2005, it was obvious that his cyclists lacked aptitude and had a lackadaisical approach to training. 'I was ecstatic when we won that medal,' Hunt says. 'It meant I wasn't going to get fired.'

His manager, however, made it clear to Hunt – a physiologist who had been promoted to national coach without any previous experience of high-performance cycling – that he still had to prove himself.

On returning to Manchester, he made the decision to dismiss the entire team, except for Emma Jones, who had won the bronze. 'I took no pleasure in it,' Hunt says. 'It's a horrible thing to do, but I'm not sure how seriously they were taking it.' With only two and a half years to go until the Beijing Olympic Games, Hunt didn't have a team.

He started looking, and found Rebecca Romero.

Romero's physique was typical of a rower: broad powerful shoulders, strong legs. She had rowed since the age of seventeen, and racing in the women's quadruple sculls at the Athens Olympics had been her favourite experience. 'It was the best crew I had ever rowed with, we were all confident to win gold,' she said. 'However, when we were in the final we messed up the first quarter of our race and that was our strength.'

To Romero, the silver medal was just a reminder that she had lost the gold. She stopped enjoying the sport. Her despondency was aggravated by a recurring back injury. She chose to retire, and was considering a career in marketing when Dan Hunt called her. A mutual friend had told him about Romero. Would she consider taking up a different sport, he wondered.

At the gym at the EIS, Hunt first asked Romero to perform a standard ramp test on the ergometer. The test starts at around 85 watts, an easy pace, and then gradually increases in steps of 15 watts every minute, until the athlete can no longer pedal.

Romero pedalled for five minutes, her cheeks flushed and her face doused in sweat. Hunt thought she had at least another couple of minutes in her.

But sixteen minutes passed before Romero collapsed off the bike, into the big pool of sweat that had trickled from her body to the floor. The ergometer registered 396 watts, one of the best results ever produced. Still gasping, Romero asked Hunt if he thought that was going to be good enough.

'I've never seen anybody do to themselves what Rebecca did to herself on the bike that day,' Hunt recalls. 'She properly emptied herself.'

He already knew that Romero possessed a superior physiology. The crucial test would start when she first rode a bike on the track, to find out whether she had the ability to adapt to it. When Romero first entered the velodrome she couldn't understand how cyclists manage to keep their balance on the steep banks. 'Riding on a cycling track for the first time can be a scary prospect,' Hunt says. Hunt taught her the basics and let her go. Within a couple of minutes, Romero was riding around the top of the steep banks of the velodrome track.

Hunt then took her to the gym to try the bike treadmill for the first time. 'Normally it takes a good ten to fifteen minutes to get the hang of it,' Hunt says. He held the saddle for about a minute and then let go. 'She just kept riding, chatting away, one-handed.'

After testing Romero, Hunt presented her case to British Cycling's performance director, Dave Brailsford. Selecting a rower with no experience of track cycling, no matter how extraordinary her potential, to the team was a huge gamble: 'We still had to justify to UK Sport that we were removing elite cyclists from the programme and now asking to fund a rower who had never track-raced in her life.' But luckily Brailsford supported Hunt.

Romero officially joined British Cycling in April 2006. On her first day, when she sat with Hunt to plan her training programme up to the Beijing Games, she made it clear to him that she wasn't there to enjoy herself. She had come to cycling for the gold medal that she should have won in rowing. She told Hunt: 'I'm going for the gold medal. That's all I'm here for.' In rowing, she had been dependent on other people. In cycling, she was in control of her own performance. If Hunt taught her how to ride a bike, she promised to show him what an elite athlete looked like.

Together, Romero and Hunt determined what power output and speed it would take her to win a gold medal. Based on her test results, Hunt estimated that Romero only needed to find an extra twenty-four watts to be in contention for gold. Then they broke it down into physical and physiological components. Every detail was part of the equation: size of the gear, drag, the humidity and temperature of the velodrome, body shape, body position.

However, Romero still had the body of a rower. For years her muscles had been fine-tuned to produce power at a cadence of around thirty-five strokes a minute for around six and a half minutes. These were big, relatively slow movements, drenched in power, suited to propelling a boat. On the bike, however, her aerobic capacity had to be moulded into an anaerobic machine, capable of operating when the muscles were starved of oxygen. She had to be capable of explosive starts and settle into a quicker rhythm that recruited her muscles at a faster pace. She would also have to change her musculature, losing upper-body strength to gain stronger legs, sculpted from muscles made of fast-twitch fibre, adapted to operate at higher intensities. Although she only needed to produce 24 watts more, she needed to express that power over 3km, at high cadence, in three and a half minutes – around half the duration of a rowing race.

Hunt was one of the coaches who leaned heavily on Murray and his crew of analysts. 'Whenever I needed to escape the velodrome, I would go see the [performance analysis] lads,' Hunt says. 'They would make coffee, banter and bombard you with questions.' Hunt shared a flat with Michael

Hughes and they would examine areas like pacing, gearing and competitor analysis.

Hughes was also involved in wind-tunnel testing. British Cycling used the wind tunnel at the University of Southampton. The tunnel had been built in 1920 and it belonged to the Aeronautical Engineering Department, where it was mostly used to test the aerodynamics of scale-model boats and racing cars. Here, British Cycling conducted thousands of tests, not only of form-fitting skinsuits and teardrop-shaped helmets, but of riders.

Wind-tunnel testing was a pretty unpleasant experience for all involved. Athletes were made to sit on a bike for hours, while being blown by a stream of cold air, experimenting with different riding positions and trying handlebars of various shapes, while analysts measured the drag. 'They needed to hold a position for about ten seconds for us to get a value. If they moved, we were buggered,' Hughes says. 'It wasn't glamorous.'

At first, there wasn't a way to communicate to the riders what their drag values were. Then Hughes installed a projector in the tunnel and a high-speed video camera that filmed them in profile. A smart screen showed the athletes where their heads and hands needed to be to provide a reference point. The projector displayed their live drag data onto the floor in front of them, and not in Newtons, but in seconds saved or lost. 'We would ask the athletes to freestyle and experiment with different positions,' Hughes says. 'They could see how much drag it saved if, say, they dropped their head. The compromise was always about being able to hold and ride in those positions.'

With the footage of the athlete's most aerodynamic positions, Hughes would then set up static cameras at the Manchester Velodrome to replicate those positions on the track. This sort of intervention was particularly important in the case of Romero, who still didn't possess the skills to ride her bike and use her body to transfer power from the legs to the pedals in the most aerodynamic way. 'It was insane,' Romero says. 'I didn't have the physiology or the bike skills. Very quickly I was being taught everything and I was going from nothing to being a member of the team and aiming for an Olympic medal.'

Romero would take notes of all her training sessions, recording what she had done, her thoughts and where there was room for improvement. 'I call it data ammunition,' she says. 'When I was preparing, we tailored all the training so that everything I was doing would lead me to be at the right point in two and a half years. We couldn't afford unnecessary training.'

In the first six months, Hunt found that his new trainee was quite distrustful of coaches, a possible hang-up from her experiences in rowing. He realised that he had to build trust between them and deliver on the things he promised to do. Over time, he got to know Romero better than anyone else. He learned to tell whether they were going to have a good day or a bad day just by the way she carried her bag into the velodrome.

'I used to worry about her because she didn't seem happy all the time,' Hunt says. 'I think when you're coaching people, you get to know them really well and I think you worry about what they are, what else they have got going on in their lives.' In time, Hunt learned that this was just the way Romero was.

The fact was that Romero was hard as nails. In training, she would visualise all the possible scenarios where she didn't win at the Olympics, and use how distressing those outcomes felt to motivate herself. To the other cyclists, she could come across as intimidating. One day, on a training camp in Newport, after a four-hour ride in freezing sleet and rain, one of the riders refused to hose her bike because it was too cold. Romero responded: 'You're not cut out for this.' It was also no secret that Romero and Wendy Houvenaghel, a rider whom Hunt had also brought into the team, weren't on speaking terms, a situation that Hunt never tried to remedy. 'As uncomfortable as it was, their desire to beat each other made both better,' Hunt says.

Hunt was clear about what it was going to take for Romero to win a gold medal. On the other hand, he was at a loss about what to make of her erratic progress. It soon dawned on him that training a rower to be a track cyclist precluded any notion of a consistent, linear improvement. 'It had never been done before, so you don't quite know what the rate of development is going to be like on a day-to-day basis,' Hunt says. 'Becks would hit a rough patch in training and you couldn't explain it. Good or bad? All of a sudden, three days later, she was amazing again in training, and we would be thinking we turned a corner. Then, three days later, it would be awful, and I would be thinking, shit, we over-trained.'

Romero's commitment was consistent and her ability to push herself to limits was unparalleled. 'Almost worryingly so,' Hunt says. 'Having people black out on bikes isn't ideal.' Hunt had never seen an athlete pass out with the frequency Romero did. She would exert herself to the point at which she would lose consciousness.

The first instance occurred during a training camp in Majorca. 'We were doing hill reps on Formentor,' Hunt says. 'She flew up this mountain, got to the top, dropped her bike, then just blacked out on the ground like a starfish in the middle of the car park.'

It happened again at the Moscow round of the World Cup, in

December 2006. This was her first international competition, and neither Hunt nor Romero knew where she would rank. The preparation had gone well, and Romero seemed happy. Two days before the race, she told Hunt that she was concerned about the gearing they had been using for a while. They sat down, looked at their notes and data, and decided to try a gear that she'd never used before. 'It was brave,' Hunt says. 'There weren't any expectations that we were going to win, and so if we got it wrong, then it would just be a learning point.'

In the race, Romero rode, in Hunt's words, 'out of her skin' and won silver in the individual pursuit, behind Wendy Houvenaghel. When she crossed the finish line she was on the verge of another blackout and had to be held up by two mechanics.

'She could barely walk straight and she was like, "I feel fine",' Hunt says.

Later that evening, they went for a celebratory drink. 'We were talking and suddenly she just hugged me. You could just feel all the relief coming out, after such a big decision of leaving rowing and the shit we'd been through. We had never really talked about it until then.' But now, all that effort had been vindicated.

In March 2007, at the World Championships in Palma de Mallorca, Romero won another silver medal. A year later, in Manchester, Romero broke both the track record and the national record to become world champion.

But then, in May 2008, Romero injured her back on a training camp. With only six weeks to go until the Olympics, Hunt was forced to redesign their training plan. Romero needed time with the physiotherapist and the strength and conditioning coaches if she was going to recover her core stability. So Hunt banned her from the track and restricted

her training to the turbo trainer: two hours of aerobic maintenance in the morning, and in the afternoon some shorter,
high-power efforts that replicated the demands of her event.
The rest of the time she would spend in bed or on the physiotherapist's massage table.

'This isn't going to happen,' Hunt thought. 'We've worked
so hard just to lose it now.' At that point, Hunt and Romero
were working together closely every day, scrutinising her
performance. 'It was no longer about the nice-to-haves, it
was about the fundamentals,' Hunt says. 'Did I know it was
going to work? No idea.' Hunt worried all the time. Doubts
crept into his mind about whether Romero deserved better
than a novice coach who didn't know what he was doing.

In June 2008, while most of Team GB were in the holding camp in Macau, the cycling team had decided to avoid
the pollution in China and convened instead at the Wales
National Velodrome in Newport. Romero hadn't been on
the track since her back injury. On her first effort, she went
faster than ever before. Hunt was nonplussed. Perhaps working on the turbo trainer had stimulated her training. Perhaps
worrying about her back had been the best thing that could
have happened, forcing Romero to train differently.

However, after they arrived in China, Romero became
stuck again. She felt and looked tired, drained by the travel,
the training, the physical and emotional rollercoaster of the
past two years, and the exacting ambition of their mission.
'Fuck. We've really got this wrong,' Hunt thought.

'We were thousands of miles away from home, stuck in a
poxy hotel, the Games were in two days, our morale at rock
bottom, and she just couldn't get the numbers. She wasn't
even near,' he says.

Hunt knew that there was only one thing left to do. He
told Romero to stop training, to freshen up and take the load

off her mind, both physically and mentally. 'I wouldn't normally do this,' Hunt says. 'There would be no coming back from it if those two days off really put her backwards, but you can't just keep training just to make yourself feel better. When in doubt, rest is best.'

On 16 August 2008, in the preliminary round, Wendy Houvenaghel qualified with the fastest time. Romero was the second fastest, to Hunt's immense relief. She was only two-tenths of a second behind Houvenaghel. On the same day, both qualified for the gold medal match, with Romero now fastest by a tenth of a second.

'I knew I had the capability to win,' Romero later said in an interview. 'It felt like I was reliving Athens all over again and all I had to do was not mess up.'

Hunt went to bed knowing that in twenty-four hours, one way or another, he would be the coach of an Olympic champion.

Usually, the coach stands on the halfway line to signal to his athlete whether she's above or below pace. In the final, Hunt decided not to walk the line for either of his cyclists. He didn't want to show any favouritism. Two other coaches would be doing that instead, while he would be sitting in the stands. He told Romero and Houvenaghel: 'I've done my job. Good luck. Race it out.'

During the race, Romero knew she was winning, but couldn't believe it. She screamed as she crossed the finish line, two seconds ahead of her opponent.

To avoid upsetting Houvenaghel, no one in the team congratulated Romero. Hunt was delighted for her, but disappointed for Houvenaghel. Afterwards, they went back to the athletes' village as if nothing had happened.

Hunt stayed until the end of the Games, but he couldn't wait to leave Beijing. 'Once my job's done, I want to go and deal with it myself,' Hunt says. 'You're there for other people. It's such an energised, energy-giving thing that I needed normality.'

Back in Manchester, Murray picked up Hughes and Hunt from the airport and they went out to celebrate. Over the next few days, Hunt began suffering from the post-Olympic blues. A week before, he had been in the Laoshan Velodrome with six thousand people shouting at him – the coach who, in the space of two years, had transformed a rower and a former dentist into Olympic medallists. Now he sat in his dressing gown on the sofa watching the *Jeremy Kyle Show*, wondering where his life had gone wrong.

'You win a gold medal and think that we'll go out and champagne will fall from the stars and it'll be amazing,' he says. 'Instead you just sit there in your house thinking if you're going to throw yourself down the stairs.'

9

THE SCIENCE OF FORMULA ONE PIT STOPS

On 25 May 2008, McLaren Formula One race engineer Phil Prew sat on the pit wall at the Monaco Grand Prix. It was the sixth race of the season. Lewis Hamilton, a young McLaren pilot in his second season, had won the first race, in Australia. Ferrari drivers Kimi Räikkönen and Felipe Massa had gone on to win the next four, clocking up two wins each.

In Monaco, the Brazilian Massa started in pole position, followed on the starting grid by Räikkönen and Hamilton. For the first five laps, Massa maintained a small lead. It was raining heavily and the notoriously difficult Monaco circuit was slippery. On lap six, Lewis Hamilton hit a barrier and punctured a rear tyre, forcing him to make a pit stop.

On the pit wall, McLaren race engineers typically follow the race through a computer dashboard developed by McLaren named MARPLE. The software visualises the race as a graph, with each car a different colour. The horizontal axis indicates the lap number; the vertical axis, the lap time. The distance between the cars is represented vertically. If a car is completing faster laps at each turn, its line ascends. When it stopped at the pit, the car line drops.

In the weeks leading up to any race, the McLaren team builds a very detailed computer model of the circuit and the performance of all the cars in the race. This allows them to simulate any possible scenario and predict the outcome. The team typically runs millions such simulations, parsing all possible permutations for different variables: timings for pit stops, number of pit stops, different sets of tyres and so on. McLaren calls this a decision-support system. 'We will have a pre-determined plan for any possible scenario,' says former McLaren race engineer Andy Latham. 'The last thing we want is to have to make any tough decisions during the heat of the race.'

During the race, engineers at McLaren's technology centre in Woking continue to run race simulations at a frequency of tens of thousands of new simulations per lap, updating the models with data uploaded from the live timing data and telemetry from the five hundred sensors fitted in each of their cars. For instance, the wheel hub has sensors that track brake temperature, brake wear, tyre pressures and G-forces. This data is first processed by a microchip inside the wheel hub before being transmitted to the electronic control unit, which relays the information across the world, via a safe network, to mission control. Back in Woking, engineers analyse this data and compare it with the data output from the simulator and computer models.

Tyres are one of the most critical factors in a Formula One race. That they are the only component of the car to interact with the tarmac, and very difficult to model, makes them the main source of uncertainty in any simulation. During every lap, race engineers usually ask their chief car strategist to update them on the tyres' performance. 'Before the race starts we know what we will do if the tyres degrade more quickly or slowly than we think, if our competitors are slightly faster than we assumed they were, or if the safety car comes out and interrupts the race,' Latham says.

During the race, engineers can see the simulation predictions on their dashboard. 'When we tell a driver to pit at any given time, we know what his position will be after the stop,' Latham says. And so, immediately after hitting the wall in Monaco, Prew was able to give Lewis Hamilton precise instructions over the internal audio feed:

'Lewis, you're coming into the pit. You make a change to the steering, the launch switch, make sure you've done that – you're going to get new tyres and you're going to get fuel.'

Shortly after, Prew instructed 'Bail out' – meaning to fuel the car sufficiently to make it to the end of the race, because no more pit stops would be allowed. The code that McLaren's engineers used to communicate with their drivers changed for every event, in case their audio channel was being tapped by other teams.

Prew again: 'Tyre set twenty-two' – a pre-determined set of intermediate tyres.

Then more silence.

The pit stop lasted nine seconds. When Hamilton exited the pit lane, he was told which drivers were behind and in front of him. Nothing else.

A puncture at the Monaco Grand Prix, a circuit where it's notoriously hard to overtake, usually means the race is lost. Thanks to McLaren's decision-support algorithms, however, the race engineers had a plan in place and were able to minimise the time lost. The moment Hamilton hit the barrier, all thirteen members of the pit crew already knew exactly what to do. The weather forecast indicated that the track was going to dry up, so if Hamilton had an accident they would have to use their intermediate tyres and refuel the car to last until the end of the race. 'Making crucial decisions that can dictate the outcome of a race still gets you in the stomach,' Latham says. 'Am I a hundred per cent confident about the decisions I make? No. I trust the computer models, but we're still human.'

With more fuel in the tank than his rivals and a set of tyres better adapted as the conditions dried out, Hamilton went on to win the race. The result took Hamilton to the top of the Drivers' Championship. Later that year, he clinched the title, becoming the youngest-ever world champion.

That McLaren sees pit stops as an opportunity to win races is emblematic of a high-performance culture, underpinned by an expert team of car designers, mechanical engineers and aerodynamicists and led by their chief operating officer, a man called Martin Whitmarsh.

Whitmarsh began his career in the aerospace industry in the eighties. He worked for British Aerospace as a structural engineer, but what he really aspired to was to design aeroplanes. He quickly learned that such ambitions were unrealistic. Planes usually had a slow, prolonged gestation period of twenty to thirty years, a consequence of heavy regulation and the globalised manufacturing process. That is, until Friday 2 April 1982, when Argentina invaded the Falkland Islands.

'We were suddenly faced with a situation where we had to maritimise the aircraft,' Whitmarsh says. 'We did it in weeks. As a young guy in the industry, I was animated by that fact. During peacetime, with the Ministry of Defence procurement process, it would have taken us years to do the same. I'm aware it's not politically correct to say this, but the necessity of war was an accelerator.'

When Whitmarsh joined McLaren as head of operations in 1989, the team, thanks to the legendary duo of Ayrton Senna and Alain Prost, was one of the dominant forces in Formula One. The sport was in the early stages of adopting new tools such as simulation software and wind tunnels.

'When I started, the cars had manual transmissions and throttle cables,' Whitmarsh says. 'Our R&D department consisted of two people.' As a business, its position was even more precarious. The company, at the time exclusively concerned with motor racing, employed fewer than a hundred people and had a turnover in the region of £19 million. It had been founded in 1963 by twenty-six-year-old maverick Bruce McLaren, who died six years later in a car crash, and had long since lost its lustre as a recognised global brand. By the eighties, McLaren had been subsumed by its sponsor, Marlboro, then one of the world's most popular brands. 'McLaren, as a brand, didn't really exist then,' Whitmarsh says. 'We were going to have to take it back, focus on developing technology and intellectual property and monetise it.'

Under Whitmarsh, McLaren began investing in its automotive business, producing new ranges of cars, and also began selling analytical software to petrochemical companies and electronic components to NASCAR.

But what really animated Whitmarsh was the frantic pace of innovation that he encountered in motor racing. It brought him back to the days of the Falklands War, when innovation was spurred by the sheer pressure of time. 'It's that stimulus that you've got to throw everything you can at it,' he says. 'It doesn't wait for you. You can't delay it. If the race is in the first week of March, it's the start of the new season in Australia, you've got to be there with the best you've got. Two weeks later, you've got to be in Kuala Lumpur, and the week after, you've got to be in China, and a week after that you've got to be in Bahrain. They're like wars. You are throwing the best that you can. You're sending your troops, racing drivers or pilots, out there and you're doing what you can to have the best.'

At McLaren, Whitmarsh saw himself as an angry engineer whose speciality was asking 'dumb questions'. 'There are hundreds of engineers who are much brighter than me, but once every three years you get a eureka moment,' he says. Whitmarsh, for instance, was the originator of mission control in Formula One. As principal of the racing team, Whitmarsh would sit on the pit wall during every race. In the eighties, the only data input available was the television broadcast. As the racing car evolved into a more sophisticated machine equipped with multiple sensors, the number of data screens in the pit increased. 'The tradition was that the principal would sit there with all the noise, heat, humidity and distraction and make high-pressure decisions second by second regarding tyre changes, pit stops, or about something that had gone horribly wrong, like the engine blowing up,' Whitmarsh says. 'It was preposterous.' Mission control was the opposite of the pit-wall frenzy. A quiet room located at McLaren's HQ in Woking, where engineers could monitor a Grand Prix anywhere in the world and relay race strategy decisions in real time.

In 1997 Whitmarsh, by now the team's managing director, had another eureka moment. One day, he took his research team to see a flight simulator at his old employer, British Aerospace, and told them: let's build one for Formula One.

Caroline Hargrove had just started working for Whitmarsh's team of engineers. She had been hired from the University of Cambridge, where she worked with complex system simulations. 'At that time, there was plenty of road testing and nobody but Whitmarsh saw the need to make a driving simulator,' Hargrove says. 'But I was like, "Pick me. Pick me!" I was really excited.'

Within McLaren, the project was received with scepticism, as yet another quixotic notion from their managing
director. 'A Whitmarsh folly,' he recalls wryly. 'My own
technical director was against it. It was against the traditional
race engineers who just didn't believe in it. "That's not how
you do it. We go out there, and we talk to the driver."' But
Whitmarsh wanted to move away from this improvised form
of car mechanics – what he called seat-of-the-pants judgement – towards analysis, simulations and physics.

Whitmarsh persevered and gradually they began equipping
the cars with more sensors and data-loggers, and developing
mathematical models for the tyres, the suspension, the chassis,
the engine, the transmission, the conditions and the circuit.
What Whitmarsh hadn't realised was that, out of all the
components that make the racing car, the most interesting
one was the driver.

'As an engineer, you tend to think physics dictates how
fast a car can go. That it's about how much grip you can
generate for contact of rubber on tarmac, fundamentally,
which determines the acceleration you can apply to the
vehicle. But then the driver comes and says, "I don't get the
feeling, I can't get the best out of it."' To Whitmarsh, this
was a revelation.

After that, understanding the cues that mattered to the
driver became one of the priorities of the simulator. There
were the visual prompts: tyres, trajectory, car. Then the steering loads, the abrupt accelerations, and the vibrations erupting
from the seat. Finally, the proportionality between the sound
of the engine and acceleration.

'He has to weigh all this and put a reliance on certain ones,
put them together in his head, compute them into where that
vehicle is, and then provide output in terms of steering angle,
throttle or brake, the three fundamental controls that he has

on the car,' Whitmarsh says. 'The fact that he's processing all of this at the subconscious level was fascinating to me.' The addition of the human element into the simulation became known as the driver-in-the-loop.

In its first iteration, the simulator was no more than a chassis with a screen. 'We had the graphics, the sounds, the steering feedback, the pedals,' Caroline Hargrove recalls. 'But we had no movement. To get the changes in acceleration you feel in Formula One, we needed to achieve very low latency and the simulators then were much too slow. We thought bad motion was worse than no motion.'

Racing drivers are so attuned to how their car behaves, a simulator must be able to give them very precise physical cues. If, for example, a driver relied on engine noise to infer loss of grip, then Hargrove had to replicate that engine noise as realistically as possible. Anything less would break the suspension of belief required for the driver to feel like he was driving an actual car.

'Drivers would say plainly when something wasn't good enough,' recalls Hargrove. 'I would ask: "Right, what's wrong with it?" There was always lots wrong with it.'

To test the simulator, engineers relied mostly on test drivers and junior pilots who were part of McLaren's young driver programme. One such pilot was Lewis Hamilton, who had entered the programme in 1998, aged only thirteen. While for him it was an opportunity to learn and impress his superiors, for the simulation team getting time with a driver-in-the-loop was a chance to hone their invention.

Hargrove's breakthrough came at the Turkish Grand Prix in 2005. The Istanbul Park circuit was a brand-new track that no driver had ever driven – except in a simulator, of course. And at the time, McLaren was the only team to have one.

During practice, McLaren's Juan Pablo Montoya went first. Drivers usually drove the first laps slowly, to familiarise themselves with the track. Montoya, however, drove it fast. To be precise, he drove it ten seconds faster than anyone else and yelled into his microphone, 'It's just like the simulator!'

'He recognised everything about the track,' Hargrove says. 'That was the seal of approval we needed.'

In its later stages, the simulator at McLaren's headquarters was a rather more complex machine than its earlier iterations, comprising a full-size car chassis mounted on a dynamic rig, with a motion system that reproduces the precise G-forces generated in a Formula One race, and surrounded by 180-degree curved video screens. Separated by a two-way mirror is the control room, containing a vast desk, five desktop computers and a huge flat screen monitor that displays in real time hundreds of parameters extracted from the simulator – steering-wheel angle, wheel speed, accelerations, engine revs and so on.

'The simulator represents everything that we think we understand about the car,' Hargrove says. 'But there might be discrepancies between our model and reality, and the drivers are our filter. They take in vast amounts of information and they can pick out anomalies really well. We often use the driver when we don't really know what's going on. If the driver drives it round and says, "Yes, that feels exactly like the track", then you know that your model is right.'

Formula One drivers and their test drivers began spending, on average, 180 days a year inside the simulator – that is, approximately seven times longer in the simulator than in the actual car. The engineers don't give them any data, to avoid biasing the driver's perception of the car's performance. Every session is a blind test.

'All the drivers hear is run one, run two, and so on,' Hargrove says. 'They are able to do thirty laps in the simulator and, at the end, talk in detail about how every single corner of every single lap felt to them.'

During a typical season, McLaren might change about 70 per cent of the mechanical components that make up its car, and again the simulator is a major tactical advantage. McLaren models and tests all of their components virtually, using the simulator to gauge the effect it has on the driver.

'Let's say you want to test a new anti-roll bar,' explains Hargrove. 'In theory, we can build a prototype, put it inside your car and test it on the road. Or you can build a model virtually and test it on the simulator. We know the size, the specs, how it behaves with physics. The program computes how this new component interacts with every other component in your car model, and that data is fed to the simulator, where the driver tests it.'

In 2007, season testing was banned by the sport's governing body, the FIA, to cut costs. Suddenly, teams with a simulator had a major technological advantage. And the only team that had one was McLaren.

That year, with the simulator completed, Hargrove was moved from the simulation department to a different company within the McLaren Group, called Applied Technologies. The company had been set up by McLaren CEO Ron Dennis in 2004, with the idea of selling Formula One's high-performance culture and working methods to other industries.

McLaren Applied Technologies didn't make any money in its first few years. In fact, it didn't make much of anything. By 2008, MAT consisted of only three people: Hargrove, a software engineer and Geoff McGrath, a mechanical engineer who previously worked in oil, gas and telecommunications.

'When we started, we were basically three people sitting at a table, wondering how to build this business,' McGrath says.

They were trying to answer the question: what would McLaren do if it didn't make Formula One cars? McGrath had a plan, at least in theory. In the abstract, the racing team inhabited a cycle of continuous improvement: simulation and simulator → pre-race analysis → live monitoring during the race with advanced telemetry → post-race analysis → design → simulation and simulator. What if they used this same model in any other industry?

'The racing car is the perfect intelligent product,' McGrath says. 'It's continuously improved upon within extreme time pressure, and is custom-built for an individual consumer, the driver. We design it in the simulator and leave the telemetry in the product for remote condition monitoring. That intelligence tells us how the product is being used.' To McGrath, the data coming off the physical product is worth more than the product itself. He calls it the meta-product. This was the philosophy MAT could sell to businesses, which were traditionally managed retroactively, by analysing the data of past financial reports. Instead, McLaren would get them to work with live data, to compete in real time and to simulate future conditions. At least that was the vision. All they needed was their first client.

Shortly after the Beijing Games, Caroline Hargrove contacted Scott Drawer, the head of R&I at UK Sport. A year earlier, she had been approached by the British bobsleigh team about conducting tests on the drivability of their sleds. They took them to McLaren, set them up on their testing rigs and analysed their dynamics.

Soon after, British Bobsleigh lost their funding and had to abandon the project. Hargrove called up UK Sport to ask whether they would be interested in the report for future reference. She was put through to Scott Drawer.

Until then, Drawer had no idea that McLaren had a consultancy arm, but he asked if McLaren and Team GB could collaborate in preparation for the 2012 Olympics. Drawer wanted to bring some of McLaren's F1 practices, such as telemetry and predictive algorithms, to other elite sports. And so the two organisations began to work together in cycling, sailing, rowing and canoeing.

'Track cycling was particularly successful,' Hargrove says. 'Of all the Olympic sports, it's probably the most akin to F1, except that, instead of an engine, they have a person.' Although all the cyclists used SRM power meters, the sprint events required more precise and accurate telemetry. McLaren built the Datarider, a small aerodynamic box that nestled under the saddle and collected data related to power, torque and bike angle from sensors on the bike. The device itself contained accelerometers, gyroscopes and Bluetooth transmitters. Previous sensors used by the cycling team could transmit information at a frequency of approximately 20Hz. Datarider ran at 200Hz.

'I wanted to make sure everything was calibrated perfectly so we did all the testing on our site,' Hargrove says. 'I saw the data from Chris Hoy, panicked, and rang them to apologise. It seemed obvious that I had the calibration wrong as the numbers were so high. They said it was fine – those were the numbers Hoy produced.'

After the Beijing Games, Stafford Murray was promoted to a new role at the English Institute of Sport, with the unwieldy title of Head of Performance Analysis, Biomechanics and Skill Acquisition. He would organise three workshops a year, where analysts, biomechanists and skills acquisition experts could meet and share best practices. One year, Murray brought in an ex-SAS operative and a musician. He also invited a comedian to teach his group how to read an audience and turn situations around. 'I invited him because there's nothing more nerve-racking than standing up in front of four hundred people and having to make them laugh,' Murray says. At the end of the workshop, the comedian told Murray that that had been the worst gig of his career. 'You have twenty-five analysts in a room and it goes without saying they are not particularly humorous people. They were just staring at him. I had to apologise to him at the end.'

Murray also took his team of analysts to visit Manchester City FC and the London Stock Exchange. 'Everyone came to London from all over the country,' Murray recalls. 'We sat in this lovely room. Big, posh room in the middle of London. They just wouldn't pass on any secrets at all. Their definition of showing us what they do was literally just giving us a walk around the stock exchange and showing us the screens.'

When they visited McLaren, following an invitation from Caroline Hargrove, Murray was introduced to McLaren's chief engineer, Dave Redding. The engineer confided to Murray that, while McLaren boasted some of the most advanced technology in the world, they had a problem: their pit crew was too slow.

'They realised that their human performance science was terrible and asked for our help,' Murray says. 'Until then, the relationship between the Institute and McLaren had been one-way. Now it became two-way. They would do hardware and software for us, and we would help them with their performance.'

Redding asked Murray if it was possible to reduce the average 4.5-second pit stop to 2.5 seconds. Murray had no idea how that would be achieved. The first thing he had to work out was why other crews were faster than McLaren's.

In March 2009, Murray attended pre-season testing in Barcelona. It was at testing events that Formula One teams unveiled new cars and trialled new technology. As part of the testing, they were also required to make frequent trips to the pit, to test how quickly they could change tyres, wings and fins.

As an accredited member of the McLaren team, Murray had access to the VIP hospitality lounge, which had a view over the paddock and the entire pit lane. He entered the building in his McLaren uniform and went up three floors to the lounge. There, he immediately went into a toilet cubicle and changed into civilian clothes. He then climbed the fire escape to the roof, set up a camera tripod on the parapet just above the pit lane and began recording the pit stops for Toro Rosso, Ferrari and Force India.

The fastest pit crew, Red Bull, was outside the range of the camera on the roof. So Murray went downstairs and sneaked into the committee room toilets. Standing on the toilet, he stuck his head out of the window and from there filmed Red Bull's pit stop with his portable camera. 'What I didn't know at the time was that I was actually in the ladies' toilets,' Murray says. 'If I knew I wouldn't have gone in there. That is God's honest truth.'

When Murray analysed his footage later that day, he was struck by how accurately other drivers pulled up in the pit box grid. They were spot on. The McLaren cars, in compar-ison, were always either a few inches short or over the line. 'If your engineer knows exactly where the car is going to stop, he can start reacting before the car actually stops. He can be proactive,' Murray says. 'The guy at the front can start attack-ing with the machine that lifts the car up. He can actually start approaching the car before it stops, because they've got confidence in where the car is going to be.'

The following day, over breakfast, Murray told Redding about his findings. Redding was taken aback and told Murray not to divulge the information to anyone, especially not to the drivers. Murray wasn't quite sure why Redding was so reticent.

He realised why later that afternoon. Sitting in the paddock, Murray was given a pair of headphones linked to the McLaren audio feed and heard a conversation taking place between Redding and Hamilton.

'Carry on. The car's fine. Carry on,' Redding said.

'No, the car's pulling to the left,' Hamilton replied.

'No, it isn't. The data's showing it's fine. The car's fine. Please carry on.'

'Hang on a minute – it is. I can feel it. I'm going to pull in.'

'Don't pull in. The data's fine.'

'Bollocks. The car's pulling to the left. I'm going to pull in.'

Murray was taken aback by how little authority the engineers seemed to have over the drivers. It was not clear why telling the best drivers in the world that they were not being particularly accurate when they stopped their car in the pit was not going to be an easy conversation.

'They're the guys driving around at two hundred miles an hour and risking their lives every day,' Murray says. 'It was amazing how much the drivers believed in the data, but questioned it all because they had the feel. Data is one thing, but data doesn't show the feel of the car. It doesn't represent the difficulty of driving the bloody thing.'

But Murray realised there was another issue. The pit crew were not simply mechanics, just as analysts were not simply geeks. These men had to be taught how to operate the wheel guns effectively – which eye was dominant, which knee they should put forward. They had to be taught how to twist and how to lunge. They had to be given workshops in mental rehearsal and jet-lag strategy. If they were supporting the athletes, they were going to have to be treated as athletes in their own right.

10

HOW TO MAKE A CHAMPION

The most basic and critical aspect of playing squash is the grip. A correct grip on the racket promotes accuracy and fine control over the placement of the ball. The grip is the foundation of the forehand and the backhand swing and its multiple variations: the boast, the drive, the counter drop, the volley. This is the technical compendium of the squash player and technique is the source from which all other elements of the game – from movement to tactics – flow.

To David Pearson, even the best tactical plan in the world could be undermined by a lack of technical proficiency. For instance, when he first diagnosed Peter Nicol's technique, he detected that the player – the world number one at the time – still had a defective grip. His forehand grip was too closed, while his backhand displayed a cocked wrist and a too-firm grasp of the racket.

The correct grip is one of the first principles players learn in squash. 'He was the best player in the world and was still willing to change it,' Murray says. 'A lot of players weren't prepared to do that. Which is why they didn't become the best players in the world.'

Pearson also realised that, at the age of thirty, Nicol was going to find it difficult to get rid of some of his most ingrained technical flaws, so they reached an agreement to leave most of those alone. 'We kept about seventy per cent of what he already did and worked on the rest,' Pearson says.

Nick Matthew, however, was a completely different matter. On his first assessment of Matthew's technique, Pearson told him that he played like 'he had a carrot stuck up his arse'. 'It was horrendous,' Pearson remembers. 'If he didn't totally and utterly reshape his technique, he was never going to achieve anything.' Nick Matthew certainly wasn't naturally gifted. He played an ugly, aggressive style of squash, which was contrary to Pearson's aesthetic sensibilities. Matthew's former coach had trained him to be a fit athlete with a strong mentality, and he had consistently been ranked among the top junior players in the world. But as a professional senior player against much stronger opponents, his physical prowess no longer represented an advantage. 'If you divide the modern game into four areas – mental, physical, technical, tactical – you can have everything in place, but what will limit you the most is poor technique,' Matthew says. 'When Pearson told me that I would say, yes, I understand, but it really took me a year to realise it. It's a very tough thing for your ego to cope with. I had been hitting the squash courts since I was eight. I'd hit millions of squash balls, which meant that my technique had been flawed for twelve years.'

One of the most elegant theories of how people acquire expertise had been laid out in a 1967 book, *Human Performance*, by the American psychologists Paul Fitts and Michael Posner. Their model posited that people go through three distinct stages when learning a new skill. They called the first stage the 'cognitive' stage. This is when the learner intellectualises the task at hand and searches for strategies to accomplish it, with the conscious part of the brain fully engaged. Take learning a language: at the cognitive stage, learners are trying to understand the basic rules of grammar, learning their first words and attempting to pronounce the different phonetic sounds correctly.

After some experience, learners reach the second stage, which the authors called the 'associative' stage. At this point, the learner has developed knowledge of what, how and when to perform an action. He or she then starts to practise and receive feedback. The conscious mind is no longer grappling with the unknown, but to become competent still requires full conscious concentration. As the learner practises, the new skill slowly migrates to the unconscious level.

At the third stage, the 'autonomous' stage, the learner stops being a learner. The skill becomes second nature – psychologists say that at this point the learner has reached a level of 'unconscious competence'. Native speakers of a language have this level of competence, whereas adult learners typically struggle to reach the autonomous stage, even when fully immersed in the language.

But even the autonomous stage does not equal expertise. In sport, elite athletes possess more than mere unconscious competence: they have an unconscious mastery. This level of skill often produces what is known as a flow experience, a mental state at the extreme of the unconscious competence spectrum that typically results in unbeatable performances.

In 1988, for instance, at the qualifying stage of the Monaco Grand Prix, Ayrton Senna, described a record-breaking lap in this way: 'I was already on pole and I was going faster and faster. One lap after the other, quicker, and quicker, and quicker. I was at one stage on pole, then by half a second, and then one second . . . and I kept going. Suddenly, I was nearly two seconds faster than anybody else, including my teammate with the same car. And I suddenly realised that I was no longer driving the car consciously. I was kind of driving it by instinct, only I was in a different dimension. It was like I was in a tunnel, not only the tunnel under the hotel, but the whole circuit for me was a tunnel. I was just going more, going – more, and more, and more, and more. I was way over the limit, but was still able to find even more.'

The opposite held true for Nick Matthew. As a case study in the science of skill acquisition, Matthew was an interesting one. At the age of eighteen, he could easily have been considered, overall, an expert player. He had been playing for more than a decade; he had won several junior tournaments and had played for the national team.

However, from a technical perspective, Pearson considered him very much a beginner. But for Matthew it wasn't simply a matter of learning a new skill from scratch. It was about modifying an existing one, dismantling habits and tendencies ingrained in his brain since he was a child and replacing them with new ones. This wasn't about getting it right the first time. It was about learning new ways to replace the old. This causes habit pattern interference, which essentially means that people subconsciously resist learning a skill that conflicts with an existing one. They forget the new teaching faster and can easily revert back to old ways.

In other words, old habits die hard.

When we think of the prowess of athletes we tend, of course, to consider only its physical manifestation. Cristiano Ronaldo, for instance, represents what might be called the complete physical athlete. He has the long legs of a sprinter and the lean physique of a middle-distance runner. He can jump approximately eighty centimetres in the air, which is higher than the average professional basketball player can. Added to his physical attributes, what makes Ronaldo a truly great football player is his supreme coordination and masterly skill with the ball. This skill is associated with fine-motor coordination, flexibility and reaction speeds, all of which are etched into muscle and tendons. What is rarely considered is that such athletes are not only biomechanically talented, but also endowed with vastly superior cognitive abilities.

Much like physiological adaptation, learning a skill can be thought of as a process of adaptation that requires progressive overloading to occur. Overloading an athlete learning a new skill can be done on different levels. One way to overload is to do the same activities with higher intensity. Take Sarah Storey, for instance, the British Paralympic cyclist. Storey was born without a fully formed left hand. She began swimming at the age of four and went to her first Paralympics ten years later, at Barcelona 1992. When biomechanists studied her stroke rate to determine which arm was dominant, despite her disability and to Storey's surprise, they found that her stroke had perfect balance. In 2005, she was forced to stop training temporarily due to an ear infection. During that period she trialled for British Cycling and was accepted in the programme. After winning five Paralympic gold medals and five world championships, she decided to see if she could do on the track what she had done in the pool. 'When I practise on the road, I can fly at 80kph, get round the corners at more than 50kph, overtake cars,' Storey says. 'But when I started I was like, "No way I'm overtaking a car".' It was a reaction that she only conquered through what she calls neurological training. Every time she went out on the track at the Manchester Velodrome, she would force herself to cycle as fast as she could. It was a year before she was overtaking cars frequently. 'It's no use if you're going at 60kph round a 250-metre track and you get dizzy and your front wheel is wobbling because it's too fast to handle,' she says. 'Your nervous system has to be able to handle the bike at speed and to send messages to the brain so that the legs turn faster.'

With more complex sports such as squash or football, with a heavier emphasis on technique and tactics, the coach can also manipulate the feedback that is given to the athlete. Sports scientists make an emphatic distinction between two types of feedback. Intrinsic feedback comes from the athlete and varies in degree – from, say, the awareness of an archer that the target has been missed, to a more attuned perception of movement, such as how much force the archer put into firing the bow. Extrinsic feedback, on the other hand, originates from outside sources, from the coach shouting instructions on the sidelines to post-match video analysis. In a sense, extrinsic feedback is what allows an athlete to compare how he or she has actually performed with how he or she thinks they have performed.

When coaching Peter Nicol, Pearson would feed the ball to him, always insisting that he took the drop shot at the top of the bounce. Meanwhile, Murray had set up a camera right at the front of the court to obtain high-speed video footage at two hundred and fifty frames a second. They would do ten shots like this and then huddle around the laptop. 'Nicol was hitting it just off the top of the bounce,' Murray says. 'I calculated his timing and estimated that he was losing about two minutes throughout the match. He was basically giving his opponents two extra minutes. This is the sort of data that we have to find. If we're not changing their behaviour and accelerating the way they learn new skills, we're failing.'

The ability to break down movements in slow motion enabled Nicol to calibrate his perception of what he was doing against what he was really doing. 'We're trying to get me to drop my racket head to the floor, but it doesn't matter how many times I said to myself I was going to do it correctly, I would always lift the racket head up at the very last minute and push the ball into the front wall. It wasn't until I saw it in super slow motion that I realised that the balls went up because of the strength and the cut I was putting on it. It allowed me to see that I could bring the racket down and still play the drop shot. I needed to see it to understand that it was possible.'

As the athlete became more proficient, the level of feedback would become more specific and focused. A study by Ian Franks and his colleague Nicola Hodges at the University of British Columbia School of Kinesiology showed that novice football players would learn faster by following general verbal instructions ('Can you pass the ball into the near-post area?'), rather than being taught specifically how this could be achieved. The lesson was that coaches need to be able to provide the smallest amount of extrinsic feedback required for an athlete to progress and to let the athlete engage in self-discovery, by trial and error. If the feedback provided is excessive, there's a danger that athletes become dependent on it to the point that they can't perform without it when it comes to competition. This fine balance between extrinsic and intrinsic feedback helps athletes to calibrate their own perception of their performance, which accelerates their learning.

Murray, ever since he had taken on his new role at the EIS, had been trying to integrate the three disciplines into one coherent approach. 'Our data analysis was the best, but unless we knew what was the best way to present data to athletes and coaches to have the maximum impact, there was no point,' Murray says. 'It was like looking through the wrong end of the telescope.' He had recruited Mark Williams, Professor of Motor Behaviour at Liverpool John Moores University, as one of his outside expert consultants.

Williams had been involved in some of the early footballing studies conducted by Tom Reilly, and was one of the country's foremost academic experts in skill acquisition, particularly visual skills like anticipation. He had looked at how elite tennis players react to the movements of their opponents. To do so, he placed tennis players in front of a large screen, onto which he projected a life-sized opponent performing a serve in a virtual court. Wearing eye-tracking goggles, players would stand on a pressure mat that could track their movements. He then had his players anticipate their opponent's action by responding physically to the film, leaving out parts of the sequence – such as by making the screen go black just before the ball was hit – to find out whether the player could anticipate the serve.

'What you find in fast-paced sports, such as tennis, is that the time taken for the ball to travel from one opponent to the other is often shorter than the combined sum of the athlete's reaction time and movement time,' Williams says. That means that athletes need to initiate a response before an opponent actually strikes the ball. Typically, they have anticipated where the ball is going to go 120 milliseconds before the ball makes contact with the racket.

By using an eye-movement sensor, Williams found that players don't even look at the ball, but predominantly at the trunk, hips, shoulders and arms of their opponent. Subconsciously, they are extracting visual information to accurately anticipate what is going to happen.

Another cognitive skill is the ability to recognise patterns during a match. Here, Williams devised a study in which football players of varying proficiency were shown a filmed simulation of an attack. 'Say you have a centre half on the edge of the penalty area and the ball is on the halfway line. What we find is that elite players will be using lots of fixations of short duration: scanning, picking up position and movements of players,' Williams said. 'They are analysing the structure of the game. Subconsciously, they are doing maths, calculating event probabilities for each given situation at every single moment, based on previous experience of the game. It's as though they have a database in their head, with a probability assigned for every play pattern that they might encounter in the game.' What sets elite athletes apart, then, is not just what they can do, but knowing precisely when to do it.

In the abstract, skills acquisition experts break down gaze patterns into three elements: tracking the object in space, aiming, and executing an action which interacts with the object.

In the specific case of the McLaren pit crew, these different phases corresponded to the start of the car movement to the car entering the box, then from the car entering the box to the pneumatic gun-on, then from gun-on to gun-off. When Murray first met McLaren's pit crew in 2010, he had them do a few trial tyre changes. In the first few runs, engineers pushed the car into the pit and stopped it right on the line. Then a test pilot drove the car into the grid at medium speed and, finally, at normal speed.

'At the beginning, I had no idea what the problem was,' Murray says. 'But I knew that a tyre change can only be as fast as the slowest member of the crew, so we analysed the difference between the fastest guys and the slowest.' To every member of the crew, typically around twenty strong, Murray gave visual tracking goggles that would continuously measure their point of gaze. They then performed hundreds of pit stops while Murray studied them.

What he found was that the difference between the fastest and the slowest came down to completely different gaze patterns. As the car was coming into the pit stop, the slowest mechanics would typically be looking at the sky, at the floor, at their feet. In contrast, the fastest would be completely focused on the relevant cues – the tyres and the wheel nuts – and got the job done in two seconds.

At the end of the project, McLaren's average pit stop was cut from four and a half seconds to two and a half seconds. 'We trained them like athletes,' Murray recalls. 'It changed the culture, not just for Formula One, but within the whole Institute.' Murray wrote a seven-page manual on the results of the project, 'Analysis of visual behaviour during a pit stop', which was classed by McLaren as confidential intellectual property until 2015. The report made it explicit that the role of tyre changer was almost a sport in itself, and so McLaren began trialling people for the role.

'Previously, they used to just pick the four strongest guys,' Murray says. 'You can't expect a grease monkey to just drop what he's doing with an engine and change a tyre under pressure. They were spending millions of pounds in technology and engineering, trying to keep up with the competition, and the thing that was holding them back was the fact that they were asking grease monkeys to do the equivalent of playing chess in two point five seconds.' The report also provided step-by-step instructions for what the pit crew should be doing at every stage and in every phase as the car came into the pit lane, when the car entered the pit box and when the car stopped.

When Murray presented the results of his work to Redding, his final slide included a recommendation to make the wheel nuts impossible to miss: 'PAINT NUTS ORANGE!!!'

Nick Matthew would train four days a week in Harrogate, where David Pearson was based. Every week, he would drive up on a Sunday evening and stay until Thursday. Like Peter Nicol before him, he became part of Pearson's squash family.

A technical session with Pearson would usually be equal parts verbal and physical. He would never plan a session. He would read the player as the session progressed and adapt his feedback accordingly. English Squash's performance director kept asking Pearson to write down everything he knew, so that other coaches could learn from it, but he refused, claiming that it wasn't possible to write down feel, or sensibility, for the athlete. To him, feel was crucial to the provision of feedback.

Murray recorded their training sessions, and to analyse Matthew's technique he also used a new software called Dartfish, which allowed him to break down movement in strobe motion, to be viewed as a continuous sequence of freeze-frames. Murray could then compare Matthew's movements with how he had previously performed them by overlaying a ghost image on the screen. He would break down the swing into its sequential parts: grip, spacing between trunk and arm, top of the swing, shoulder-blade rotation, drop of the racket head, extension of the elbow, firm wrist, rotation of the forearm, extension of the shoulder, recoiling to the T.

The problem, it became clear, lay mostly in Matthew's backhand. Dartfish clearly showed that Matthew was mostly using his wrist, rather than his whole body, when taking a backhand drive shot down the wall.

'I had a break in my elbow and a break in my wrists. Both collapsed when I hit the ball,' Matthew explains. 'I was always flicking the ball from behind me with a broken wrist. I was using a lot of wrist instead of using my arm and my body. The body should go into it first; the subtleties should come from the wrist. As a result, I couldn't generate much power.'

Every day, Matthew would spend around four hours on court, just practising his technique, never breaking a sweat. 'I would sleep for twelve hours at night because I was exhausted,' Matthew says. 'I was probably working areas of the brain that had not even been tapped into yet. It was like learning to walk again.'

Matthew would hit a dozen balls and then look at the monitor. Pearson would feed him the ball slowly, as if he were a beginner. If he hit a bad shot, the coach would come to the front of the court and demonstrate the correct technique, getting Matthew to extend his arm right out. 'Like this,' Pearson would say.

Matthew practised his backhand over and over again. Frequently, the ball would go horribly astray, straight onto the floor or smack into the ceiling lights. 'I had been playing since I was a kid, and now I was learning how to hit a ball from scratch,' Matthew recalls. 'I felt a lot of self-doubt. I kept thinking, Do I really need to go through this? I'm already a good player. It was the hardest thing I've ever had to do.'

A few days before a tournament, David Pearson would stop the technical sessions. Just go and play squash, he would say. 'He was always verbal about it,' Matthew remembers, 'because feedback can become a crutch, something that players lean on too much. It can drive you mad.'

At first, Matthew had found himself going into tournaments thinking about his technique. 'Mentally, it was a lot of baggage to take into the game. You get analysis paralysis.

I would feel really happy with my progress during a session and then go into a game, and as soon as I was put under a bit of pressure, my technique would just fall to pieces.' In those early days, his ranking stalled, his confidence was shattered and his work-in-progress swing began to look ridiculous.

This was not unconscious competence. Matthew was still far too aware of how his body was moving and of when he was releasing his wrist. He was still at the cognitive stage. 'People appreciate how hard you have to work physically, but they don't understand the attention that goes into detail from a scientific point of view,' he says. 'The endless hours to change one per cent of the angle of your swing – that might make the difference between playing a drop shot into the nick and just missing it.'

Yet what Matthew describes is not a failure of willpower or of talent. Unconscious competence does not just happen. An athlete reaches it by forcing themselves to remain in the cognitive stage: they have to practise the skills which they are not yet competent at, making their training mentally strenuous. 'The best athletes always practise at the edge of success and failure,' says Mark Williams.

In September 2002, Nick Matthew was training on his own when, for the first time, everything felt just right. Elated, he immediately phoned Pearson to tell him. 'During that session I felt I could have put a fifty-pence piece on the floor and hit it every time,' he recalls.

By January 2003, Matthew was ranked in the top thirty. A year later he had climbed the board, making it into the top ten players in the world. In 2006, when he met Peter Nicol in the Commonwealth Games semi-final, Matthew was ranked number nine in the world and Nicol was number seven. Matthew had always been inspired by Nicol – by his work ethic and his commitment. Even though he lost to

Nicol in that match, he didn't leave Melbourne deflated. He left inspired, especially after Nicol's final against David Palmer, one of the most entrancing games of squash he had ever seen. The new version of Nick Matthew was a product of the system, a player who had been exposed to performance analysis since his very first day as a professional.

'I would say we cut the learning curve down by half,' Pearson says. He estimates that he modified approximately 80 per cent of Nick Matthew's swing. The process was akin to dismantling a machine and reassembling it using a different blueprint. He taught him about footwork, how to use his large wingspan to his advantage, and how to move with grace.

It was not something that every athlete would have the willpower to do. But the results of this new approach were evident. Matthew finished 2009 as world number two. In 2010, he started the year by winning thirty-five matches in a row, including the North American Open and the Australian Open. He dethroned the Egyptian Ramy Ashour from the number one spot in June 2010. He was now, according to Stafford Murray, playing at the same level as the great Peter Nicol.

11

SKELETONS ON ICE

One day in October 2002, Amy Williams was halfway up an ice track, lying face-down on an old sled. About to be pushed down the track for the first time, she didn't know what to expect and was clueless about what she was supposed to do.

The winter sport of skeleton involves athletes pushing a bony-looking sled for thirty metres flat before flinging themselves onto the sled and sliding down a track head-first, their faces just a few inches from the ice. Williams was at the Lillehammer Olympic Bobsleigh and Luge track, a meandering, 1365-metre course made of artificial ice, with sixteen turns and a vertical drop of 112 metres – enough to accelerate sliders with a force similar to that experienced by jet pilots.

Williams had been a 400-metre runner, but her budding athletics career had been interrupted in her teens by shin splints, which caused excruciating pain. In 2002, unable to train properly, she had begun looking for an alternative sport. She started modern pentathlon while at the University of Bath. The sport suited her – 'Any excuse to pursue a sport that would allow me to go riding horses,' she says – and she proved a natural at fencing and shooting.

One day, while at the gym, she struck up a casual conversation with a group of athletes who happened to be skeleton sliders. Williams tagged along to the push track at the University Sports Training Village, a concrete track where the sliders worked on the push-start part of the sport. 'It wasn't very impressive,' Williams says. 'They had an old shed, the track and little else.' They would push a sled along a set of metal runners and down a concrete slope, then were stopped by a bungee braking system at the bottom.

Williams found the experience odd but enjoyable. Later that month, she was persuaded to enter the World Push Championships in the Netherlands, where she won silver. Simon Timson, the performance director of British Skeleton at the time, encouraged her to go on the novice training camp in Lillehammer and try an actual ice track. 'I needed my student loan to pay for it,' Williams says. 'It was something like two thousand pounds – a lot of money for two weeks. I had to get myself out there and do it on my own.'

At the camp, the novice sliders started halfway up the track and then gradually made their way to the top, as they grew accustomed to the speeds, the oscillations and the corners. 'They didn't really tell you how to navigate a basic sled down a very steep ice track,' Williams says. As she sped down the track for the first time, she felt as if she was tumbling around inside a washing machine. She bit her tongue and crashed repeatedly against the track walls. Everything was acceleration, a blurred sensation of ice and speed. When she got to the bottom of the track, Williams was first engulfed by a rush of adrenalin, then she felt shocked, then scared and then, finally, she burst into tears.

'There were these beefy girls and big bobsleigh guys that I

was scared of,' Williams recalls. 'I wasn't going to be this girl who's going to be a wimp and go home crying.' So she went up for a second attempt.

After a couple of runs, she was swollen and puffy, her arms and legs black and blue. Gradually her senses began adapting to the speed, and she was managing to count the corners and registering the gradients of pressure in her body, which allowed her to manoeuvre the sled.

After that winter season, in March 2003, Williams was faced with the dilemma of either committing to skeleton or returning to pentathlon. Although Pentathlon GB would grant her funding to train as a full-time athlete, competition for a place in the national team would be stiff. Skeleton, on the other hand, offered no money but offered better odds of representing her country. 'I had no Olympic dreams,' Williams says. 'I just wanted to represent Great Britain and do the best I could. My mum always said that when I was a kid all I wanted was to do a really good job and not get told off. I hated being told off.'

She left university, moved back to her parents', and got a part-time job in a café. 'I was scooping ice cream, serving hot chocolates and making coffees all day. Not ideal for an athlete,' Williams says.

Over the summer, she was at the gym at 6 a.m. every day and again after work in the evenings. During the winter season, which started in October, the British skeleton team competed on the international skeleton circuit.

Great Britain was one of the few countries without its own ice track. They also didn't have a full-time ice coach to teach them about the technical aspects of sliding. They hired someone on a part-time basis who, according to Williams, wouldn't bother to turn up if he was in a bad mood. 'He once abandoned me at a track,' Williams says. 'I had to get a lift and a ride with another lady all the way through Germany so I could get to the next track.'

With minimal training and scant support, Williams would turn up at races with an ill-fitting sled that had been made for a man and so was too big for her. She would arrive early in the morning, before the scheduled training sessions, and walk down the side of the track, taking notes, studying the turns and planning how she was going to tackle them. Competitors were only allowed two runs a day. 'There was a lot to learn in those runs, when sometimes you have up to nineteen corners to learn,' Williams says. 'You had to accept that you couldn't learn every corner to perfection, so you just had to pick the major corners, learn them as quick as possible and then piece them together.'

In 2006, the low ranking of the British skeleton team meant that only one female athlete could represent the country at the Winter Olympics. Shelley Rudman was chosen for the team, with Williams as reserve. Williams was, however, invited to go out to Turin as a commentator for BBC Radio 5 Live.

Rudman surprised everyone by clinching the silver medal, the best-ever result for British Skeleton. Williams swore never to watch the Olympics from the sidelines again. 'It was really tough,' Williams says. 'Missing out put a fire in my belly. That was it: I was obsessed.'

As Britain has no ice track, the programme had to focus on training at the push track and in the gym. Danny Holdcroft's mandate, as the newly appointed start coach, was to create the best starters in the sport.

When Holdcroft arrived, he noticed that the team's overall approach to training was somewhat lackadaisical, as expected for part-time athletes. They would come in whenever they liked, train individually and make up their own training programmes as they went along. Holdcroft upped the number of sessions from four a week to sixteen. He told them they needed to start working as a team, come into the gym at set hours every day and work much harder. When athletes began complaining that the sessions were too long, he would reply, 'We're trying to get a gold medal. This is the way it needs to be.'

Holdcroft had a diverse background. He had been a footballer in his youth, playing for Plymouth Argyle and Crewe Alexandra. Following that, he had coached football in Ohio, and worked as a strength and conditioning coach at a national tennis youth academy in Bath. There he met a sports psychologist called Simon Timson. Timson was also the performance director of British Skeleton. When Timson offered him a job, Holdcroft still had no idea what skeleton was. He accepted, regardless.

Typically, in skeleton, athletes would have an ice coach, who would accompany them throughout the winter season and work with them on the fine skills of ice sliding, and then run complementary track and field-style training sessions two or three times a week during the summer. There had never been such a thing as a dedicated start coach in the sport, even in other countries.

Holdcroft spent hours looking at video footage, analysing different movement patterns. What became clear was that, during the start sequence, athletes had to exert a force that created a forward acceleration while running bent over. And from what he could see, the way the athletes were training had no discernible connection to what it would take to make them better starters.

'Everyone was saying that they needed to do Olympic lifts, cleans, jerks. I asked them why,' Holdcroft says. He removed them from the programme and introduced gym exercises that better emulated the movement patterns of the push start, like slide board work and lunges. He told his athletes that they had to stop running upright, because they didn't run like that in competition.

Holdcroft received a lot of criticism for the changes, but not all athletes complained about the new regime. Amy Williams enjoyed training. She liked getting strong and would turn up to training forty-five minutes early. After she had missed out on Turin, every decision had become a binary option. Even when making trivial decisions, she would ask herself: 'Will this get me to the Olympics?' 'Will this slice of cake make me faster?' No, so she wouldn't eat it. 'Will going out make me a better athlete?' No, so she would be in bed by ten every night.

'What do I need to do? Tell me what I need to do, and I'll go and do it,' she would say to Holdcroft. 'She wanted to be Olympic champion and understood the sacrifice that was needed, who did everything that you asked,' Holdcroft says.

As a coach, Holdcroft wasn't scientifically driven. He wouldn't spend much time reading the latest literature. Instead, he would observe and experiment, trying new approaches that made sense in his head. That was just how his brain worked.

For instance, in the winter of 2007, when he sat watching his team warm up at the World Championships in St Moritz, what he was witnessing didn't make much sense to him. The sun was out, but it was cold outside. The British athletes would come out of the changing rooms, tinker with their sleds, chat with the coach, do a brief warm-up, strip down to a 2mm-thick Lycra race suit and then race.

'Our warm-ups aren't great,' Holdcroft thought. 'There's no intensity. They are going outside exposing themselves to the cold. Why? Isn't this all basic stuff?'

On returning to Bath, Holdcroft broached the issue with Scott Drawer. Drawer knew just the person to help, a physiologist called Christian Cook, who had just moved from New Zealand to be a special adviser at the EIS. When Holdcroft and Cook met, the two men hit it off. Holdcroft asked Cook if he could see anything wrong with hanging around in the cold as preparation for sprinting down a skeleton slope. 'Well, it's 5°C and your athletes are standing around outside for three or four minutes before they race and they've only got a Lycra race suit on,' Cook replied. 'Of course there's something wrong with it.' Warm muscles are able to contract much faster, Cook explained, so an effective warm-up increased the explosiveness of the athletes at the starting point – a 4 per cent increase in power output per degree Celsius increase in temperature, to be exact. A warm-up at moderate intensity could produce an optimal temperature increase of three to four degrees after ten minutes. But by the time the athletes reached the start line, their temperature had dropped and their muscles were cold again.

Holdcroft asked Cook to introduce the idea to his athletes: 'You're the renowned scientist. It will have more impact coming from you.'

First, they bussed the athletes to the EIS centre at Bisham Abbey, to use the cold chamber there. They measured how fast their temperatures dropped after a warm-up. The standard warm-up protocol lasted twenty minutes and consisted of a combination of jogging, sprints, calisthenics and stretching. The warm-up usually started thirty-five minutes before the race. The athletes would then strip down to their race suits, weigh themselves to ensure they were within the weight limits, wait in the pre-race call room, and then go to the starting area five minutes before the start of the race. Over several weeks, they experimented with different warm-up protocols, varying the timing and intensity of the exercises and the interval until the start.

They found that a warm-up with 30 per cent more intensity and a fifteen-minute interval until the race improved performance by nearly 5 per cent, a marginal gain that, at the Turin Winter Olympics, for instance, represented the difference between first and second place.

They also discussed with the athletes the optimal procedure for leaving the changing room and standing in the starting block just before the race.

'You're walking out six minutes before your run starts. Why are you there so early?' Holdcroft asked.

'We want to see what the sleds look like,' was the reply.

'No – in. The coach will tell you. If you need that information, ask the coach.'

Two minutes to the start was the earliest that Holdcroft allowed them to go out. 'And when you go out, you need to wear clothes.'

'But it takes so long to get them off.'

'No, you think it does. Take your clothes off now. I'm timing,' Holdcroft would say.

It took twenty seconds.

'Really?' the athletes replied. 'That's not too bad, is it?'

'They hadn't thought about it,' Holdcroft explains. 'We got the protocol down to a real structure. Warm-up inside. Precise timings. Boom. Optimal as you get.'

Drawer, Cook and Holdcroft also experimented with heat pads, the idea being that they could warm the athletes' legs while they waited in the changing room. Holdcroft volunteered to be the guinea pig. They were trying pads that could heat up to 90°C. Holdcroft placed them on his thighs, turned them on and felt nothing. 'It's not working,' he said. Then they started heating up. He ended up with two square burnt patches on his legs. They opted instead to try survival jackets that could retain body heat. The jackets had puffy plastic sleeves and lurid colours. Not all athletes opted to wear them. 'Do you want to wear that?' Holdcroft asked Amy Williams. 'Because you'll look stupid.' Williams's response was predictable: if it made her faster, of course she would wear it.

In 2006, Scott Drawer emailed his collaborators at the University of Southampton to ask whether they would be able to find a PhD student to work with the British Skeleton team. One of the students they put forward was an engineer called Rachel Blackburn.

Blackburn was a former competitive sailor, who had studied ship science and came with a recommendation from the technical director of the Olympic sailing programme. She had never heard of skeleton before, so in the evening before her interview she did some perfunctory background research.

'What do you know about skeleton?' she was asked at her interview.

'They go down a bobsleigh track,' she replied.

'How?'

'Feet first?'

'No, that's luge,' Drawer replied. 'How heavy is the sled?'

'Five kilos?'

'More like thirty.'

Blackburn had the distinct feeling that she had botched the interview, but afterwards she was told that she had been selected for the programme, along with James Roche, who like Blackburn was a competitive sailor and had read ship science at Southampton. The two students were to undertake the project as part of their PhD work. Their salaries were effectively a graduate scholarship – or, as Blackburn says, 'They basically wanted people to do it on the cheap.'

The project involved the design of a new sled for the Sochi Winter Games in 2014. They divided it in two, with Blackburn in charge of the sled's design, and Roche working on the aerodynamic components, from helmets to skinsuits. They called it BlackRoc, a portmanteau of their surnames.

In 2007, Blackburn and Roche travelled with the British skeleton team for the first time, joining them at the World Championships in St Moritz. 'I took my sailing boots, thinking it would be a good idea,' Blackburn recalls. 'I spent the best part of three days slipping on the ice of the Swiss mountains.'

At St Moritz, Blackburn learned how the sleds were prepared for competition and how they were looked after and inspected before a race. She had brought her camera and attempted to take a few pictures of the sleds in action. 'They were so fast all I got were photos of an empty track,' Blackburn recalls. At the end of the event, she met performance director Andi Schmid and ice coach Mickey Grünberger. Both had just recently joined the programme and bombarded her with questions and opinions about what could be achieved with the new sled.

Over the winter season, as Blackburn spent more time with the team, she began overseeing the maintenance of the sleds. Skeleton sleds are typically flat 1.2-metre trays made of steel. The athlete lies on the sled, face down, head first, cradled in a saddle covered with adhesive tape. A pair of bumpers jut out at the sides, as protection against collision with the ice walls of the track. Underneath the sled are two long strips of stainless steel, the only point of contact between sled and ice. These runners can be bowed to decrease the area that touches the ice, making it faster. The sharpest parts of the runner, the blades, dig into the ice, providing grip.

During a run, a sled undergoes intense vibration. It became

Blackburn's job to check that the components remained intact and free of rust patches. She would also check that the runners were bowed according to the coach's specification and the saddle was fitted properly, and ensure that the sleds were levelled horizontally. Depending on the weight of the athlete, she would have to drill holes in the sled, move the saddle forwards or backwards, and fit them again to make sure the sled was levelled. 'The athletes were changing sizes by several inches between the end of the season and the start of the winter season,' Blackburn says. 'It was all [Holdcroft's] fault.'

Back in Southampton, Blackburn set herself to finding out what made a sled both fast and stable. She got her hands on four different sleds, including the one used by the British team, and equipped them with a variety of sensors, from strain gauges to accelerometers. 'Given that I had never wired anything before in my life it was quite a challenge,' she recalls.

Blackburn had to obtain permission to use other countries' ice tracks in order to run her tests. Nations like Germany had three ice tracks and the luxury of testing their sleds with twenty athletes over the Christmas break. Blackburn had to content herself with a few hours a day on a track in Austria during the pre-season, in the last months of autumn, when the ice was still thin and bumpy. 'Normally they would have twenty-five track workers scraping the ice to make it smooth,' Blackburn says. 'We had only four, sweeping it with a brush.'

Schmid and Grünberger volunteered as Blackburn's guinea pigs. The two Austrians were former world champions and had been sliding together since their teens. They had experience in designing their own sleds and had strong opinions about it, which were mostly intuitive and lacked objective technical insight. What Blackburn needed were quantitative facts, not opinionated Austrians.

She made the two coaches do as many runs as they could every day, using different sleds and varying parameters such as the bow of the runners and the weight of the saddle. To receive some form of systematic feedback, Blackburn tried getting them to fill in a questionnaire after their runs, but the coaches complained that they were too tired to do it after sliding. Instead, she provided them with Dictaphones so that they could simply record their thoughts after a run. 'Their English wasn't great,' Blackburn says. 'They kept saying, "I'm totally naked". I asked them what they meant by that. They were trying to say "knackered". I had to break it to them that they meant quite different things in English.'

Blackburn also compiled a questionnaire for the athletes. It took two hours to complete and had hundreds of questions about all aspects of their sleds, from controllability to the tape used on the handles of the saddle. From the feedback, Blackburn realised that Williams was the one athlete who didn't want to look inside a sled. 'Some athletes are control freaks but she just didn't like to know,' Blackburn says. 'She just wanted to be given the sled and told it was as fast as it could possibly be.'

In March 2008, Schmid told Blackburn that there had been a change of plan regarding the new equipment. British Skeleton was now looking to compete in the 2010 Winter Olympics with new sleds and was planning to sign a contract with a commercial sled manufacturer. Blackburn was to carry on pursuing her project on the side, but she told them that there would be no need: she would deliver new sleds in time for Vancouver. She secluded herself in an office at defence tech company BAE Systems, who were collaborating with UK Sport, and, armed with the sled data sheets and the athletes' feedback, completed the new design in six months. Blackburn then gave a two-hour presentation to Caroline

Hargrove, who Scott Drawer had asked to evaluate the new sled design, at the McLaren Technology Centre. 'I was so nervous I don't remember what the feedback was,' Blackburn says. The project was green-lighted. Four weeks later, three prototype sleds had been built.

The sleds were taken to the Igls ice track in Austria for their first run. The two coaches made a bet about how fast the new sled would be, down to the hundreth of the second. Schmid was optimistic about its performance, while Grünberger was sceptical that a student who'd never driven a sled could design one.

'I was terrified,' Blackburn says. 'I really hoped my maths was correct. I didn't want to kill someone halfway down the track. I just wanted them to get to the bottom in one piece.'

The Austrians took turns, and Schmid won the bet. Grünberger had to take a two-minute ice bath as a forfeit.

The new sleds were made in two sizes: one for female athletes and a larger version for men. They incorporated a saddle designed to fit the individual athlete. They also made them modular, allowing athletes to customise the sled by removing or adding components, with a chassis that could be adapted to different track geometries and driving styles. In theory, a stiffer sled was a faster one, but that somehow never applied to Amy Williams. She preferred one that she could manoeuvre. There was a weight limit for all competitions, dictating how much the sled and the athlete could weigh. For women, that was 92kg, with a limit of up to 29kg for the sled. Often, Williams would have to cut bits out of her sled or spend forty minutes in the sauna dehydrating herself to make that limit. Having a saddle that actually fitted her, and the option of subtracting weight from the sled, was a boon.

Williams always named her sleds. Her previous one had

been Flat Stanley. She christened the new sled Arthur. 'I've got to look after Arthur,' she thought, 'and he will look after me.'

By early 2010, Rachel Blackburn had manufactured the new sleds for all but two of the athletes in British Skeleton: Shelley Rudman and her fiancé Kristan Bromley. Rudman and Bromley operated independently from the rest of the British skeleton team. Bromley, whose nickname was Dr Ice, had a PhD in skeleton dynamics and made his own sleds through Bromley Technologies, the company he had founded with his brother Richard. The company had supplied sleds to British Skeleton, but Bromley would often refuse to share the newest designs with the rest of the team, keeping them for Rudman and himself.

The relationship between Rudman and Williams, at first amicable, had been deteriorating since 2005, when it became clear that only one of them could qualify for the Winter Olympics. 'Every race, you knew you were trying to beat the other girl, not athletes from other countries,' Williams says. 'It didn't matter if you were tenth, as long as your teammate was eleventh. It created a lot of bad feeling within the team.' By this time, they were barely speaking.

Williams also felt that the ice coaches treated her differently because Rudman was the favourite to win a medal. According to Williams, she would never be asked for her opinion, making her feel that she was very low in the pecking order.

During that winter season, away from home and friends, Williams had struggled. In training, she could beat anyone and would often break records. She was, by then, one of the world's fastest push-start sprinters. But in racing, she floundered. Grünberger called her the training champion. She had never won a race in competition.

'Her stress levels were very high during competitions,' Cook says. 'Amy used to get too aroused, and that arousal cost her in terms of energy across the four races.' Many times she thought of quitting, and many times she told the team director that she was finished with skeleton. Williams, a naturally gregarious person, thrived on the camaraderie of the many friends she had made among the international athletes. She enjoyed the banter and the distraction. During competitions, restricted to socialising with her own team, she found the environment oppressive.

'The coach would always tell me that I wasn't concentrating because I enjoyed chatting with people,' Williams says. 'Everything was serious, deadly silent and no one spoke to each other. I hated that silence.' She wasn't even allowed to meet her then boyfriend, a Czech bobsleigher, in the lobby of the hotel for a hot chocolate. 'We would sneak out to the car park for half an hour and that was it,' Williams says.

Her only solace was the presence of Rachel Blackburn, with whom she had struck up a friendship. 'You are in close proximity with two Austrian coaches whose English isn't great and two athletes who don't want to talk to you, and there's absolutely nothing for miles but woods,' Blackburn says. 'Amy was definitely glad I was there.'

Williams began seeing a psychologist, who eventually discerned that the reason she wasn't performing was simply because she wasn't happy in competitions. She needed to recreate her happy environment. 'I was never brave enough to say anything when I felt I was being mistreated and make my true feelings known. But I needed to be firm. This was my dream.'

The Whistler track was considered the fastest in the world. It had a snap 180-degree turn towards the end of the run, hitting sliders with a sudden acceleration nearing 5g. Even though Williams wasn't too enthusiastic about the high G-forces, she seemed to do well on these types of tracks. One leg of the 2008–09 Skeleton World Cup had been held at Whistler, where Williams won silver, her first international medal. 'I think that from that World Cup I knew: hang on a minute, me and this track do get on. We do like each other,' she thought.

Preparation had been going smoothly for Williams when, two weeks before the Olympics, at the Olympic holding camp in Lake Placid, she was given a new set of metal runners for her sled. The runners had been manufactured by a team of researchers at University College London, under Rachel Blackburn's supervision, and in theory would make the sled a lot faster. Trialling the new equipment, Williams crashed several times, breaking her sled and injuring herself. She hadn't crashed in years.

'It scared the life out of me,' Williams says. She couldn't adapt to the new runners and felt that she wasn't going to have time to get used to them. According to Williams, she was pressured to use the runners at the Olympics, given the large investment that had been made in them, but Williams stood her ground. Feeling in sync with her sled was paramount to her. 'It's like when you get in your car, and the seat and the mirrors are set up just right and you drive home and you don't know how you got home,' she says. 'I had to feel at one with my sled.'

So Williams's confidence was already shaken when, on 12 February, the opening day of the Winter Olympics, she was told that a Georgian luger, Nodar Kumaritashvili, had just died after a crash at the ice track. During a training run, the out-of-control slider was ejected from the track at one of the bottom corners and smashed into a metal support post. He was airlifted to hospital, where he was pronounced dead.

It was not clear at first whether the culprit had been Kumaritashvili's sled or if the track itself was unsafe. As a precaution, sliders were granted an extra practice run, scheduled for 5 a.m., to allow them to get better acquainted with the track. Williams and an Italian slider were the only people to show up. 'I just had to get rid of my nerves,' Williams says. 'I wanted to do that one run and know that I wasn't going to die.'

After that session, one of the ice coaches walked with Williams down the side of the track, helping her visualise the corners. 'It helped me become friends with it,' Williams says. 'I probably learned more from him than the rest of the day.' It was the same coach who had abandoned her at a track once. At the end of the walk, he gave Williams a delicate copper Olympic rings necklace that had been blessed by Buddhist monks for luck.

Later that day, Williams was putting on a sock when she felt one of the discs in her spine pop. The pain was agonising. She couldn't bend over. She asked her physiotherapist to give her as many painkillers as she was allowed to take.

On the day of the race, Williams followed her usual routine methodically. Three hours before the race, she went to the gym to do leg presses, an exercise that had been prescribed by Christian Cook to prime herself for competition. Then she prepared her sled.

A few minutes before the race, she began warming up. Everything was timed precisely. She knew, from tests in the Bisham Abbey cold chamber, that exactly twenty seconds after she had got down to her skinsuit her temperature would start to drop, so she would need to be sprinting down the slope before that deadline. She had sewed Velcro to her shoes and trousers so that she could undress quicker. She heard her name called over the PA system, and walked out, having donned her bright pink survival jacket. She felt uncomfortably hot, with sweat trickling down her back – a sign that she was at an optimal temperature.

Holdcroft was standing at the gantry over the track next to one of the coaches, watching the warm-up, when the song 'I Gotta Feeling' by the Black Eyed Peas came on the PA system. 'We just looked at one another and had a feeling, like it was going to happen,' Holdcroft says.

In the first run of the competition, starting positions were dictated by world ranking, so Williams went fifth. She sprinted down the straight and launched herself onto the sled.

Williams always tried to get herself into her ideal position on the sled as quickly as possible. She had learned this after spending countless hours at the Southampton wind tunnel, trying out different helmets and skinsuits, aching so much that she would be crying inside her helmet, her body so cold that she would always be ill for a few days afterwards. She hated the wind tunnel, but it was there that she learned how to shape her body in the most aerodynamic way. This involved rounding her shoulders, but not excessively, keeping her head as low as possible, her elbows tucked in and her hands pressed flat against the saddle. Williams held herself in perfect tension, her feet together except when she occasionally used them to steer.

Williams had decided that during the competition she didn't want to know how the other sliders were performing. She was going to avoid looking at the television or the time sheets. If something needed changing, her coach would tell her. 'I'd literally have my fingers in my ears,' Williams says. 'Knowing wasn't going to make me faster.'

The rules dictated that on the second run the slowest slider would go first. Williams went last. At the end of the first day of competition, Williams was wilfully ignorant of the fact that she had a 0.3-second advantage over second-placed Kerstin Szymkowiak of Germany. The United States, Canada and Germany had filed a protest regarding Williams's helmet, which had small ridges incorporated around the back. In theory, James Roche's design could give Williams a 0.01 per cent gain if her head was in a certain position. The International Bobsleigh and Toboggan Federation dismissed the complaint.

On the fourth and final run of the competition, the fastest slider would again be last to go. Williams was in the changing room alone, unaware of how well her competitors were doing, awaiting her call.

She was the last to be called. She walked to the starting block. After that, everything happened far too fast for her to remember much. She was aware that she made mistakes. When she reached the bottom of track, she saw Schmid approaching. She asked him what her final position was.

When she was told she was Olympic champion, she didn't know how to react. She had broken the track record twice and won by more than half a second. She kept her helmet on, feeling dazed. 'I wish I had reacted in some other way,' Williams remembers. 'I just felt really shy.'

In the meantime, Rachel Blackburn had been called into the jury room where Williams's sled, Arthur, was to undergo a full inspection. The top six sleds are always taken for inspection, in the presence of a team member. Blackburn was asked to dismantle the sled. The thought that Amy Williams could have her medal taken away because of something she had done to the design of the sled petrified Blackburn. Had she missed any rule? Did she screw up the measurements? It was the most stressful experience she had ever endured. She was shaking so much that she struggled to undo the bolts on the sled. 'It's okay, Rachel,' a member of the jury told her, 'I can do this one.' Blackburn's ordeal lasted thirty minutes, while the jury inspected each component. To her immense relief, they didn't find any fault.

Williams remembers wanting to hug her coaches and her parents after her race, but she couldn't see them anywhere. She was directed to the media zone and then to doping control. 'I was being pulled around,' Williams remembers. 'Then I had to go for a meal out with all the posh people of British Skeleton and the Olympic Association and all these people that I didn't want to be sat having a meal with. I wanted to be sat with my team and I wasn't allowed.'

Williams was beyond tired. She didn't know what to eat, she couldn't even make out what the menu said. It was like she had hit a brick wall. She went to the toilets and locked the door. Then she just cried. Her initial feeling was relief. Then pride that she was bringing a medal home, that she was part of history. She remembered how she had always been disappointed, how she had never won a race. Forever the training champion. 'Finally, girl, you did it,' she thought to herself. 'Take your time. Finally, you've won a race.'

12

THE WINNER EFFECT

When two animals square up in anticipation of a fight, they experience a rise in testosterone levels. Given that testosterone is a natural anabolic steroid, these rising hormone levels are essentially a self-doping mechanism that prepares the animal for competition. When it floods into the bloodstream – excreted from the male's testicles or the female's ovaries – it increases the blood's capacity to carry oxygen, quickening the speed of reactions and amplifying the body's strength as a result. Testosterone also affects the central nervous system, increasing an animal's fearlessness and appetite for risk.

This reaction is not restricted to the anticipation of a challenge. In the aftermath, winners can emerge with a tenfold increase in the amount of testosterone circulating in their bodies, whereas losers' testosterone levels can be suppressed by the same order of magnitude. This doping effect can sometimes last for months, and increases the winner's probability of winning the next confrontation. Nature primes winners to keep on winning and losers to keep on losing. Biologists have termed it, appropriately, the winner effect.

The winner effect has been observed in numerous species, from insects to reptiles, from cichlids to rhesus macaques, but it is not exclusive to the wild. The same effect has also been observed in humans, predominantly in sport: fencing, tennis, even chess. If, for instance, a judoka wins the first bout, the likelihood of winning the subsequent bouts increases. The winner effect also explains statistical anomalies in sport such as home advantage and the hot hand, and why fans of winning teams, as well as the teams themselves, experience a post-victory spike in testosterone.

Christian Cook remembers that, in the early noughties, testosterone was still widely considered to be a hormone whose main effect was to facilitate the growth of muscle. 'We still had the stereotypical vision of the balloon-muscled man injecting a hundred times his normal physiological levels of testosterone into his body,' Cook says. 'It biased our thinking and people assumed that testosterone only made muscle.'

The discovery of the winner effect shattered that notion. Although steroids catalyse reactions that produce muscle, it became clear that, within a normal biological range, testosterone's main role was behavioural. It was not that testosterone gave you something extra for free, Cook found, but that it allowed you to express more of what you were capable of.

'If you have higher levels of testosterone, you can jump higher and lift more weight, not just because you may have more muscle power, but because your hormonal levels allow you to express that power more freely,' Cook explains. 'Testosterone gives you more confidence and motivation, and that makes you work harder, which indirectly influences muscle growth.' He speculates that this is the reason athletes become addicted to steroids: because of the confidence boost they get from artificial testosterone. This is why Christian Cook tells athletes and coaches that testosterone is not a molecule of the muscle but, fundamentally, a molecule of the mind. He is also keen to emphasise that testosterone is a part of a complex system that dictates how athletes respond to stress imposed by training. This he knows from his own research, which took him from experiments on lab mice to working with one of the top rugby teams in the world.

In the late eighties, as a physiology student at the University of Auckland, Cook was captivated by the ideas of Robert Sapolsky, who spent nearly thirty years studying the social behaviour of baboon troops in Kenya. Baboon troops have rigid hierarchical structures, where the social rank of males is dictated by brutal one-on-one fights. Losers are not only subjugated by the alpha males and relegated to the bottom of the social rank: Sapolsky observed that these males are also more prone to sickness and mental disease.

Whereas Hans Selye is widely considered to have discovered the stress response, Sapolsky is regarded as the first to make the link between stress hormones and the social environment. 'Selye was a visionary, whereas Sapolsky was an explorer,' Cook says. 'He bridged the laboratory research to the real world.' In 1989, Cook attended a lecture by Sapolsky, and left the room feeling inspired. He thought: 'This is what I want to do. This is what, in the long term, is going to answer many questions at the core of who we are as humans, from the moment we are born.'

By then, endocrinologists had mapped out the complex hormonal web that mediated Selye's general adaptation syndrome. In the most simple terms, when people feel stressed their brain triggers the release of cortisol, a hormone that puts the body in a heightened state of alert. Cortisol mobilises nutrients into the bloodstream, rapidly increasing its glucose levels and providing muscles with a burst of energy. Cortisol also shuts down all non-essential bodily processes, such as the digestive and reproductive systems. It is also a natural anti-inflammatory. 'If you take a hard blow in rugby you will have an elevated level of cortisol for twenty-four hours,' Cook says. An acute cortisol response to a challenge is fundamental to survival.

However, this stress response is designed to be short-lived. Problems therefore arise when stress does not go away, and cortisol builds up in a body over months and years. In the seventies, neuroscientists found that when lab mice are repeatedly exposed to uncontrollable stressors, such as electric shocks, after a while they will fail to leave their cages even if the door is left open. Biologists call this state learned helplessness. It's a stark illustration of the extent to which high levels of cortisol can dramatically change our brain and subsequently our behaviour: you feel you no longer have control over your own fate, even if a way out is right in front of you. You become risk-averse and despondent.

'If I put you under huge stress for a week, it wouldn't do anything too detrimental to you,' Cook says. 'But if I put you under huge stress for a month, you probably would start to lose weight and lose sleep. If I continue that for fifteen years, you might develop heart disease, type two diabetes, obesity and symptoms of dementia.'

Cook initiated his research career in paediatrics at the University of Auckland, investigating how stress affects the foetus in utero. Like Sapolsky, Cook began his investigations by observing animals in their habitats. He studied how human encroachment affected polar bears. He concerned himself with the ethics of animal domestication. When working with lab mice, Cook would create rich universes for them, complete with wheels, mazes, ladders, see-saws and treats, finding that these animals, as adults, grew up to be more resilient to stress and more functional socially. 'You could argue that's what the wild looks like anyway,' Cook says. 'Most domesticated animals inhabit far blander environments.' Cook always felt that, as masters of their domain, it was their responsibility to make their lives better.

Then, in 1997, after delivering a talk on how stress made critical-care patients more susceptible to septicaemia, Cook was approached by a coach from Team New Zealand, which in 1995 had won the America's Cup, the oldest and most prestigious sailing competition in the world. Cook was asked if he would be interested in studying the stress responses of sailors in training.

'Although it sounds idyllic, being out and about at sea on a sunny day, they were doing eight hours of demanding sailing drills regularly,' Cook says. This collaboration with Team New Zealand subsequently led to an opportunity to work with the All Blacks, then coached by the legendary Wayne Smith.

The nature of primal hormonal responses to challenge and danger is ingrained in rugby. 'In the rugby scrum, you have eight men on either side, and each is dependent on the physicality of every other one of those men,' Cook says. 'That scrum is related to something that's long been ingrained in human history, when our far-flung ancestors were hunters and gatherers that depended on each other for survival.'

Cook was now studying stress not as something relative to disease, but as something that underpinned human performance. That connection, of course, had previously been made, linking stress to physiological adaptation. But Cook went one step further, linking it to behaviour on the pitch.

The roots of this theory came from a deeper, more challenging idea: that many of the decisions that we assume are conscious processes are strongly manipulated by signals from our bodies. This was something that Cook first noticed when he worked with Wayne Smith and the All Blacks. Smith was particularly interested in how the players were influenced by what he said and the way he said it.

In rugby, there is a huge reliance on the people playing in the team, and a clearly structured hierarchy. Cook was amazed by the influence a coach had on what the players felt about their performance. This took him back to Sapolsky's big idea: the notion that the social environment deeply affects each person's physiology.

The fundamental lesson was that there was no such thing as pure human intellect, untainted by the hormonal waves and other signals that arise from the rest of the body. ('Physiologists often don't think about the brain and neuro-scientists often don't think about the rest of the body,' Bruce McEwen, a pioneer in the study of neurophysiology and stress, says. 'People have to realise that hormones are not only controlled by the brain, they act on the brain. They affect all sorts of behaviours.')

Performance and its associated concepts of adaptation, stress and recovery turned out to be far from purely physical phenomena. They were also processes of the mind. 'What we found in rugby is that you could be recovered physically but not be ready to compete,' says Cook. 'Recovery is far more than the ability to physically perform. It's also the ability to mentally make yourself perform. The power of the brain and the power of the muscle are not really separable, and to go down that line is probably a non-productive way of exam-ining athletes.'

This optimal state – what Cook called readiness to com-pete – is dependent on the player's hormonal balance and appropriate physical recovery. Training programmes are designed to be intermittently stressful. Any kind of physical exertion is accompanied by a release of cortisol in the body. Once that stress response is switched off, the body turns on a testosterone response to cope with the stress and rebuild its energy stores. In this way, the body adapts to physical stress through a rhythmic alteration, a period of physical loading followed by a period of recovery and adaptation. That adaptation increases an individual's capacity to handle stress.

Elite athletes have an unusual ability to cope with challenges: their initial stress response is strong, but abates quickly. The two hormones are not necessarily antagonistic: high volumes of cortisol require high volumes of testosterone. By tracking the testosterone-to-cortisol ratio, Cook found a biochemical performance indicator. A high ratio indicates a positive recovery, whereas a low ratio signals over-training. Monitoring an athlete's testosterone and cortisol responses, Cook found, could provide him with a reliable diagnosis of an athlete's readiness to compete.

In 2005, Cook made his first trip to the United Kingdom, to deliver a lecture. It was there that he was told that he absolutely had to meet the head of the Research and Innovation programme at UK Sport, a man called Scott Drawer.

When Cook met Drawer, the two men immediately hit it off. Drawer saw how ground-breaking Cook's research was, so he invited the New Zealander to move to England and pursue his work under the sponsorship of UK Sport. London had just been selected as the host of the 2012 Olympic Games, and the prospect of working with Olympic athletes in the run-up to a home Games was a singular opportunity. 'Scott was telling me that he wanted to be innovative, to think differently to see what happens,' Cook says. 'The thing about Scott is that he gives people so much freedom creatively, then he gets out and finds the money to get stuff done.'

Cook accepted the offer, and in 2006 moved to Bath to take up a position in the Sports Science Department at the university. Drawer introduced him to Danny Holdcroft, at the British Skeleton team, and to other national squads around the country, including British Cycling, where Cook began a collaboration with the 2005 world champion Victoria Pendleton.

Cook also collaborated with Chris Gaviglio, the performance coach of Bath Rugby. The club became a de facto laboratory for Cook to continue his experiments and to test the ideas that he had been pursuing with the All Blacks. When it came to Olympic sports, Cook worked with athletes who seldom competed all year round and whose performance cycle ran over four years. With rugby, on the other hand, Cook had thirty experimental subjects who played week in, week out. Furthermore, rugby was the ideal ecological setting for Cook to investigate his notion of readiness to compete. 'Rugby is a combat sport with a high degree of aggressive interaction,' Cook says. 'Believe me, you have to be mentally prepared for a game of rugby. If you have 120-kilo men running at you, you want to be prepared.'

When preparing athletes for competition, most sports scientists began at a macro level, designing a periodisation plan for a competition year, or even across the four years to an Olympic Games. They then concerned themselves with the day-to-day detail of what would happen as they approached the competition. At Bath Rugby, Cook and Gaviglio opted to reverse-engineer that process, working backwards from the day of competition.

For his first study, Cook recruited twenty-two male professional rugby players and took saliva samples forty minutes before a game and fifteen minutes after. From these samples, the players' cortisol and testosterone levels were measured. During the period of the study, the team played six games, winning three and losing three. Cook then compared the hormonal data against the match outcomes. A performance score ranking was also devised, from 1 (Bad loss: 'Due to amount of points lost by poor skill decision making and execution during the game') to 6 (Good win: 'A dominant win. Reflected usually by the quality of the opponent (good) and the score, including intermediate scores that accounted for unlucky losses in the last few minutes or good performances not reflected by the score line').

When he compared the pre-game testosterone concentrations with the performance indicators, Cook realised that hormonal levels predicted how a player would perform that day. This surprised him. 'The hormones that we measure first thing in the morning don't usually correlate with an awful lot,' Cook says. This meant that, prior to competition, there was indeed an anticipatory rise in the testosterone levels that predicted how competitive the athlete was going to be.

In a second study, Cook measured the hormonal responses of the players to a training session in the middle of the week – three days after their regular Saturday match and four days before the next. Again he observed that, before going on to win the Saturday match, the players were already presenting a significant increase in their testosterone responses to a workout. On the other hand, if their testosterone response was weak, the likelihood that they would lose the upcoming match was much higher. 'We've gone back three days from a game now, and we already had the ability to strongly predict how well they would play on Saturday,' Cook says.

These findings suggested that the testosterone response to a workout was a way to monitor an athlete's readiness to compete, with a high response suggesting that an optimal state had been reached. By methodically tracking players' testosterone responses, Cook was essentially mapping out the neurophysiological recovery that bridges the interval between one game and the next. 'In that initial phase following a game, you are recovering and dealing with whether you won, lost, how you played,' Cook says. 'On Monday, you're still coming off a game, so it's too early to have that response.' The turning point seems to happen somewhere around the middle of the week. 'If you're on the right track, you become far more responsive to a stress that's imposed on you. But if you don't have that by Wednesday, it becomes really hard to be right by Saturday.'

The question for Christian Cook then became: what could be done in the first few days after a game to manipulate the players' hormonal state and aid their recovery? On Mondays, the coach usually held a debrief. Cook found that coaches could often be extremely critical of their players, focusing too much on the negative aspects of their performance instead of praising their efforts.

Cook suggested a different approach. He gave the coach a shortlist of standard phrases from which to choose, such as 'You did that poorly, why couldn't you do that right?' or 'Well done, that's how you do it, you performed really well.' Half the group received positive feedback, with the coach positively reinforcing things that were done well, whereas the other half listened to the coach negatively reinforcing things that had been done badly.

Players who received positive feedback had a 30 per cent higher testosterone response than those who received negative feedback. This effect lasted several days, right up to the next match, when the players who had had positive feedback performed better than the players who were criticised.

'You get to a competition, your athletes prepared physically as best they can,' Scott Drawer says. 'That coach–athlete interaction can make or break that environment. Psychologists talk about it, but what we're trying to do is measure and understand it. From the perspective of the coach, what buttons they push, how they push them, how they set up that brief and debrief environment is really crucial.'

Cook designed a different kind of intervention for Sundays, the day after the game, when the players usually got together socially. They were presented with an hour-long video montage of their mistakes and successes from the match the day before. He had one group watch the video in the presence of strangers who were larger than they were; another group with strangers who were smaller; a third group watched it with friends who were larger; and a fourth group with friends who were smaller. When the groups were assessed three days later, all registered an augmented testosterone response. Surprisingly, the players who had watched the video with larger friends registered the strongest testosterone response before the match six days later. Although Cook had expected that larger companions would pose a threat to dominance, he later theorised that, in the context of rugby, dominant males might actually be perceived as supportive.

In a similar study, the players were shown several four-minute videos. These included a gag from the *The Big Bang Theory*, a clip of starving children in Africa, a clip featuring exotic dancing, a motivational clip featuring UFC fighter Brock Lesnar and a clip of major aggressive rugby moments. With the exception of the clip of starving children, all of the videos generated an increase of testosterone in the players, which then translated into improved performance when doing squats fifteen minutes later.

These findings neatly corroborate the animal studies on the winner effect. But when it comes to humans, Cook's work makes another, subtler point, which is that testosterone is not related to winning. It is in fact related to our *perception* of winning: 'What you thought about your performance in the game, irrespective of whether you won or lost,' Cook explains. 'That can be used to put athletes in a much better state both physically and mentally at the start of the next week.'

Many factors impinge on our hormonal reactions: a message from a coach; the content of a video; the context of social interactions. If used appropriately, these can prime athletes to recover faster and perform better. Similarly, ignoring them can have deleterious effects on performance.

The elegance of these pioneering studies was that they cut through the messy complexity of human physiology and identify clear relationships between objective performance indicators and the interior hormonal world. These studies mark a conceptual leap forward from the abstraction of Selye's theory and the one-size-fits-all periodisation templates of Soviet sports science. Hormonal tracking not only provided a deeper understanding of stress responses and physiological adaptation, but also of the individual.

'People's bodies respond differently,' Cook explains. 'A lot of our training is wrong because it enforces the same programme for everyone. There may be athletes who, if they were trained in a different way, would have succeeded. Instead, we're setting them up for a cycle of continual failure from day one. It's survival of the fittest, but it's not necessarily survival of the best.

13

A BITTERSWEET VICTORY

The first symptoms of Stafford Murray's torturous relationship with food showed at the age of two, when he started vomiting up any fruit or vegetables that his mother tried to feed him. He was a fussy eater. Only much later was he introduced – by Mike Hughes – to something he actually enjoyed: curry.

To Hughes, beer and curry were essential to living the good life. It was also over a beer and curry that analysts bonded with coaches and gleaned vital information from athletes. When Murray worked for Hughes at UWIC, they would dine every night at the Himalaya, a curry house in Cardiff. The Himalaya sponsored the university squash team and would offer them a special price: curry and a naan for £2.50. 'We were probably the first-ever sports team to be sponsored by a curry house,' Murray says.

Hughes would ask the chef to make his curry as hot as he possibly could, while Murray would ask for a chicken korma, requesting the chicken and the rice in separate bowls, along with a portion of chips. 'It was sacrilege,' Murray says. 'The first time I went to a curry house was in

Cardiff, and I thought curry was the sauce that you got on the chips.'

For three years, Murray exclusively ate chicken korma before transitioning to chicken tikka masala. By his late twenties, he had been on a consistent diet of four crumpets with Marmite in the morning, a bacon sandwich for lunch, six pints of beer at the pub after work, followed by a curry for dinner. If his dinner companion happened to be David Pearson, who had adopted the eating habits of his analyst, they would have, on average, three portions of naan and five poppadums to share, and four pints of beer each. To top it all off, Murray also had a habit of smoking eight Café Crème cigars a day. 'Absolutely disgusting,' Murray recalls. 'I've no right to be alive.'

By the time his back exploded while playing a recreational game of squash and surgeons had to fuse two of his vertebrae, Murray weighed twenty-one stone. Certainly, his history of squash training involving seven-mile runs in a pair of plimsolls and playing on wooden floors laid over concrete – not sprung, as modern courts are had damaged his back, but, as his doctor pointed out, his obesity was placing undue strain on his already weakened spine.

He knew that he had to change his dietary habits, but that wasn't a straightforward proposition. He was the type of person who became anxious when invited to eat out with other people, and usually made excuses not to go simply because he was so picky about what he ate. Once, in New York, Pearson walked out of a restaurant after Murray kept badgering the waiter to make sure there were absolutely no herbs in his chicken pasta. Pearson told him he had had enough of his stupid ways, and left. 'I stayed there and had my pasta without the bits of herbs and David had steak next door.'

It was only after his third back surgery that the precarious condition of his health finally dawned on Murray. It happened following a bizarre incident on a sunny Sunday afternoon in the autumn of 2009. Murray was in his back garden, sipping a beer and painting his shed, when he heard a blood-curdling scream. He looked over his fence and saw a woman crying in panic. Her baby was hanging from the jaws of a pit bull terrier.

Murray jumped over the fence and swung a kick at the dog. The terrier dropped the baby and bolted. Murray, despite being out of shape and overweight, gave chase across a nearby football pitch. The two eventually came to a dead end, at which point the dog turned around, growling and foaming at the mouth. 'Oh fuck,' Murray thought and sprinted back to his garden, the dog now in pursuit. He jumped over his fence, tripped and hit his back on his wooden decking; he damaged a nerve, which caused him to evacuate his bowels. Murray lay on the ground in his soiled trousers, immobile, waiting for an ambulance. At hospital, he was told his disc had collapsed and that there was a waiting list of twelve weeks for surgery.

The period that followed was a blur. For weeks, Murray could hardly move. He was only comfortable when lying down. During the first few months, his analysts would go to his flat for meetings. Murray would conduct these meetings from his bed, his team sitting at the end of the bed, updating him on their various projects. It was the same for the first meeting with any new analysts who joined the team. 'They would come in to my room and I would be in bed,' Murray says. 'I'd be like, "Hi, I'm your new boss."'

When Murray returned to work he was still in excruciating pain and needed to lie down for at least a few hours each day, which he would do under his desk. Whenever they had to attend a conference, his team would transport him in the back of a van, lying on a mattress.

Murray also spent much of this period experiencing intense hallucinations from the opioids the doctors had prescribed him. He would often wake up crying in the middle of the night after dreadful dreams. One day he received an email from England Squash, congratulating him on a successful application for the role of team manager for the 2010 Commonwealth Games in Delhi. Murray looked at the email, puzzled. He had been so spaced out he couldn't recall applying for the job.

On 7 January 2010, Murray and Pearson met the England squash team in Manchester to kickstart their preparations. Murray, now both lead analyst and team manager ('They called me the manalyst'), had planned the 268 days up until the Games in October. The final team would be selected by 31 May. There would be preparation camps at which former gold medallists and world champions would give motivational talks, including Martin Johnson, captain of the England rugby team in 2003, and the Olympic track cycling champion Sir Chris Hoy.

A special sports science programme – dubbed Project 2010 – was put in place to ensure that everything was provided, from motivational DVDs to acclimatisation in a heat chamber, and from psychological interventions to individual needs analyses. Sixteen players had been selected, from which five women and five men would go to the Games. Of those ten, all but three had a top five world ranking. They were products of the system created by Murray and Pearson over the previous decade, and were the strongest national squash team ever. Pearson, in particular, had high expectations. Topping the medal table, and their highest-ever medal tally, seemed well within reach.

Pearson had, however, been in prolonged talks with England Squash over his contract. One of the points of contention was the new administrative requirements, which included the compulsory reporting of all training sessions and written justification of decisions made. This was anathema to Pearson. He was a maverick, someone who coached instinctively and who rarely planned ahead. He had never kept any records or micro-managed his performance programmes. 'The new performance director didn't allow that,' Murray says. 'They wanted every decision recorded and justified. They saw DP as a threat.'

England Squash told Pearson that they were willing to let him continue as national coach until the Commonwealth Games, but he would have to step down after the competition. Pearson, indignant at the decision, sued them.

After protracted negotiations, Pearson and England Squash settled the case out of court.

Pearson was to resign from his position with immediate effect. He would be paid a year's salary, in addition to his salary as Jenny Duncalf and Nick Matthew's coach. He would have to serve a two-year gagging order, and stick to the narrative that he was stepping down from the job due to illness.

Murray had been the only one who had been kept abreast of the situation from the start. Shortly after the settlement, one of the directors of England Squash phoned him to ask him to relay the news to the players. Murray argued that the message should be conveyed by someone from England Squash's directorate. They disagreed. He was told the news would be better received if it came from him. Murray felt he was betraying Pearson. Part of him just wanted to pull out. Part of him wanted to say, 'You know what? You can deal with it yourself, thank you. You've shattered my mate – you can get stuffed.' Murray had never seen such a mockery in sport in his life.

In May, Murray travelled with the team to the European Team Championships in Aix-en-Provence. Pearson was notably absent. While the men's team, led by Nick Matthew, won, the women suffered their first defeat in the history of the tournament. Jenny Duncalf, Pearson's stepdaughter, unexpectedly lost her match and England caved in to the Netherlands in the final. When Murray went to console the players, he found them desolate, in tears. Two told him that they had lost because the chief executive and performance director of England Squash had been watching the game from the stands. These were the guys who had sacked their coach, and having them there threw them off.

'No, girls, you can't say that. You can't blame the fact that they were sat there. You're professional players. That isn't a good attribution of loss,' Murray stammered.

'Well, you can believe it or not,' they replied.

In his debrief report to England Squash, Murray reported what the players had told him. One of the factors that contributed to the women's team defeat was that they couldn't concentrate in the presence of the chief executive, he wrote.

On 13 July the England team gathered together for their second preparation camp in Manchester. Murray acknowledged that there were rumours flying around about Pearson's situation. England Squash had reviewed the role of national coach, Murray informed them, and decided that Pearson – one of the most successful coaches in the history of the sport – was no longer fit for purpose. Pearson agreed with this, Murray continued, but it had been a shock and he was currently on sick leave. Pearson also wanted them to forget about this unfortunate situation and crack on with the job, Murray concluded. 'The players weren't stupid, but I had to carry the official line,' Murray says. 'They were like, "What do you mean, he can't go to the Games? He's been to the last four. He is the Commonwealth Games."' They were angry and upset. They had just been informed that they were going to compete at the most important event of their careers without their coach.

Murray was distraught, angry, and disgusted at how Pearson was being treated. 'I wanted to tell the system to fuck off.' But he couldn't let the players down. He couldn't let his emotions take over. He had a job to do. Every night he called Pearson and apologised. 'I asked David for permission to proceed as normal,' Murray says. 'He understood. He told me to do what I needed to do for the sake of the team.'

At the holding camp before the Games, Murray gave the players a breakdown of the Games' venues and facilities. Murray had first gone out to Delhi in May. As team manager, it was his responsibility to conduct a reconnaissance. When he had visited the athletes' village, it was still under construction, but the model apartments on display were outstanding. They could expect a safe, comfortable, high-quality environment, Murray told the players. He reiterated that this could be the most successful England team ever. The players pledged to do it for England, and for David Pearson.

'I thought if you beat on your chest and kissed the badge everyone would be motivated,' Murray reflects. 'Some people afterwards told me that they hated that. They hated the fact that we were doing it for England and for other people, because the truth was they were only doing it for themselves.' On the outside, Murray was keeping it together. Inside, he felt treasonous, stressed and completely out of his depth.

*

On arriving in Delhi, the English team were met with chaos. Traffic was infernal, the sporting venues were shambolic, ticket sales disappointing and the athletes' village still looked like a building site. In some apartments, water was coming out of the electrical sockets. The wall of one of the toilets was smeared with faeces. 'The plumbers at the time weren't getting paid, and they were being treated like slaves to get the job done,' Murray says. 'When they finished the room, they literally wiped shit on the wall as a form of retribution.'

Between the village and the athletes' shuttle stop was a one-mile buffer zone where no traffic was allowed. It took an hour to get through security and athletes were advised not to leave the village during the Games. It then took the shuttle hours to travel the three miles between the village and the squash centre, due to the heavily congested traffic.

Nick Matthew had also been affected deeply by what had happened to Pearson. He was upset that he had been left to prepare for the Commonwealth Games without a coach, and upset by how Pearson was being treated. Like Murray, he was one of the people determined to win it for Pearson as much as for himself. He wasn't overly verbal about it. Murray would occasionally bump into him in a corridor and Matthew would give him encouragement. 'Come on. Let's do this,' he would say.

'That's where me and Nick got really close,' Murray says. 'He was a huge ally and helped me immensely during that period. He was more mature, a leader.'

In Delhi, Matthew advanced through round after round with ease, and without losing a single game. He was being assisted by an analyst called Will Forbes, who would work through the night, profiling Matthew's opponents. Murray, his usual analyst, was too busy with other matters. Such as, for instance, dealing with a blocked toilet on the evening of the men's semi-final. 'One of the boys flushed it and it literally exploded about a metre in the air,' he recalls. 'The bathroom was covered in other people's poop.' Murray gave the players his bedroom and waited until five in the morning for a plumber to arrive to fix it.

On 13 October 2010, the men's singles final took place between Nick Matthew and his compatriot James Willstrop. Matthew controlled most of the game. On match ball, Willstrop played a forehand boast from the back of the court. Matthew responded with a backhand drop shot, slamming the ball perfectly into the nick. This was exactly the type of shot that Pearson and Murray had taught him. It was also Pearson's personal favourite. Matthew dropped his racket and lifted his arms in celebration. He remembered all those training sessions with Murray and Pearson, the long hours honing his technique.

'I think the general public can relate to a session where you come off and you are sweating, dripping from head to toe, and you've worked really hard, but they can't maybe quite relate to one where you come off after an hour and a half and you've not even raised your heart rate to eighty beats a minute but you've still achieved something great,' Matthew says. 'You create a bond with those guys because you are dissecting your personality as well as your technique in those sessions. You trust them with your livelihood. They are the sessions you remember when you win, not necessarily the one when you got the best sweat on.'

Pearson, of course, wasn't there to witness his pupil's greatest achievement. Neither was Murray. He was sitting in the empty stands of the adjoining badminton hall, getting the score via text from his wife, Sarah, back in England. With this final victory, England topped the squash medal table for the first time. It was a bittersweet feeling. Pearson wasn't present, but the man who had sacked him was. Afterwards, Murray was proud of himself for managing not to punch him in the face. He sat alone, crying his eyes out, feeling both joy and anger.

After the Commonwealth Games, Murray received an email from England Squash, notifying him that his services would no longer be required. 'Not even a phone call,' Murray says. 'I had always made it clear that I was on David's side, I knew I had put the nail in my own coffin. I was bloody done then, but the hypocrisy was too big.' Murray would never work for England Squash again.

Back in the UK, Murray visited Pearson. The protracted legal wrangling had plunged Pearson into a deep depression and post-traumatic stress, and the coach looked a shadow of his former self. 'He was a mess,' Murray says. 'I was absolutely disgusted by the way he had been treated.'

All of this was weighing on Murray's mind when he was driving back to Manchester on the M6 one evening in December 2010. He was proud of what he had achieved, but had been left with a sour taste in his mouth.

His thoughts turned towards the Olympic Games. He had thirty-five analysts going this time. Never before had they sent so many. Murray was asking himself what they could achieve with that sort of workforce when his phone rang. It was Dave Reddin.

After nearly ten years with England Rugby, Reddin had joined the British Olympic Association as head of perfor-mance services. He had been invited by his old boss, Clive Woodward, who had been hired as deputy chef de mission for the 2012 Games. The remit of the BOA was to provide logistical support for Team GB during the Olympics, and

Woodward and Reddin wanted to make home advantage count. They were willing to invest serious money in the most ambitious performance analysis project that had ever taken place during an Olympic event. Was Murray interested in heading that operation?

'Fuck yes,' Murray replied.

They met at the British Olympic Association's London offices the following week. Reddin was familiar with Murray's outfit of analysts and told him that the BOA was committed to exploiting home advantage in terms of performance analysis. The only question was how.

Murray explained that the biggest challenge would be to capture and provide different teams with high-quality competition footage with a fast turnaround. Unlike most international competitions, the Olympic Games imposed strict restrictions regarding accreditation, how many team members were allowed inside venues, and even permission to film some of the events. Every sport had different constraints, and not all would be allowed to have analysts embedded in the teams. Adding analysts to the teams inside the accreditation zone was out of the question.

'Analysts are the sneakiest group of people,' Reddin says. 'They always find a way, whether smuggling cameras through back doors or cables into the back of the truck. But the Olympics are different from other competitions. In most sports, you're not allowed any equipment in the venue or, unless you're accredited, you can't even get access.'

They could, however, assemble their operation outside the accreditation zone. During the Games, the BOA would lease an entire floor of an office block at the Westfield shopping centre in Stratford, adjacent to the Olympic Park. They called it Team GB House. It was to be the BOA hospitality and media centre, and it would also function as accommodation for extra support staff. To capture footage of the events, they considered using the Olympic Broadcasting Services feed.

The Olympic Broadcasting Services was established in 2001 by the International Olympic Committee as the Games' official broadcaster. It adhered to a broadcast standard that ensured that radio and television coverage was unbiased and equal for every country. This feed, named the World Feed, was distributed as a service to international television and radio broadcasters.

However, if Murray was to use the World Feed they would need to hardwire Team GB House with a data-transmission cable. The OBS feed cable was located in the Olympic Village, on the other side of the Olympic Park, so this was a massive logistical undertaking. They would have to physically split the OBS cable and create a secondary stream to Team GB House, where the feed would be available to stream via twelve Ethernet ports.

But if they did somehow make this work, it would be the first time centralised performance analysis was deployed at a Games. Murray didn't know if it was going to be prohibitively expensive, feasible or even legal. But in any case, he was going to need some analysts.

This was already looking like a bad idea. Murray had always maintained that hiring new analysts specifically for major competitions was out of the question. The Games weren't the time to try something different, he would argue.

On top of this, since all the analysts were engaged with their teams, he was going to have to pull the whole thing off mostly using students. Murray had contacted the three top university departments for performance analysis – Chester, Middlesex and UWIC – and told them he had a singular work experience opportunity. But he wasn't interested in the best students academically. He wanted people who would work eighteen hours a day, could work when frazzled and under pressure, and keep their cool when an incensed coach called them in a fit of rage, asked where the fuck was the match data and repeatedly told them to fuck off, loud and clear.

14

WOMEN ON THE VERGE OF GOLD

According to his players, Danny Kerry was 'miserable', 'grumpy' and 'unapproachable'.

Kerry was thirty-four, lean and bald, with a circumspect and courteous demeanour. He was also a naive, inexperienced hockey coach who believed he could defeat any team through 'knowledge and process'. Most of the time, he was glued to his computer, analysing video, devising strategies, planning and reviewing. He was obsessed with his players' performance, but he didn't show much concern for them otherwise. He wouldn't socialise with his players, or engage in any light-hearted banter, or comfort them after demoralising defeats. He wasn't aware of how they were feeling, and whether they were coping with the pressure, because he seldom asked them.

Kerry's philosophy of 'knowledge and process' was not only alienating his team, it was also making them predictable on the pitch. 'We were more prescribed to and told what to do, rather than expected to learn as a group and rely on each other,' defender Crista Cullen says of that time. 'As a result we became easy to read. The opposition knew what we were going to do.'

Going into the Beijing Games, the British women's hockey team was ranked eleventh in the world, and had modest expectations. In their first match, on 10 August 2008 against Olympic champions Germany, Great Britain were demolished, losing 5–1. They finished the Games in sixth position after losing the playoff against Australia.

By then they were a broken, fractious group. 'We fell into a blame culture,' Cullen says. 'We weren't connecting as a squad, we were sporadic. We didn't have unity. We were just made up of little groups without a common goal.'

After Beijing, UK Sport asked the players to complete a survey. When he received the feedback, Kerry was stunned to see some of the epithets that his own squad had chosen to describe him.

At first, he felt hurt by their brutal appraisal. He asked his wife if the man it portrayed really sounded like her husband. UK Sport had already confirmed that Kerry would continue as coach: after all, he had delivered a sixth place at Beijing, which was above their world ranking and a marked improvement on previous tournaments. Nevertheless, he thought of quitting. 'Personally, it was a trying time,' Kerry says. 'The feedback was harrowing.'

Instead, Kerry began to make a conscious effort to change, to have a relationship with his athletes that wasn't limited to coaching them on tactics and technique. Being more human: asking about their relationships, asking about their weekends. 'He made himself vulnerable, and that was a brave thing to do,' Kate Walsh, the then captain, says. 'I imagine it was quite tempting for him to say no and say that it was going to be his way. But he knew he couldn't do that. He knew he needed to get buy-in, and he needed the players to go with him. That was empowering.'

After the Beijing Games, the players decided to commit

to training full time at their base at Bisham Abbey. In previous years, most of the players had been scattered around
the country, working and studying part time, playing for
their clubs at the weekend and only gathering as a national
team at training camps before major tournaments. With the
announcement of the London Games, investment in the sport
had increased and a centralised programme could be afforded:
athletes could train full time, in one location, with a support
team of specialist coaches and sport scientists. 'When we were
first asked about it, there were definitely people in the room
thinking, I'm not sure I want to do that,' midfielder Helen
Richardson says. '[But] I was like, Oh my God, I can do this
as a full-time job? Sign me up.' In the end, the majority of
the players voted to centralise.

From now on, Kerry decided that the players would take
collective ownership of the programme, not the coaches.
A leadership group was chosen, of senior players including
Helen Richardson and Kate Walsh. The players would be
empowered to make decisions about all aspects of the team's
performance, from their day-to-day training to their long-
term vision.

Agreeing on that vision took months. In one meeting, the
team psychologist gave each member of the team a piece of
paper and crayons, and asked them to draw a picture that
illustrated their vision for the London Games. Some drew
themselves and the team on the podium. Others drew tro-
phies and medals. 'Our normal assumption is that everyone
has the same view, but it becomes very clear very soon that
they're all there for a whole different bunch of reasons,' Kerry
says.

Kerry thought they should aim to make steady progress,
climbing one world ranking place each year, but he wanted
the athletes to take ownership of the strategy. Because with

that ownership came responsibility. What he didn't want was to drag his team to aim for something they didn't buy into. If the team wanted to be medal contenders in London, they would have to accept the sacrifices and the tough decisions that came with it. They were the ones who would have to miss weddings and skip holidays and train twice on Christmas Day. They debated what would be their collective vision for London 2012. Both long sentences and punchy statements were suggested.

Helen Richardson was getting fed up with the fluffy talk. She was set on what she wanted to achieve and wasn't prepared to take anything else. In fact, she believed quite a few others wanted the same but were afraid to admit it.

'Why can't it be just one word?' she said. 'Why can't it be just "Gold"?'

Now that the team was centralised, Kerry knew the importance of hiring support staff that had actual experience with a full-time team. 'When I came in, they were coming from a programme based around four-week camps before major events to one where they were training twice a day, six days a week,' David Hamilton says. 'No one was sure about how to schedule the week.'

As their new fitness coach, Hamilton was to play an essential role in honing the women's hockey team. Kerry knew that favourites like Argentina and the Netherlands had a deeper pool of talented and technically proficient players. England had to become a team that could overpower, physically and mentally. That was Kerry's plan. That was the only plan.

At his first meeting with Kerry, Hamilton asked to see how their current training schedule looked, and what fitness testing was in place. The programme didn't include many sessions dedicated to physical preparation, and their conditioning tests didn't make much sense to Hamilton. They included a test called the double doggy, time completion tests, and some endurance tests.

'They were just training them in the hope that they'd be successful,' Hamilton says. 'There was nothing that was quantifiable. It was a very mixed bag.' He asked Kerry to understand that the current tests weren't a reliable method to measure athletic improvement. 'I can't judge whether I've made them fit or not because I don't even know what these numbers tell me,' he said.

At first, Hamilton's relationship with the head coach was professional, and occasionally frosty. When Hamilton entered the coach's office to suggest something, Kerry's barriers would go up. 'He would challenge me and decisions would be delayed for future discussions,' Hamilton says. 'It was clear that he had been burned before.' He soon learned to avoid approaching Kerry when he was sitting behind his desk. Those circumstances seemed to trigger a less receptive response.

Hamilton's friendship with Kerry began when the two started meeting on the squash court to play for a few hours at the end of the day. Hamilton noticed that, afterwards, Kerry would seem transformed. 'He wasn't under pressure to be somewhere else and his barriers were down,' Hamilton says. They could chat as friends, rather than colleagues, and when Hamilton suggested something Kerry seemed to listen unreservedly. Hamilton was also comfortable enough to tell Kerry what he was thinking – for instance, that the team should be spending a lot more time in the gym.

Hamilton had compiled a report on the physical performance indicators typical of elite female athletes. From previous studies, he collected numbers on the speeds that athletes should be able to achieve over different distances, which gave him an idea of how quickly his players should get to the ball and how often. He also had measures for strength, from bench press to back squats, which indicated how quickly they could change direction. He had aerobic metrics, such as repeat sprint ability and the 30–15 intermittent fitness test.

He devised a simple traffic-light system for the test results, with green as good and red as a concern. When he first tested the team, in October 2009, 62 per cent of the players were in the red. It wasn't promising.

Hamilton decided to introduce a periodised training programme, rather than one based around training camps. He would work the players hard for three weeks, and then remove hockey playing in the fourth week, allowing them time to recover. To monitor their recovery, every day before training he would ask the players to perform a drop jump: they would step on to a box, drop on to a mat and then jump back up vertically. Timing how long the players spent on the ground and how high they jumped gave an indication of neuromuscular fatigue. This provided Hamilton with a very simple indicator of how hard they were training, how well they were adapting and the impact on their ability to perform.

He could now see what effect the training was having on the players, who was coping with the training load and who was struggling. They were a side who recently had struggled to perform when it mattered. Now, with a centralised pro-gramme, they were starting to understand what it was going to take to realise their vision of gold.

Kerry collaborated on many projects with Scott Drawer. One of Drawer's first ideas was to use drones to film training sessions. Kerry was concerned about players getting injured by a falling drone. This project was abandoned the following day, when Kerry read a newspaper story about a drone that had fallen from the sky.

Other projects followed: a top-secret recovery drink made at the University of Oxford and funded by the US Army ('It didn't taste good and we couldn't make it taste nice, so it didn't really work'); a new hockey stick model ('In the end we decided we'd spend a huge amount of time and energy and if the rules changed it wouldn't be worth it'). 'We did all sorts of weird projects with Scott,' Kerry says. 'Sometimes we would be like, okay, we're going down a rabbit hole here.'

That was not the case when Kerry and Hamilton asked about female physiology and Drawer put them in touch with Christian Cook.

Cook had been pondering the question for a while. He had observed how Danny Holdcroft – who he considered to be one of the best coaches he had ever worked with – and Amy Williams had forged a successful partnership based on the belief that athletes rarely fulfil their potential under a generic training regime. Rather, they thrive when they are treated as individuals.

His follow-up question was what he calls an 'aha' moment: 'Shouldn't we consider the fact how different the male and female physiologies were?' Then it really struck him: 'We just train women like they're small men,' Cook realised. 'Are we actually doing a disservice to our female athletes by not fully understanding the physiological advantages they surely have? How much do we actually know about them?' When he searched the academic literature, he realised that the answer was not much at all.

There never had been a study, for instance, on the concentrations of testosterone and cortisol among elite female athletes and how these hormone levels responded to training. So Cook enlisted eighteen athletes, including skeleton sliders, swimmers and cyclists, and for a period of twelve weeks, every Wednesday before training, collected saliva samples from which he measured their hormone levels. It was known that women produce, on average, about 10 per cent of the amount of testosterone that men generate. In a normal man, about 5 per cent of that testosterone is free. The rest is bound to albumin protein circulating in the blood.

'Such an analysis has not been conducted in females, but would provide an important first step toward understanding adaptive potential in the female athlete,' Cook and his co-authors would write in the resulting paper. The study showed that elite female athletes had more than double the concentration of free testosterone compared with national-level athletes, a much more significant difference than among male athletes.

'The typical thing that gets thrown out there is that females have one-tenth the level of testosterone of men, so testosterone can't be important to them,' Cook says. 'Actually, their responses were really strong. If you have a one per cent change in a man it probably doesn't do much, but if you have a one per cent change in a woman, from a relative perspective it's a large change.'

Cook began to speculate that, over time, they were going to find that from a behavioural perspective testosterone may be even more important in women. When looking at the physiological difference between men and women, the menstrual cycle was an obvious starting point. Women's menstruation means that, unlike men, their internal hormonal state changes regularly over an approximately twenty-eight-day cycle. What Cook didn't accept was the notion that the menstrual cycle disadvantaged women. In fact, he believed the opposite was true.

When Cook and Hamilton presented the idea of a project to investigate the effects of their menstrual cycles on performance, the players felt that finally someone was acknowledging their biological reality. 'It's a social taboo to talk about menstrual cycles, but it's a biological reality and you ignore it at your peril,' Kerry says. To the players, of course, the subject wasn't taboo. They would talk about it between themselves and they knew, at least anecdotally, that their cycles affected how they felt. 'You would also hear people saying that, oh, during your menses your ligaments are more lax,' Helen Richardson says. 'Stuff that you didn't really know whether it was true or not. You would hear all sorts.'

From October 2010, whenever a player got her period she would send a text to David Hamilton, saying 'Day One'. Hamilton would log the information into an Excel spreadsheet to track the menstrual cycles of his twenty-eight athletes, noting also who was on the pill. He also recorded testosterone and cortisol levels, and every morning, before doing their drop jumps, the players logged into an app called Restwise and entered their resting heart rate, oxygen saturation rate (measured with a pulse oximeter), urine shade, muscle soreness, appetite and energy level, and the app would output a recovery score.

As the data accumulated, Hamilton began to see patterns. He noticed, for instance, that on particular days he would get an unusually high number of 'Day One' texts. 'His poor wife was probably like, "God, not another one",' Kate Walsh says. The menstrual cycles of players sharing a flat seemed to synchronise, following the pattern set by the perceived alpha female of that group. Hamilton and Cook also found that drop jump results correlated with levels of testosterone; those on oral contraceptives had lower testosterone and tended to make a few more errors in the game; while athletes with a longer training history were less affected by their cycles relative to newer athletes.

After accumulating data for a few months, Hamilton and Cook compiled a comprehensive matrix that related menstrual phases, hormonal levels, physiological and psychological differences, and effects on training. From this, they could create training prescriptions for each menstrual phase. During the late luteal phase, hormonal levels, including testosterone, were low. As a result, the player was more likely to be affected by mood changes, which could result in higher stress and had a higher propensity to suffer mishaps in training. That week should therefore be focused on recovery. During ovulation, on the other hand, testosterone levels peaked, making it ideal for strength training.

For Cook, this research proved to be a conceptual shift in how menstruation was perceived. For around ten days in the menstrual cycle, women have a heightened ability to deal with stress. 'They've got this double churning,' he says. 'They're putting nitrous oxide into the engine, and then they've got another extra tube of nitrous oxide they can put in when they head towards ovulation. They have this ability to respond stronger and better.'

When Danny Kerry took a psychometric test, he wasn't surprised by the result.

The test, called Insight Profiling, was based on personality theory, which can be traced back to Carl Jung and his model of four psychological types: the fiery reds (extroverted, high energy, action-oriented), the cool blues (introverted, precise, analysts), the earth greens (relationship focused, democratic, reliable) and the sunshine yellows (extroverted, radiant, gregarious). The test, in which one has to choose the statements that best apply to specific situations, took a few hours to complete. People could answer questions like 'When I am working in a team and we encounter a difficulty of some kind, I am most likely to say . . .' with 'Lighten up! Just go with flow!'; or 'The thing someone could say that would have the most positive impact on me is . . .' with 'You are fantastic!' The questionnaire generated a profile based on the four Jungian personality tendencies.

Kerry's report, for instance, described him as a highly analytical, introverted individual who lived inside his head: a typical cool blue personality. David Hamilton, in contrast, was found to be equally cool blue and sunshine yellow – a rare combination of polar opposites.

The players were predominantly gregarious sunshine yellows and caring earth greens, and Kerry's cool-blue persona was, for this group of caring and extroverted individuals, a source of much misunderstanding. He soon realised that he had to understand himself and how his emotions were interpreted by his players. And he had to remember to smile more.

During matches, Kerry could be inscrutable. He would grimace, clutch his head, scowl. He found it difficult to hide his emotions. And yet these outbursts didn't mean he was angry at his players. They were simply an outward expression of Kerry's thought processes. It was decided, for his own good as well as that of his players, that Kerry would no longer sit on the bench during games. Instead he would sit in the stands, leaving the in-game communication to his assistant coach, Craig Parnham. From his vantage point, Kerry could work on tactics, communicating with Parnham via a radio link-up. 'Somehow, I could still tune in and literally listen every word he said,' Kate Walsh says. 'Sometimes he would be angry, banging his clipboard, shouting. Which sometimes was a good thing, because I was able to pass the messages on.'

Eight months before the start of the London Games, Kerry and his team of coaches stopped mentioning players' weaknesses at team meetings. During meetings or when around players, the coaches were only allowed to mention the athletes' strengths. 'There was one player in particular who always had issues about her technical ability under pressure,' Kerry says. 'What we found was when we stopped talking about that weakness of hers and started talking about all of the strengths that she brought and focusing only on that, the technical problems disappeared.'

By then, their vision – encapsulated by the word gold – had taken on a life of its own. For instance, any of the leadership group could stop a training session if they considered that standards were slipping. 'You could stop a session and say, "Is what you're doing gold?"' Walsh says. If a player's attitude in training was consistently lacklustre and didn't live up to the gold standard, she would be summoned to a meeting with the rest of the team, called the forum, where they would sit in a circle and discuss that player's behaviour.

One player left as a result, concluding that such an environment wasn't for her. Another recognised that she was responsible for her sub-par performance and promised to improve. 'This wasn't being driven by the staff, these were the athletes themselves saying that someone wasn't living up to what they were about,' Kerry says.

In January, the team started training once a week at the Riverbank Arena, the hockey venue in the Olympic Park. The Riverbank Arena had high stands surrounding a blue pitch nicknamed the smurf turf. The team played friendly international games there, so that the players could familiarise themselves with the surroundings and the atmosphere. The coaches assumed that during games, with a fifteen thousand-strong crowd shouting for Great Britain, they wouldn't be able to hear each other. So they forced the athletes to look at each other more frequently, to raise their hands to visually acknowledge that they had heard what was being said; the team were not allowed to talk to each other during training. They also realised that as the media centre was just next door to the pitch they were more likely to be accosted by reporters, so they brought in former tabloid journalists to give the players extensive media training in how to deal with any unexpected questions.

This was all part of a plan to minimise distractions and surprises. Players would be sharing rooms in the Olympic Village, so a team psychologist matched them according to their psychological profiles. The players also agreed to restrict time with their families during the Games, only allowing themselves a forty-five-minute period after matches. 'Families often travel to major events and they will want to see their daughters during the competition,' Hamilton says. 'We tried to minimise as much as possible the influence of parents. It pulls us apart as a group and athletes will start scheduling things that aren't a priority to the coaches and to their performance. Parents sometimes critique how they are performing and we don't want that feedback. We're trying to get over the game, moving on to the next game, and parents will still want to talk about the game. It never helps.'

Hamilton had delivered on his promise to Kerry and produced a team who were in their best-ever physical condition. Not only had he implemented a periodised programme, he was individualising according to the players' menstrual cycles. The drop jump scores were the highest they had ever been. At the Beijing Games, the average distance covered per player during a game had been 5500 metres. Now they were capable of covering more than a kilometre extra per game. Because hockey uses fifteen field players in rolling substitutions, that was the equivalent of covering an extra fifteen kilometres every game. The percentage of time spent walking was reduced from 56 to 30. Sprinting went from 6.5 per cent to 20 per cent.

'I used to really struggle with fitness,' Helen Richardson says. 'It was something that did not come naturally to me. I'm very skilful, but when jogging I used to be always at the back, chasing the other players. But now my sessions were individual, and the distances were worked out from your fitness test. It wasn't that everybody was running the same distance. Even though I would be running less, it would be just as hard for me as it was for others. That was really motivating.'

As the Olympics approached, Hamilton used the drop-jump data to determine how much the programme needed to be adjusted. He also extrapolated the menstrual data to find out where in their cycles the players would be when they arrived at competitions. Kerry very much wanted the players to understand that this was information derived from a medically informed position, not the whims of some maniacal head coach. They wanted the athletes to have good strategies going into the most important performance of their lives. 'We did have one or two athletes who chose to double up on their contraceptive pill through that period of time, to ensure they weren't in a bad space in terms of menstrual cycle,' Hamilton says. 'It was the athletes' choice, it wasn't forced upon them.'

To win at the Olympics, it wasn't enough for the players to play one game in peak condition: they would have to play seven – five pool matches, a semi-final and a final. A hockey game is made up of four blocks of fifteen minutes, and for most of that time players would be sprinting repeatedly in an extremely low position at high intensity, with unbelievable hand–eye coordination. In football, a player might cover 150 metres per minute. In hockey, the average is 250 metres per minute. This would then be repeated for seven matches over thirteen days. The players were only going to have, at most, forty-eight hours to recover before the next match.

The team sat down with Christian Cook and hatched a flawless recovery plan. Straight after the game, they would perform six minutes of active cool-down exercises and take bespoke nutritional supplements. Then they would immerse themselves in an ice bath at 12°C, as the cold temperatures accelerated the healing of muscular tissue. Afterwards, they would put on medical-grade compression socks and apply a Firefly for six hours. This was a device worn behind the knee that delivered painless electrical impulses to increase blood circulation in the lower leg, reducing muscle soreness after a high-intensity game.

Cook also suggested they try a new method of hormonal manipulation, called 'priming'. Priming consisted of a short workout which accelerated recovery. 'The premise was that if I give you a workload and then I give you a day off, it's not until the end of the day that your body goes, "Oh, right, I should have probably started to recover." And it goes into recovery mode,' Cook explains. 'As a result, when you then go to perform the next day, your body's still trying to recover. Whereas if you were to give it a stimulus on the morning of that next day, when you have to play in the evening, you've re-engaged that system.'

The priming workouts varied according to the player. Cook had worked out four different athletic profiles: elite power velocity, elite power force, elite endurance force and elite endurance velocity. Players with a power velocity profile, for instance, responded better to short high-intensity sprints. Athletes with endurance force profiles were more suited to longer and slower strength workouts.

The priming workout was voluntary. 'It goes back to how testosterone works,' Cook says. 'If I tell you to do something

and you don't like it, that's not going to create a positive testosterone response. We had to make this voluntary, getting
buy-in to want to do it, because if they like it and they buy
in, we get a better response.'

In the last five months before the Games, Hamilton noticed
that the players were consistently complaining about the
training regime and how tired they were. 'It got frustrating
for us coaches, because we were in a heavy training phase
and the players were pushing back,' Hamilton says. Besides,
all the data suggested that the players were doing just fine.
Hamilton continues, 'What they were actually suffering
from was more just monotony of training. The day-to-day
grind of coming in and the repeatability of everything was
making them cognitively fatigued, but physically they were
okay.'

Hamilton wanted to reset their understanding of what
tiredness was. So he devised a workout, which he called
'dislocation of expectations'. It started as a normal ninety-
minute training session. Kerry called the players into a circle,
as he usually did at the end. At this point, they believed
that they were almost done for the day. As usual, Hamilton
asked them to line up and perform a number of drills – from
sprints to calisthenics – at maximum aerobic speed. When
they had done the usual twelve repetitions, he gave them a
three-minute break. Then he told them to start again. The
more extroverted athletes started protesting. They had no
idea when the session was going to end, no way of pacing
themselves. Their arms slumped, their heads went down,
their bodies drooped. But individual pain then turned into
collective support. Players began shouting words of encouragement rather than words of frustration. 'Come on, guys,
keep going!'

After twenty-one repetitions, Hamilton told them it was over. The players, without exception, collapsed on the ground. Hamilton had wanted to emulate what the players would potentially feel if, in the last minute of a final, exhausted after a long game, they would still have to find something extra within themselves to clinch the game.

'You all want it to be over and they just don't tell you how long you've got to keep going for,' Crista Cullen says. 'You're all hitting the wall. You're all feeling sick. The only thing you want to do is stop. Then, just because you're part of a team and you're all in it together, you're still able to find that reserve that you didn't think you had. No one gave up, everyone kept running. That in itself was a statement of togetherness.'

On 18 May 2012, Danny Kerry was at a press conference at the London Stock Exchange to announce the sixteen women who would represent Great Britain at the Olympic Games. Twelve of the players who had been part of the centralised programme for three years would not be competing. They had been informed ten days earlier via email, an approach they had opted for as a group. At the conference, Kerry looked distraught and drained. He was a different man from the coach who had been accused of not caring for his players four years earlier. He had met the players who hadn't made the cut, one by one, to give them an opportunity to speak their minds and receive an explanation. When asked by a journalist how difficult those meetings had been, Kerry broke down in tears.

15

HOME ADVANTAGE

On 28 July 2012 Stafford Murray gathered with his team at Team GB House. The day was bright, the weather mild. It was 6 a.m. In two hours, the first full day of the Olympic Games would kick off.

The Team GB space included a press conference room, a sponsors' lounge and a dedicated area for athletes' friends and families. The main room was a large office where the logistics, legal and management teams would sit. In the far corner was the so-called nerve centre. Murray had demanded that secluded space for his team, so that they could concentrate on the task at hand. He and his team would spend the entire duration of the Games in the nerve centre.

Murray had arrived a few days before this to set up the room. Engineers from Dartfish were called in to sort out a few connectivity glitches. A white table with laptops was set up in the middle, and Murray had organised the laptops in a perfect straight line, with exactly five centimetres between the edge of the laptop and the edge of the desk, where his analysts could neatly place the agenda for the day. 'As my brother would say, if it was a rock band it would be called OCDC.'

Murray had arranged an exclusive partnership with Dartfish for Team GB. In the nerve centre, they had sixteen computers configured with Dartfish software to analyse and tag the videos they received, according to templates of performance indicators set up by the coaches of the teams competing in the Games. Six other computers would send these videos back to the coaches via Dartfish TV, a cloud service that functioned as a kind of private YouTube. The software engineers at Dartfish also wrote a patch to split the Olympic Broadcasting Services video feed into forty-one different channels.

'We were bending the rules,' Murray says. 'Each nation gets an OBS feed, which you can then split amongst your sports. But you cannot record it. That was a copyright violation. We got around that by claiming that we weren't sharing it, just distributing it.'

On the wall was a large whiteboard with a complete schedule of the Games, the analysts assigned to cover each event, and respective laptop numbers. Below it were three lockers with five spare laptops inside, turned on and ready to go in case one of the other machines crashed. Murray had also secretly stashed bottles of beer in there.

On the opposite wall was another whiteboard, displaying important contact numbers and a list of specifics on how every sports team wanted their data disseminated, how and when. Above it was a red LED digital clock. This clock was synchronised with the watches of every Team GB analyst at the Games. Every second would matter.

That day began with preliminary events in archery, badminton, basketball and beach volleyball. Sixteen laptops were capturing the OBS feed for the first time. For three minutes, everything was running smoothly, then someone said 'Black Hawk Down.' The room erupted with cries of 'Black Hawk Down'. One by one, laptop screens went green, then black.

In February 2012, the first cohort of performance analysis students had met at Sportcity in Manchester for two days of testing. Murray and Reddin had arranged for a room similar to the one they would be occupying at Team GB House in London, with laptops configured for Dartfish TV. From eight in the morning until midnight the software broadcast competition footage collated from previous events, emulating the output of the OBS feed.

'Dave played bad cop,' Murray says. 'Well, we were both bad cops. But Dave is a World Cup winner and a big character, he carries a lot of clout and gravitas. That added pressure, instead of being just me there.'

Throughout the day, the analysts were presented with unexpected scenarios. Scenario one: Laptop 7's feed has gone and the analysts have just got a call from a beleaguered coach who wants the data in fifteen minutes. What are you going to do? Or scenario two: Laptop 11 is broken. What are you going to do?

This pressure testing allowed Murray to suss out who could hack it and who couldn't: 'You could tell by their faces and by the way they reacted to the scenario.'

He told his team that they had to plan for all contingencies. Things will go wrong, he said, and they will crash and they will fail, so they had to pre-empt failure and engage in a creative exercise of negative 'what if?' For hours, they would go through a list of contingencies:

What if two PCs break at 2.30 a.m. when we have multiple things going on at the same time?

What do we do if the schedule changes all of a sudden, because that does sometimes happen?

What do we do if one of our staff ends up being ill and they can't come in?

What if your laptop gets stolen?

What if you start feeling the pressure and you can't handle it any more?

What if the coach can't handle it any more and gives you an absolute bollocking for no good reason?

What if your parents want tickets and they're in your fucking ear all the time?

What if you're at a venue and there's no food and you start feeling hungry and you're sweating and shaking?

That was the first lesson that Murray tried to inculcate in his new team: the Olympic Games were akin to a soap opera, and all of these things were going to happen. The pressure was going to be bigger than ever, the coaches angrier than usual, the athletes more nervous, and what the analysts had to do was not get caught up in the drama. The point, Murray said, is that being an analyst was not just about analytical skills. It was about relationships.

In 2011, all the EIS analysts had taken the Insight Profiling psychometric test. Stafford Murray thought it was a load of mumbo-jumbo. But when he received his twenty-two-page profile, his wife told him that the report knew him better than she did. It said, for instance, that 'Stafford is outgoing and makes things more fun for others by his pure and unreserved enjoyment of the moment . . . Will tend to be influenced by the last person he speaks to . . . When communicating with Stafford, DO NOT: appear slow, sluggish or too formal . . . His constant ready socialising can interfere with the job at hand and get him into trouble.'

'It was so accurate, it was spooky,' Murray says. As expected, most of the performance analysts leaned heavily towards the cool blue quadrant, as analytical, introverted types. Of all the analysts, Murray was the only yellow–green. At first, he perceived that as a negative. But then he reflected that it was the job of an analyst to communicate and to forge relationships with coaches. It was not the analyst's prerogative to complain that coaches didn't understand the data. 'It's our job to teach them,' Murray says. 'We have to learn to speak their language; we have to learn to put ourselves in their shoes; we have to walk in their footsteps. Coaches and athletes are important because they're strong, opinionated people and a lot of them are very stuck in their ways. So we can't question them being stuck in their ways, we have to work our way around it. We have to look in the mirror before pointing our finger at them.'

In July 2012, a few days before the start of the Games, Murray's team had travelled to London for a camp at Team GB House to run through more scenarios.

For five days, they tested everything to death. Murray felt prepared.

They had run through all possible scenarios, and for each they had established a contingency plan. For instance, because a few of the teams required the hand-delivery of hard drives between competitions, their delivery timing had to be flawless. They travelled from Stratford to the Olympic venues across the city, to estimate how long it would take to get to their destinations using different means of transport. They also established a protocol to follow if a laptop crashed: the analyst would first say 'Black Hawk Down', followed by the laptop's number. Then the team leader would get up, fetch a new laptop from one of the lockers, swap it for the malfunctioning computer and plug the OBS feed back in. Everyone else was to remain seated and continue as normal.

'What happened in the practice run was that when someone

shouted "Black Hawk Down", everybody would try to help at the same time and we were getting in each other's way,' Murray says. As a result, they thought it best to leave the task of switching the laptop to the team leader, while everyone stayed put. They rehearsed this countless times and estimated that if a computer crashed they would, at most, lose twenty seconds of footage. 'The guys in my team were bored of me talking about it by the end of it,' Murray says. 'I said, don't get bored, because this is time in the bank.'

They prepared for every single contingency. Except one.

'We "what if-ed" it to death, but one thing we didn't "what if" was, what if all the computers crash at the same time?' Murray says. They had five spare laptops in case one or two of them crashed. But they didn't have sixteen in case they all crashed. And that was exactly what had happened.

'It was just like a *Monty Python* sketch,' Murray remembers.

What if this was it? What if the laptops couldn't hold the entire OBS feed? Murray remained silent, almost in a daze. 'You know how everything becomes slow when shit hits the fan?' he recalls. He felt like he was underwater, passively watching everything unfold in slow motion, voices muffled, chaos unravelling in front of him. 'Almost half a million pounds,' he thought. 'I'm in charge and everything has crashed.'

He started mentally running through the list of coaches overseeing the teams currently competing. He was thinking about how many of them were going to be absolutely distraught. He counted three. Three isn't that bad, he considered. He had been in worse situations than this. It wasn't as bad as, say, being covered in faeces at the Commonwealth Games. It wasn't as bad as telling people that their coach had been sacked three months before a competition. It wasn't as bad as digging holes in the snow as a pipe-fitter, at six thirty in the morning in the middle of December. This wasn't the end of the world. Besides, everyone else was in a state of utter panic. He had to remain the cool, rational guy. 'Which wasn't very me, as I'm normally the biggest panicker going.'

'Right, everyone just turn your machines off and let's just start again,' Murray said to the group.

Ten minutes later, the laptops finally rebooted. What had happened was that the OBS feed had gone down, due to an excessively high bit-rate, which then caused the laptops to crash. 'That gave me a bit of solace, because it wasn't our fault,' Murray says. 'I now felt more comfortable calling the coaches and saying that we had lost the first ten minutes of the competition.'

Shaken, Murray went downstairs for a cigar. 'Fucking hell, that was stressful,' he thought, trying to compose himself.

The mission of the central team of analysts was to analyse the footage, categorise it, tag it and deliver it to the teams when they needed it. Each analyst looked after four sports at any one time. Eighty per cent of their job comprised capturing video footage. Most of it was then transmitted via Dartfish TV, but a few teams required other methods of delivery.

Boxing and the equestrian events were in venues where the Wi-Fi was particularly slow, so they required the footage to be cut up into different files and delivered on a hard drive. The team would also upload a low-resolution version onto Dartfish TV, in case the analysts needed to appeal immediately against a referee's decision.

In the case of track cycling, analysts would normally stream the footage from the performance analysts' platform in the stands, but the Wi-Fi at the velodrome was painfully slow, so the analysts had practised alternative methods. One was downloading the footage onto a USB stick, cutting a hole in a tennis ball, placing the USB stick inside and chucking it across the track.

In modern pentathlon, competitors draw lots for their horses an hour before the start of the show-jumping phase. The horses were schooled at the venue the day before, so analysts sneaked in with a camera to film the session covertly. On the day of the competition, as soon as they knew which horses had been drawn by the British athletes, they picked the corresponding footage and analysed the horses' behaviour.

Murray also knew of a biomechanist who had volunteered at the Games, so he could covertly set up one of his video cameras near the track. 'I can't name names,' Murray says. 'There he was in a bloody purple outfit, measuring stuff down at the track.' There was also a rumour that an analyst was using sunglasses with in-built cameras that transmitted footage straight into a laptop carried in their rucksack.

Squash analyst Mandy deBeer took over the project management side of things in the nerve centre and Murray focused on managing his team of young analysts, which was mostly just telling them stay calm. He would make sure that they went home after their shifts and got some rest, instead of staying to watch the rest of the day's events. He was also the designated deliverer of bad news, the one in charge of making difficult phone calls to inform coaches that their footage was lost, mixed up or unavailable. Three times he was called a cunt by enraged coaches. Once, when one of his analysts missed her rendezvous to deliver a hard drive at 7 a.m. because she was hung over, Murray told the seething coach that it was his fault, and that the data had been corrupted.

Paul Brice, the athletics analyst, had to resort to espionage because filming was banned inside the stadium. Instead he purchased regular day tickets and watched the games from the stands. In the interval between sessions, Murray had an approximately one-hour window to deliver footage to Brice. With the clock ticking, he would first download the files onto a USB stick and then double-check that the video file could be read on a different machine. ('You're better off being late with good footage than being early with bad footage,' Murray says. 'That was a lesson learned the hard way when I took a hard drive to an analyst across town and then found that the files were corrupt.') He would then sprint across the Westfield shopping centre plaza to the stadium.

Brice, wearing a baseball cap and shades, would be waiting outside for Murray to hand him the USB stick as inconspicuously as possible. Brice would then dash back into the stadium, change out of his civilian clothes into his Team GB official kit, don his accreditation lanyard and head to the changing rooms, where the athletics coach awaited the footage. 'He had befriended some of the stewards, so he would ask them to guard the access to the dressing room at particular times so that they could let him in without hassle,' Murray says.

On Day 6 of the Games, a BBC journalist interviewed Murray at Team GB's media zone, as part of a live broadcast from Team GB house.

In the previous four days, Team GB had underperformed. Rumours began circulating that this Olympics was going to be the biggest flop ever. On Day 5, 1 August, the deluge of medals began, when rowers Helen Glover and Heather Stanning won Team GB's first gold.

Things were looking up. Murray, dressed in the official Team GB outfit, a red and blue polo shirt with an upturned collar, had a wide smirk on his face, his eyes darting nervously from camera to reporter.

'One of the fascinating things you learn is the amount of analysis that is done of these sports,' the reporter said, before turning to Murray and asking: 'What do you actually do?'

'It's a good question, and I ask myself that every morning,' Murray replied. 'If we go right back fifteen hundred years ago, Sun Tzu, the Chinese warrior, said if you know your enemy as you know yourself, you need not fear a battle. So that's really what we're trying to do. Every battle we go into, every event, we need to know where our opponents are strong and where they're weak, so we can tactically beat them.'

'Which are the sports where this is most important?' asked the reporter. 'Because one would assume that for something like the hundred metres you can't really provide much advice other than run as fast as you can.'

'And in the four hundred metres run as fast as you can and turn left occasionally. It's obvious the open-skilled sports or the tactical lead-based sports is where it would be most beneficial. No sport is a complete science, so there's always an art side to it as well. So we're not telling people exactly what to do but we're just guiding them the way that they should go.'

The following day, 3 August, would become known as Super Saturday. That day, Team GB won six medals, three of them within a single forty-six-minute period when, in one of the most extraordinary moments of British sporting history, Mo Farah, Jessica Ennis and Greg Rutherford all won gold in the Olympic stadium.

Next to the main room in Team GB House, there was a staging area with a large screen where staff and visitors could watch the action. If there was an Olympic final involving a British athlete, the analysts would determine who would get to watch it by playing scissors-paper-stone. Celebrities also made regular appearances. 'You can't get star-struck. You got royalty, literally, walking through every now and then. Dermot O'Leary comes tapping you on your shoulder and you're like, "What? You're really standing in front of me?" It's like, "No. Focus. Back to work. This is what we've got to do. That is what we're here to do",' deBeer says. Coaches from winning sports started coming in, bearing coffee and a box of doughnuts, to say, 'Thanks, guys, your footage was so useful, we couldn't have got a medal without it.'

Murray's eighty-one-year-old grandfather called him afterwards, in tears. 'Bloody hell, son, I can't believe it,' he said. 'I'm so proud of you, son. I'm glad I fought for my country for this to happen. I'm so proud to be British.'

A few days after Super Saturday, another British medal favourite faced a crucial match: it was the women's hockey semi-final.

Until then, the team had been inconsistent. They had started as planned, winning their first game against Japan. Late on in that game, however, Kate Walsh was caught across the jaw by an opponent's stick. 'I was right behind her and I knew it was bad,' Crista Cullen remembers. 'She just collapsed on the floor. Kate doesn't do that. She'll just shrug it off and crack on.' When Crista reached her teammate, she immediately saw the extent of the trauma. Walsh's jaw was broken, and she was taken straight to hospital for emergency surgery.

At that point in the competition, there was still the possibility of bringing in another player to replace Walsh. Danny Kerry met with the team to solve the dilemma: replace Walsh, or hope that the surgery went well and she would be able to return in time for the rest of the tournament? Because hockey has rolling substitutions, with the eleven players on the field being able to be substituted by one of the five on the bench, having one fewer player, especially one as crucial as Walsh, could significantly dent their performance.

Kerry asked the team for their sincere opinions. They opted to play with one player fewer until Walsh was able to return, not knowing if she was going to be able to do so. Helen Richardson stepped in as captain. 'It was tough, but we knew as a group what we needed to do was do the best thing for Kate, and she would expect us to put our game faces on and get out there whether we were a pair of legs down or not,' Richardson says. 'It just happened to be our captain.'

In the next two matches they beat South Korea and Belgium. Walsh returned to action in the fourth game, against China, with a plate in her jaw and wearing a protective mask. Kerry and Hamilton had predicted that this match would dictate who would finish second in the pool, assuming that favourites the Netherlands would top the group. They had done an extensive analysis and built a game plan that revolved around beating China. In training, they used to split the group into two teams, with one team emulating the Chinese style of play. 'People would mix in between each, so we would know intricately what the Chinese do because we trained as them,' Hamilton says. 'They run a lot lower to the ground. They tackle in a certain way. They play in a certain formation.'

The team expected to win against China. They had played them many times in the lead-up to the Games, and beaten them every time. But that day they lost. Hamilton says that even though they had been learning a lot about the Chinese, the Chinese had obviously been learning a lot more about the British.

Another factor also contributed to their defeat. From GPS and drop jump data, Hamilton noticed that having played two games with one player fewer had taken a toll on their performance. On average, each of the players was doing 7 to 9 per cent more work to compensate for being a player down, and they were beginning to tire.

With their qualification for the medal round now hanging by a thread, they prepared to face the Netherlands, while China played Japan. Great Britain lost but, unexpectedly, so did China. This left Team GB in second place in the pool, and going through to the semi-finals, where they would face Argentina.

Argentina were the number two side in the world, but the British were confident they could beat them. 'The belief was through the roof,' Hamilton recalls. They had been preparing for this moment for three years, during which they had beaten every team in the world. 'We were sure of our ability.' Within six minutes, Team GB were a goal down, after a penalty corner conversion. The British dominated possession but lacked composure at crucial moments in front of the goal. In the third quarter, as they chased the equaliser, the Argentinians scored. In the lead-up to the goal, however, an Argentinian player had obstructed Crista Cullen, allowing the player with the ball to sprint unimpeded towards the goal. It was a so-called 'third-party obstruction' and illegal. The umpire, however, waved them to play on.

Cullen would replay that moment in her mind, vividly, for the next four years. 'I really struggled not to hold a grudge against it,' she says. It was an umpiring error, but she still blamed herself. 'I should have made more of a big deal. I should have ploughed through her. Do what I needed to do, which was stop her, whether that meant I ended up carded or whatever. Stop her no matter what.'

The game ended 2–1. After the whistle blew, the British players collapsed to their knees in tears. On television Kerry, visibly shaken and tearful, vented his frustration. Millions of television viewers, sixteen thousand people in the crowd and twenty-two players on the pitch saw the obstruction, he said. Everyone except one person.

In the dressing room, no one spoke. Their dream of winning a gold medal was gone. Their vision of gold had been vanquished. They returned to the Olympic Village and had dinner. Few slept. Next morning, they were quiet at breakfast. Then they took a shuttle bus to a local school for their pool session, one of the recovery rituals after a game day.

These sessions had been another of Christian Cook's ideas. The concept went back to the importance of a social debrief among players, getting them to spend time together in a relaxed manner, which expedited recovery and increased testosterone levels.

At the Beijing Games, they had been a structureless team, whereas in London they would always meet at 7 p.m. to walk to the dining hall, where they would sit and eat together. Phones weren't allowed. The players used to joke about it, and called it compulsory fun, but there had been a gradual, but definite shift towards these social occasions. 'It's such a fine balance of having those fun times but not it being like, "Oh, let's go and have some compulsory fun",' Walsh says. 'It evolved over time, so it's given people space to take ownership of that. Rather than it being the team leaders saying, "Okay let's play volleyball outside now, or go for a pop quiz," it would be like, "Oh, yes, let's go." It just grew on you.'

Pool recovery sessions were meant to be relaxed and fun. 'There was always a certain amount of abuse given to Dave, because the pool was normally quite cold and nobody wanted to get in,' Walsh says. 'There were always people screaming. It's generally quite a buoyant, vocal session.' These sessions would include easy, silly games like tag or shark. Hamilton would sometimes throw a float into the pool and get the players to race each other to it. Or he would instruct them to close their eyes and spin around, then try to work out their way back to the float with their eyes shut.

That day, the players entered the pool silent and depressed. Hamilton got a water ball out, and they started to play volleyball. Almost despite themselves, they began to enjoy it, laughing, forgetting. 'It started to be like, "Oh, we can laugh, it's okay, we can smile",' Walsh says. 'It just helped break down a lot of barriers.' They had prepared for this situation as part of their contingency planning. In case of defeat, they would give themselves until the end of the pool session to get it out of their system, to deal with it. Until then, they were allowed to be upset and frustrated. After that, they would draw a line under the experience and move on.

The following day, Great Britain played New Zealand for the bronze medal. Kate Walsh remembers the stark contrast between the two teams as they came out onto the pitch and lined up for the national anthems. 'The body language was insane. We could see the players on our bench standing, the shoulders are back, chests are out and we are all looking at each other.' Helen Richardson recalls that it was the strongest they'd felt as a team. 'The looks I was getting back from the others was fire.'

That game was fiercely fought and competitive. New Zealand hit the post once and had plenty of chances to snatch the game. But the British players knew that their opponents had already lost. 'It just felt no matter what they threw at us that day, we were going to win,' Walsh says.

During the London Olympics, Stafford Murray's team analysed 2500 hours of footage. The project cost around a quarter of a million pounds to run but, according to Murray, at least four gold medals can directly be attributed to it. When all the results were in, Team GB was third in the medal table, above their direct competitors − Australia, France, Italy, Germany − and even above Russia, an achievement previously considered unthinkable.

During the closing ceremony, Murray went to a local pub he had been frequenting. Pubs were a second home to Murray − though his wife contends that they are actually his first home. He had been going there every night on his own, wearing plain shorts, flip-flops and a Hawaiian shirt. He would speak to other customers about anything but the Olympics, drink a couple of pints and smoke a couple of cigarettes.

That day, he went there still wearing his EIS kit. Although he was not officially allowed to drink alcohol while wearing the official uniform, he had a few beers and smoked a cigar. He watched the closing ceremony on the television, in silence. It had been two years since he started planning the Team GB project. He called his mother, his brother, David Pearson and finally his grandfather.

Then he sat in silence for another hour, thinking, 'Shit, that just happened.'

16

WHAT IT TAKES TO WIN

In August 2012, during the London Games, Isabelle Gautheron, the performance director of the French cycling team, gave an interview to the press. The track cycling competition, which includes ten different events, had finished the previous day. Topping the table was the British team, who came away with seven gold medals. France, in third place, had won just one gold.

Gautheron was visibly at a loss to explain the extent of Britain's dominance. 'Have they found a new training process based on certain energy pathways? I am not talking about any illicit product, because anti-doping tests are so strong,' she said. 'But we are looking a lot at the kit they use. They hide their wheels. The ones for the bikes they race on are put in wheel covers at the finish. Do they really have the wheels of Mavic, the official supplier? We know they work with McLaren.' The British, she claimed, were using 'magic wheels'.

Scott Drawer is a tall, handsome man, with neatly parted hair and a sheepish grin. He speaks in a steady cadence, leaping between diverse topics with polymathic ease and the infectious enthusiasm of a young postgraduate student. He's a restless networker whose motto is 'the only sustainable advantage is to learn faster than your opposition'.

Drawer has a PhD in injury epidemiology, applying risk management to footballers' health. In 2000, he joined the embryonic Technology and Innovation team at UK Sport. There, he was tasked with scouting out new sciences and technologies that could be applied to sport. Three years later, he was heading the Research and Innovation programme, with an annual budget of approximately £150,000.

Olympic sports were then, by and large, relatively unsophisticated in applying science and using technology. On the other hand, Great Britain was home to some of the world's best universities and engineering companies. Drawer treated his project like a start-up. 'The mentality was you just go out, try stuff and learn though doing,' he explains.

Drawer didn't have that much time. He had to transform unsophisticated teams into early adopters, accelerating and moulding the employment of technology into four-year Olympic cycles of development, testing, adoption and refinement. He was aware that the transfer of fundamental research into real-world applications was painfully slow. He wanted to shortcut it.

In his first six months in the job, Drawer travelled the country, visiting universities and companies, building a network of contacts and identifying talent. It was talent scouting, but instead of athletes, Drawer was looking for scientists and technologists, experts in fields as varied as aerodynamics, material sciences and human physiology. The government stipulated that any project had to be processed via a formal tender process, so Drawer would proactively ask people to submit proposals. He would test them out on small projects first, to evaluate whether they were a good fit for his network, assessing how big their egos were, and if they genuinely wanted to be a part of the Olympic project for the right reasons.

British Cycling were early adopters. Andrea Wooles recalls first meeting Drawer just before the Athens Games in 2004. She had been struggling with the ingestible thermometer pills that they were using to gauge the riders' temperatures, a crucial part of their preparation as the Athens velodrome was expected to be sweltering.

'Your brain gets protective and stops you from producing power, which isn't really what you want in a race,' Wooles explains. 'It was crucial to stop people reaching that point, hence the thermometer pills. In theory, the riders ingested them and a handheld scanner could tell you the temperature. But they were drinking cold fluids that were wreaking havoc on the measurements. We were getting really ridiculous readings.'

Drawer arranged for Wooles to meet with the British military, who told her that they had stopped using the pills thirty years ago and had returned to a tried-and-tested method: 'The thermometer up the bum,' Wooles recalls. 'I said there were limits, even for a female physiologist.'

Drawer, according to Wooles, soon earned a reputation for innovations and ideas that were consistently excellent: 'If he was bringing you an idea, it was worth it. You would get all sorts of people coming up to you with all sorts of crap. With Scott, it was never fluffy.'

In late 2004, Drawer held a 'Boffins Day' on the aerodynamics of cycling at his alma mater, Loughborough University, in a large room set up with several round tables. A group of twenty aerodynamicists, bike engineers, computer scientists and software engineers were invited, and joined by staff from British Cycling, including the men's team pursuit coach Simon Jones and the former Olympic champion Chris Boardman. Drawer had no idea whether this was going to change everything or prove a massive waste of everybody's time. He was, as he later put it, 'shit scared'.

Drawer screened a few clips of cycling competitions and then asked his audience: how can we make these people go faster? Several ideas emerged, from optimally designed aerodynamic skinsuit fabrics to pear-shaped helmets with a pendant dangling in front ('It was based on fundamental aerodynamic theory, that says if you've got a small object in front of a big object you can actually divert the air away,' Drawer says. It was also totally impractical).

That was the first of many 'Boffins Days'. Often, only the members of this restricted group were privy to the ideas that emerged from such meetings. As concepts materialised into new equipment and training methods, riders would be then kept in the loop. Dan Hunt, vexed by the secretiveness of the group, gave them the moniker 'the Secret Squirrel Club'. The name stuck.

In 2005, when the International Olympic Committee designated London as the host of the 2012 Games, Drawer's team received an infusion of cash and personnel. With £2.5 million a year to play with and a team of fifteen sports scientists, Drawer scaled up his operations, dividing them into five major programmes: competition equipment, training science, coaching tools and technology, athlete health and the Paralympics.

At the London Games, the French performance director was accurate in stating that the British team collaborated with the McLaren Formula One team. In the case of equipment, the collaboration with McLaren was only one of many. At the Manchester Velodrome, BAE Systems had developed a timing system that used lasers and bar codes on the cyclists to give exact identification, split times and velocity data. The team were riding bikes fitted with instrumented cranks that captured force measurements, velocity and acceleration. The data was logged in real time via a system developed by McLaren and performance analysts to stream the video of the cyclists' workouts directly to the coaches' iPads.

The ambitious R&D undertaking wasn't restricted to cycling. The analysts at British Canoeing were using data-logging sensors developed by BAE Systems and McLaren to collect real-time acceleration and power data. Biomechanists within the athletics team had their Laveg laser guns, for calculating horizontal and vertical velocities in the triple jump and working out the optimal speeds before take-off. Boxing analysts were using the bespoke software iBoxer, with its detailed tactical briefings on over twenty thousand international boxers. These were just some of the hundreds of sports science and analysis projects taking place across the British teams that year.

This painstaking attention to accruing performance advantages, no matter how small, via research and innovation, became known as 'performance by the aggregation of marginal gains'. This organisational principle, which originated in British Cycling under Dave Brailsford but was applicable across Team GB, reflected the principle that by breaking down athletic performance into various components and improving each by 1 per cent, the resulting increase would be significant. As a philosophy, it was akin to a widely known business concept known as kaizen, and popularised by Toyota, which requires the implementation of a culture of continuous improvement. In fact, the word 'marginal' came to Brailsford as he was reviewing some studies on marginal costing he had done during his MBA. In cycling terms, it meant breaking down everything that goes into riding a bike and looking for the 1 per cent shifts that would make a difference. It seemed obvious to Brailsford that going after big ideas was difficult to do on a daily basis, but small gains, which were often overlooked, could regularly be aggregated to create meaningful change.

'Marginal gains came out of the magnitude of change required, in terms of where we were and where we wanted to get to,' Brailsford says. 'And then, equally, I know this sounds a bit contradictory, the margins of victory. You could win a race by one-tenth of a second. And you're thinking, "Okay, if we could win a race by one-tenth of a second, all these little things over here could equate to one-tenth of a second. So why won't we do them?"'

With the unwritten assumption that the difference in talent and training methodologies was indistinguishable at the elite level, the competitive advantage that the British seemed to have could be found in the details, in the margins, in the milliseconds.

In the case of equipment, for instance, much like physiologists periodising an athlete's training programme, Drawer and his collaborators had periodised technological innovation itself. In a four-year Olympic cycle, they experimented with and tested different technologies in training, but seldom in international competitions. They would then only implement the new technologies when it mattered. At the Olympic Games, therefore, British athletes not only peaked physiologically, but technologically, too.

For Drawer, innovation was a weapon. But the culture surrounding innovation was perhaps an even more powerful force. 'Once we got this process right, we noticed the aura and the fear we created,' Drawer says. 'As soon as others are thinking about your performance and not their own, you've already won.' And to him, marginal gains was the biggest

smokescreen going. He was bemused by how people perceived and misinterpreted the concept. The notion gained
traction in the press – anatomical pillows! peeled bananas!
rounder wheels! – but the fact was that few understood it.
'They thought it was about one great new idea that was going
to make a tiny little difference,' Drawer says. 'It's got nothing
to do with that.' Instead, according to Drawer, all those little
differences that added up to records and medals and Olympic
glory were the consequences of something far bigger, far
more fundamental.

He compares the situation to the classic psychology experiment on inattention blindness, in which subjects are asked
to pay attention to a video clip of a basketball game. When
tested, the subjects largely fail to notice a person in a gorilla
suit wandering around the court mid-game. Drawer cites
another study, which repeated this experiment with radiol-
ogists. They had spent years honing their ability to detect
small abnormal nodules in tissue imagery, yet in the test, 83
per cent failed to notice a nodule forty-eight times the size
of an average one, even though they looked straight at it. 'It's
the same principle,' Drawer says. 'Everyone thought it was
about the tiny differences, and fundamentally forgot about
the process that was in place.' That process was a rigorous,
methodical approach to performance planning that covered
all the elements, from the mental to the physiological, that
resulted not in small, but in the biggest possible gains in
human performance. Drawer had even come up with a catchy
name for it: What it Takes to Win.

And in the case of the British Olympic team, What it Takes
to Win was the gorilla.

Murray had assumed that after the Olympics there was
going to be some downtime. The London Games had ended

on Sunday 12 August. Murray took the Monday off, and returned to work on Tuesday. 'I thought it was going to be easy street for a while,' he says. 'You know, get a pat on the back, sit back and reflect on the success.' Instead, everything changed.

From UK Sport came rumours that there were going to be personnel changes across the board, and that a new organisational structure would be put in place. Many people who had been essential to the London success, like Scott Drawer, left the EIS. Analysts who had worked with Murray, like Mandy deBeer, also moved on.

'It was a stressful time, which was disappointing,' Murray says. 'I thought it would be a funfair, bunting everywhere, but it wasn't.'

The position of Director of Science and Technical Development was advertised, and Murray applied. He was one of the EIS's most senior and experienced members of staff, and everyone was saying that he was the strongest candidate. He made it to the final three, but didn't get the job.

This knocked his confidence – 'a real kick in the balls', as he puts it. For a while, Murray contemplated changing his demeanour. Being more serious. Maybe even wearing a suit. He confided in a psychologist friend, who made him see that, for non-conformist types like himself, there was probably a ceiling on how far he could be promoted. 'I can't fundamentally change who I am,' Murray reflected. 'I can't be a bloody boring suit. Life's too short.'

He began pondering whether the time had come to leave the British system. He had plenty of job offers coming through. Canada wanted him. Australia wanted him.

Dave Reddin, who was now performance director at the Football Association, asked Murray to consider becoming the head of analysis for the England football team. Murray was somewhat allergic to the world of football, but he respected Reddin. They met four times to discuss the future structure of the FA, and how analysts would be integrated within the team. Before his final interview with Reddin and a panel of executives from the FA, Murray pulled out. His maternal grandfather had just died, and the interview was on the same day as the funeral. 'I had to do the eulogy for my granddad. That was more important to me at the time,' Murray says. He called Reddin and apologised.

He made the decision to leave the EIS one evening, in a taxi. He had just received a technology award for the Team GB project collaboration with Dartfish during the London Games. As he looked out the taxi window, Murray contemplated his successes. 'Do you know what? It's time to step down. It's not going to get any better than this,' he thought.

A few days later, Murray received a call from Mark Jarvis, one of the directors at the EIS. The Institute was about to roll out the 'What it Takes to Win' model across all the Olympic teams. Although the model was already common practice in some teams, the EIS wanted to formalise it and ensure it was part of every team's performance planning. Jarvis was putting together a dedicated team of performance scientists to liaise with coaches as they adopted and adapted to the new process. He needed Murray to help him run it. 'I bit his hand off.'

To Murray, What it Takes to Win was, in a sense, what performance analysts had been doing back in 1998, when, with David Pearson and Mike Hughes, he created the first elite templates and performance profiles for squash; and in 2005, when his group of analysts and cycling coaches began methodically deconstructing performance on the track.

In the early days of the EIS, when sports scientists first entered the system, their support would regularly be siloed and uncoordinated. 'It was a bit hit and miss,' Andrea Wooles says. 'You would have a trainer trying to build up an athlete's muscle, while the dietician would try to make them skinny. If they don't work together we end up undoing each other's work.'

At the British Cycling programme, different specialists gradually converged on a unified view of performance. This was no doubt facilitated by the quasi-deterministic nature of track cycling, a sport that is highly measurable and quantifiable, where the race to win gold can be summed up as a battle of physics against physiology, with a considerable complement of biomechanics and tactics thrown in.

With cycling, the entry point was usually data captured by the analysts, who would break the target time down into lap splits, speed and cadence. They would translate this into the physical determinants of a rider, such as power-to-mass ratios, and then convert these into physiological measurements – including strength, body mass and aerobic conditioning – and commission individualised research projects covering aspects like warm-ups and aerodynamic drag reduction.

Mark Jarvis remembers how, in cycling, they use to plan by doing what he calls 'performance-backwards'. 'A common habit in anybody, in any sphere of life – certainly sports – is that you go, "I've got some stuff that I do and I know that I need to get better. So if I do these things I'll improve, which means it's working, right?"' Jarvis says. 'That feels like a sensible way of working, but they step-changed that mindset. They would set a target, for instance, of taking eight seconds off the world record. Hugely ambitious target. Now, what do we need to get there?'

And that, on the surface, is the simple concept behind What it Takes to Win – what do the best in the world do? How good are my athletes? How are we going to get there?

This idea, of course, only describes the destination. It doesn't necessarily prescribe how to get there. Mark Jarvis describes the problem as follows: if you put in room a physiologist, a psychologist, a biomechanist, a nutritionist, a strength and conditioning coach and ask them what is the best way to improve performance, they will come with four different plans and countless interventions that improve performance. 'If I'm a strength and conditioning coach my answer to all your problems is squats,' Jarvis says. 'We call that "ology goggles".'

With the constraints of time and money, successful Olympic programmes distinguish themselves by prioritising the right things with the right people at the right time. And that's what What It Takes to Win aimed to provide: a flexible, adaptable, planning strategy that ensured that all scientists, coaches and athletes involved focused on the interventions that would make the biggest possible difference in performance.

Consider, for instance, the men's hundred metres. To win that competition one simply needs to be the fastest. A reasonable assumption to make is that a runner that could beat the hundred-metre world record – 9.58 seconds – would probably also be the fastest on the day. However, that is not enough to guarantee a medal. In a competition, the hundred-metre runner would also need to consistently perform over three consecutive days, sometimes with a semi-final and final on the same day of the tournament. There's a difference between preparing an athlete to run one race in one day versus running four races in three days. These are two distinct performance goals that require a different kind of training.

The next step is to break down the performance goal into its different components. These are the abilities – mental, physical, psychological – required to reach the goal. In the case of the hundred metres, this might include the ability to react to the gun in 160ms, running thirty metres inside 3.9 seconds, and reaching a peak velocity higher than 12.2 metres per second.

These performance indicators can be further broken down into the so-called headline goals. Broadly described, these are the components of the performance that can be trained and learned. They might include strength and power profiles, and the robustness required to tolerate the training. For each, a list of technical indicators is produced: a counter-movement jump higher than 60 centimetres, a barbell peak power higher than 4000 watts, a reactive strength index higher than 3.8.

Once this forensic process is concluded, the athlete's journey is mapped out throughout the Olympic cycle, from training camps to performance milestones.

The model itself is fluid. Its content varies across the range of sports, in a spectrum that runs from the determinism of physiology-driven sports like cycling and running, to the complexity inherent in team sports like hockey and combat sports like boxing.

It was in the latter cases that the biggest misconceptions about the model emerged, with some coaches and performance directors thinking it an attempt to reduce everything to deterministic modelling and performance indicators. 'Some people would say, "We can't do that for our sport, we're not cycling,"' Jarvis recalls. 'They thought it was a narrow-minded exercise that didn't understand the theory of complexity. Nothing could be further from the truth.'

If in the case of the hundred metres, one can objectively quantify the time, the speed, the power, even the necessary physiological attributes to beat the world record (and, by extension, the competition) how does one even begin to tackle the problem when it comes to a complex sport like football? This, of course, is a problem that has occupied generations of performance analysts since the time of Charles Reep, with varying degrees of success. But none would dispute there are myriad ways to win a game, and none are infallible. In such cases, What it Takes to Win is really more 'What it Takes to Increase the Probability of Success'. So here the expertise and belief of the coach takes precedence. It was the job of performance leaders like Murray and Jarvis to talk to the coach, understand their modus operandi, and codify this knowledge into a framework that sports scientists could understand. This coach-led model was then scrutinised by the analysts, who would seek out objective evidence to support or falsify the assumptions of the coach.

Consider, for instance, judo. 'There are a million different ways one can win in judo. They are different fighting styles, different weights. How do you decide what you are going to train? If you can't say what is going to make you more likely to succeed, how do you decide how to run a training programme?' Jarvis asks. 'As opposed to a big fishing exercise with big datasets and looking for patterns, in judo they started the process by talking to the coach, capturing their philosophy and beliefs. Then they validated it through data. It's not about the perfect plan, it's about a plan that works and that everybody in the team freely adopts as their own.'

Nigel Donohue, the performance director of the British Judo Association, and his coaches created a What it Takes to Win model based around five technical trademarks: Throw for Ippon (the equivalent of a knockout), Win in Newaza (a specific grappling technique), Dominance in Kuminaka (a gripping exchange), Contest Management (from defending a lead to managing the space and tempo of the contest) and Fight Without Fear (which was self-explanatory).

These became the pillars of the judo programme. They were printed on the back of the players' T-shirts and were on the wall of the dojo in Walsall. Every session targeted a particular trademark. Throughout the Olympic cycle leading up to Rio, each athlete was evaluated every six months on the five trademarks, scoring between a 10 (gold) and a 1 (red), with a rationale given for each mark. These trademarks also shaped the education of new fighters entering the sport. Junior fighters who went to tournaments were instructed to focus on displaying the trademarks over winning a contest. The characteristics that made them junior champions were not the trademarks that would make them champions in the future.

'Obviously, they would prefer them to win,' Murray says. 'The point was that you can win the junior world championships, but there's no correlation really between that and being an Olympic gold medallist in the future.'

The new model aligned all the scientists, so that they adhered to the same performance indicators. As Murray put it, 'If you stopped a member of staff at any time in the day and asked, what are you doing? Doing this. Why? Because it fits to that bit of the model. Even the person cleaning the toilets, they know they need to keep the toilets clean so the athlete is not going to get ill, therefore they can train more. Everything is related to the What it Takes to Win model.'

It's like that story of John F. Kennedy's visit to the NASA Space Center in 1962. When the President asked a janitor sweeping the floor what he was doing. 'Helping to put a man on the moon,' was the reply.

17

TICKLING THE DRAGON'S TAIL

Shortly after the Beijing Games, a poster affixed to a notice-board at the University of Gloucestershire caught the attention of nineteen-year-old Lizzy Yarnold. It featured images of Rebecca Romero and Shelley Rudman in action, and read:

THE SEARCH IS ON FOR ATHLETIC GIRLS WHO HAVE WHAT IT TAKES TO WIN OLYMPIC GOLD Are you a GIRL4GOLD? UK Sport and the English Institute of Sport (EIS) are searching for highly competitive sportswomen with the potential to become Olympic champions in cycling and other targeted Olympic sports (bob skeleton, canoeing, modern pentathlon, rowing and sailing) in time for London 2012. GIRLS4GOLD is the single most extensive female sporting talent recruitment drive ever undertaken in Great Britain.

If you are . . .

- Female, aged between 17 and 25 years old
- Competing in any sport at county/regional level

- Fit, powerful and strong
- Mentally tough and competitive
- Up for a once in a lifetime opportunity to become part of Britain's sporting elite

. . . then we want to hear from you!

This new campaign, Girls4Gold, seemed to be targeting athletes just like her, women who had competed since childhood in a given sport and who might have untapped potential in a completely different one. Yarnold had competed in javelin, shot put and heptathlon. She was a competent athlete, but not good enough for the Olympics. Her sister, Katy, had previously applied to a similar programme, called Tall&Talented (she is 6ft 1in), and was selected for handball. Yarnold was thinking, 'Hold on, I'm the one who's always been very talented at sport. It was supposed to be my future.'

Yarnold and her friend Gemma were among the nearly nine hundred athletes who signed up for Girls4Gold. Later that month, the two women drove up to Loughborough University for their talent assessment trial. Yarnold had applied to study sports science at Loughborough, but hadn't been accepted. She felt strange being there again, being tested for the opportunity of a completely different life.

At registration, the clerks stamped a number 53 on Yarnold's hand. As they asked her to face a camera, she was thinking, 'I need to make this day count, because this is serious.' Yarnold says, 'It felt like a *Sliding Doors* moment.' Of the six sports the talent search focused on, Yarnold desperately wanted to be selected for modern pentathlon. When she filled in a short questionnaire, she claimed that she was very good at swimming and long-distance running – 'All a lie.'

The young athletes were split into groups. They were

weighed and measured, and performed different physical tests at stations around the sports hall: standing vertical and long jump; pulling and pushing at maximum force; three-minute spin tests on the cycling ergometer; and a thirty-metre sprint. As Yarnold was doing the sprint, she saw Gemma struggling on the bike. She ran over and, just as she fell off the bike, grabbed her friend, who then proceeded to vomit all over her.

A few weeks later, Yarnold received a letter congratulating her. She had been selected for the second phase of trials in skeleton. Her superior thirty-metre sprint performance made her well-suited to the sport. Enclosed was a DVD of Shelley Rudman's silver medal performance in 2006 and one of her appearances on a television talk show.

Yarnold was invited to the second phase of trials at the University of Bath's Sports Training Village a month later. She got lost in Bath and arrived very late. When she looked at her competitors – one hundred women were present that day – she felt disheartened. Yarnold was a heavier athlete, given her background in javelin and shot put; the others looked fit and toned and powerful. She thought, 'How am I going to compete against this? That girl has a six pack. That one is really quick.'

Danny Holdcroft doesn't really recall meeting Yarnold that day, but she remembers him well. It was a sunny day and Holdcroft was leading the group at the top of the push track. Yarnold offered him her sunglasses. She also had some Jelly Babies, and went around offering the sweets to the group.

She made sure she listened attentively to everything Holdcroft was saying. Being a javelin thrower, she was used to running with her torso turned sideways, much as in skeleton, so she soon took to the push start. Still, she thought the whole routine was somewhat embarrassing. 'You just collapse onto the sled – your legs are left behind you and you're flat on the sled like a pancake.' Yarnold says.

Over the next four months, the initial group of a hundred athletes was culled by further trials to fifty, then twenty, then the final ten. 'It was weird because you'd do the tests and then go away, and after a while an email would arrive saying you'd made it to the next stage,' Yarnold says.

In March 2009, the British Skeleton coaches took the ten novices to Lillehammer for a three-week ice camp. Yarnold had been told to bring a foam camping mat, which was to be cut up and gaffer-taped to her elbows, knees, hips, ankles and wrists for padding. On arrival, the athletes were given a sled and a map of the track. Yarnold shared a cabin with three other athletes, and the night before their first run on the ice track they took turns practising. Three of them would lie face-down on the floor, and a fourth would read out the corners and the direction of the steers so they could try to memorise it.

Yarnold had no idea what to expect from the ice track. She just tried not to be as petrified as everyone else seemed to be. 'All I was trying to do was deal with what was in front of me and get through the six packs who were facing me down,' Yarnold says. 'I had to try and just get a pass to the next trial.'

The following day, she found herself lying on a rudimentary sled, with her running spikes on, ski goggles taped to a crash helmet. She was let go from the third corner, and as she descended the ice track she started counting the corners. She lost count by the fourth turn. The G-forces pushed her helmet firmly onto the surface of the ice, emitting a deafening crunching noise. By then, Yarnold was just holding on the best she could.

'How was that?' the coach asked her at the end.

'Painful,' Yarnold replied. 'If I take some of the corners better, I will be faster.' And she went back up.

One athlete had broken her leg, and five others dropped out after the first run. Some said they were never doing it again and left early. Yarnold had to psych herself up to continue. She wasn't going to be the one who didn't do it.

The second run was much worse, as Yarnold now knew what to expect. As the athletes improved, they moved up towards the top of the track. Yarnold was the last in the group to get to the top.

After Lillehammer, Yarnold went to Uganda on a university trip. It was there she received a call informing her that she had made the team. A group of two men and four women – including Yarnold – joined British Skeleton in the summer of 2009. They were going to receive generous funding from UK Sport, and all athletes would be supplied with the latest BlacRoc sleds. This level of support was unheard of in a talent programme.

Danny Holdcroft intended to make an Olympic champion out of these new recruits at Sochi 2014. 'That didn't go down well with some of the senior athletes. We had a lot of athletes in the programme already and this was a challenge to their place in the programme,' Holdcroft says. 'But that's the way it is.'

The foundation of the skeleton programme remained the push-start sprint. Holdcroft revisited his understanding of what it took to win, and asked Scott Drawer to sponsor a PhD student who could spend four years studying push-start performance. Holdcroft had a formula based on coaching instinct, but now wanted data to quantify his theories. Data suggested that a 0.1-second advantage in the initial fifty-five metres was the equivalent of a 0.25-second advantage by the end of the run. A technical model was developed for pushing the sled, emphasising force production with exercises like leg press, squats and deadlifts.

The crux of the talent programme, however, was a grand experiment to redefine how athletes were trained. Traditionally, skeleton, as was the case with many other sports, followed a linear periodisation model. Before the start of the competitive season, athletes returning from holidays would first undertake a training block focused on building a foundation of general fitness and strength; this would be followed by a heavy strength-training period, and then a block of power and speed training.

'It's this idea that you build an engine, then you fine tune it, then you race,' Christian Cook says. This intense conditioning was then followed by a phase where technical skills and tactics were prioritised.

Different sports use variations of this template, according to the priority given to each of the components – power, speed, skill. In skeleton, sliders typically trained hard in the gym during the summer months, between June and October. They would then travel to tracks around the world to practise their sliding, at which point they would forgo gym work. 'That part of the season was focused around hopping on the sled and going down the ice,' Cook says. 'Which is great because, obviously, skill components are extremely important, but what you find doing this is when they come into competition they're not as strong, they're not as powerful as they were before.'

This was the tradition that Holdcroft wanted to change. Instead of training for power, speed and skill in separate six-week blocks before race season, he wanted to train for them all at once. Instead of the continuous cycle of physical improvement in the summer and decline in the winter, he wanted not only to work his athletes even harder in the summer, but to maintain their fitness with extra gym sessions in the winter. He saw each year as a stepping stone of gradual improvement, reaching a peak at the Sochi Games.

Furthermore, the new development group comprised athletes who had never competed on a skeleton track before and were going to go up against athletes with more than a decade of experience in the sport. It wasn't enough to have a well-defined training programme. If they were going to win, their progress would have to be accelerated. Holdcroft wanted to push them harder than he had ever done previously. The question was how to do that without breaking them.

At the time, Christian Cook had been reconsidering his understanding of stress and physiological adaptation. 'People talk about resilience to stress with the implication that we are managing in spite of stress,' Cook says. 'I wasn't interested in seeing adaptation purely as a process of resilience. I was interested in using stress to thrive.' He had been particularly interested in theories of ecological dynamics and adaptive complex systems. He read the works of Nikolai Bernstein and about predator–prey co-adaptation. 'Predators and prey can evolve rapidly in a complex and dynamic environment,' Cook says. 'You might view the stress response as an evolutionary response that shares the same features.' This suggested to Cook that when it came to promote quick physiological adaptations in athletes, linear periodisation programmes were potentially inferior to programmes that were non-linear, complex and dynamic.

This new way of thinking was aligned with Holdcroft's crazy notion of accelerating training. If they were going to try it, Cook said, they needed to monitor how the athletes were adapting along the way, so they could pull back or stop training when it became clear that they were pushing the athletes over the edge.

Cook began daily monitoring of the athletes' testosterone

and cortisol levels that summer. In the most intense periods, this could mean taking four samples per athlete per day. They also used the Restwise app, tracked heart-rate variability – a well-known measure of stress – and monitored the athletes' perception of their moods: were they excited about training? Were they enjoying mixing it up? Was it boring?

As planned, Holdcroft didn't go easy on his new recruits. He expected them to follow his instructions with commitment. That was non-negotiable. When they stepped into the gym they were expected to deliver, no excuses. 'We weren't messing around,' Holdcroft says. 'We were shifting big weights. We basically threw the kitchen sink at them for May, June, July, then repeated it.'

Yarnold remembers those excruciating training sessions. Dragging herself into the leg press machine, lifting, getting out and crying. 'Then I knew I had ten seconds before I had to lift again,' Yarnold says. 'It was horrible, training under extreme fatigue. We were going into this dark place. We had to get to the bottom of this trench to bounce back out of it.'

Holdcroft created a mindset called Own the Gym. He wanted his team to step into the gym as a squad and own the space. He wouldn't allow joking and idleness between sets and reps. 'When we go in, we lift. We break. We lift. Metronome, tick-tock, tick-tock, tick-tock, deliver and get out,' Holdcroft explains. 'We don't mess about.' If athletes from the other sports that shared the facilities didn't comply with those rules, Holdcroft would tell them that they were affecting his session and politely ask them to leave. 'We would do the same among ourselves,' Holdcroft says. 'If we had someone coming in who wasn't quite on it, we'd say, "Look, mate. You come in, this is what we expect. If you're not on the page today, go and train outside."'

By the third month of their first summer season, Holdcroft

noticed that his athletes were starting to flag. 'They started breaking. I don't mean breaking muscle and bones, but becoming prone to colds and minor illnesses.'

Holdcroft saw his athletes' illnesses not as a negative, but as a natural human reaction that signalled a need for recovery. 'Yes, they're tired and fatigued, but that's what their normal is,' Holdcroft explains. 'This is a typical training adaptation. You put them into a hole and you bring them out until you get a spike.' It was his job to find out how deep that hole was, that fine threshold that provoked an optimal adaptation. 'What is an athlete's breaking point? People don't like going underneath this line. Once you know it, you push the envelope.' At that point, Holdcroft would give the sick athlete some time off. When they returned, sure enough, the sliders would register a personal best on the push track.

To test their new approach, they didn't include any gym work at their first winter-season camp, in Igls, and tracked cortisol levels to get a sense of the stress that an ice session imposed on the athletes. They were low, nowhere near the levels observed during the summer. For the second camp, they added extra workouts on top of sliding. This was an experiment – skeleton athletes had rarely mixed ice training with strength work. Cook and Holdcroft found that they were able to continue improving the athletes' strength and power without a detrimental effect on their ability to learn ice skills. Their stress levels remained the same.

And yet, athletes began complaining of the extra load and how tired they were feeling. Holdcroft would say, 'Guys, you handled this in the summer and now you are telling me that you are doing too much. Think about it.' Besides, they had the data to prove that everything was going well. Holdcroft continued to schedule gym workouts every day. Cook called this approach tickling the dragon's tail.

The expression was first used by the physicist Richard Feynman referring to a nuclear experiment in the forties, when physicists would drop small spheres of plutonium into a radioactive sphere to keep it near a critical point. Cook knew, from previous experience, that athletes who underwent a period of heavy training prior to the start of the season typically had lost a significant part of those strength gains by the end of it. Athletes who still trained every seven to ten days, on the other hand, were able to maintain their initial strength.

'If you want a dragon to blow fire, you should tickle it so that it keeps knowing how to blow fire,' Cook says. 'It was this idea that a very small thing can make a big impact.'

In February 2010, Amy Williams won gold at Vancouver. After the Winter Olympics, Holdcroft and two of the coaches flew from Canada to Cuba for a week's holiday. Then they went to Lake Placid, where the talent development team were meeting for an end-of-season camp and to compete in the North American Cup.

In competition, all of the women registered start-sprint times that would put them inside the top eight in the world. 'We blew all the other nations out of the water,' Holdcroft says. 'I could see the other teams going, "Oh shit. These guys are coming."'

To everyone who knew her, Lizzy Yarnold had a double personality. In everyday life, she was genial, sociable, smiley. 'I was very much about the group and about the team,' Yarnold says. 'Making sure everyone was okay.'

In training, however, she was focused, intense, single-minded. This other side of her persona was nicknamed The Yarnold. She wouldn't smile or talk to other athletes. If her boyfriend happened to pass the gym while she was training, she would ignore him. One of her mantras was 'Don't be shit.'

She was very conscious of this metamorphosis. 'It was really exhausting to have those two personalities. When I was the athlete, I was making sure I did everything in the correct way. I think it got to a point where I was trying so hard in competitions, expecting nothing less of myself than to win, that it took so much energy to get there. Outside of training, I'd cry and become emotional because of that.'

That relentless perfectionism, accompanied by the expectations that the team would deliver a gold medal, was affecting her performance. 'I mean, they didn't need to explicitly say that that was the expectation,' Yarnold says. 'I wanted to go to the Olympics, and I certainly wasn't going there to get a T-shirt.' Yarnold had been identified as one of the new talents with the highest potential, but her numbers placed her near the bottom of the pack.

With Yarnold, Christian Cook explains, they had to look beyond the sport and examine how she dealt with life in general. As a chronic over-achiever, Yarnold was a person who demanded a lot from herself in every single sphere of life. 'They have a whole list of things in life that they want to be the best at. They don't often stop and think of the consequences of this, and that leads to an accruing of stress that affects them. Performance is not just what you do in the gym or on the track; it really is how you orientate your life towards that goal,' Cook says.

Yarnold began culling extraneous concerns from her day-to-day life, making sure she wasn't adding unnecessary stress. In November 2010 the women's team competed in a round of the Europa Cup at Cesana in Italy, their first event as professional athletes. The expectation was that the four women would come inside the top ten. Yarnold, on the first day of the event, came eleventh, the lowest ranking among the British women. Holdcroft and Mark Wood, her ice coach, took her aside and asked her why she was eleventh and not tenth. What was going on?

'I really felt like I'd been yelled at and I was like, "I'm literally doing my best",' Yarnold says. 'It's the first time I've ever done this. Hello? I'm trying really hard.' She was angry about how harshly she was being treated.

What happened next, she calls her cliff-edge moment. 'I basically was hanging off this cliff edge, being yelled at. I've come eleventh, and been really rubbish. At this point, when you're under stress, what do you do? You either fall and give up or you just climb back up and try and save the situation.' The following day, she placed fifth, above two other British women. At the Europa Cup in Innsbruck two weeks later, she won two races back to back. She understood then that change could come from within – that she could be calmer and more in control.

'I think what's really common for people that are hugely successful and hugely driven is their perception that they can handle everything, but the reality from a biological perspective is that nobody can,' Cook says. 'Your hormones don't lie.'

Yarnold first realised that she had total recall for ice tracks in November 2012, after she blacked out during a training session. Yarnold was competing in the World Cup at Whistler, and was in her second season as a professional. On the first two practice runs, she was still trying to work out how to steer the track and was hitting all the walls on the way down. On the first run of the second day, she slid faster than most of her competitors. Going into the final corner of the next run, her brain, crushed by 5g accelerations, switched off and Yarnold lost consciousness.

She was taken to hospital for observation, and to be checked for any signs of concussion. The following day, she was cleared to race. 'I asked the TV commentators not to say anything because my parents didn't know I'd been toast,' Yarnold says. At the race, she took it easy during the first round and finished safely. On the second run, she went for it, and was the second fastest, placing third overall.

She surprised herself by being able to overcome a potentially traumatic incident so easily. On reflection, she realised she was no longer petrified of the track. It had taken two years for that fear to abate. She no longer felt the out-of-control panic that used to assail her in the early days. Her perception of the speed, of the forces pushing and pulling her, and of the nuances of the tracks had assumed a very different nature. They were now vivid, visual memories. When, for instance, she faced a difficult turn like the one in Whistler, she would identify the type of corner and associate it with one she had experienced before. Then she would extract all the information about the geometry, the speed, the ice, her sled and the runners. It was all in her mind, in a sort of exaggerated mnemonic of ice and shapes, a total recall designed specifically for the purposes of navigating skeleton tracks at top speed.

As with most mnemonics, the way Yarnold memorised the tracks involved a complex form of storytelling. In her system, every track was a different character. For instance, Igls, the beginners' track in Austria, corresponded to a child. The track itself is short and relatively easy to navigate, and for that reason Yarnold associated it with children's learning processes. Lake Placid was an old man: 'It can be okay sometimes, but also it can be really difficult and challenging. It can come back at you. You never know what's going to happen. Every corner in Lake Placid has a long story.'

In Yarnold's mental universe, every corner of every track has a story. She tells these stories not only using the material of her own experiences, of how she acted and how the track reacted to her, but also from watching her rivals: 'When you go around a corner you can go round safely and simply, just trundle around the bottom. How much space is there? When you come into a corner, it's a single oscillation. You rise, you fall. You could come in and steer hard, and then release. You could do a graded steer. You could steer, hold up and then squeeze out. There are millions of different things you could do. You could wiggle the whole way through the corner or do nothing. What do I need to do to exit the corner? To get into the corner, what's the line? And then you need to work out what the fastest line is, that no one else is doing. As I'm going into the track physically, I need to then translate what is going to happen. What's it going to do with me? What does this translate to?' She calls it an inverse game of snooker, as if she was reconstructing the trajectory of a ball with time running backwards.

In her mental representation, every ice track is in a different book on a mental shelf. There is a separate shelf for books about relating corners from different tracks. It is in this inter-connected hyper-dimensional mindspace that Yarnold finds her strategy for coping with ice tracks. At the start of a season, she might be slower and more forgetful. But as the season progresses, she practises her recall through visualisation. She tries to visualise the tracks increasingly fast, several times a day, a different track every week.

'There are so many tracks around the world and they're so different,' Yarnold says. 'You might race on the Friday; Saturday you pack up, you fly and then you're at the next track on the Sunday. In my mind, I have put away the last track and opened up the book for the next one.' If there's a new track, she first chooses three aspects of three corners to focus on. Never more than three. Once she has done that, she will keep improving and iterating, adding to the book about the track.

When she visualised the Sochi Olympic track, Yarnold would close her eyes and start rocking from side to side, mimicking the body movements that steer the sled – gentle, delicate nudges of shoulders and knees, head, toes. She called this dancing. To the outside observer, it looked as though she was in a deep trance. In her mind, she was standing at the top of the ice track, inside a teak building, open and airy. She saw fluttering shutters and the room awash in white light. She saw herself walking out and standing at the top. It was three minutes to the start, so her coach was standing there with her sled. She heard the crunch of the ice underneath her shoes. Had she got any ice in her spikes? If so, she cleaned them. She fastened her helmet and stood ready at the starting block.

Then she sprinted. She would always aim to execute her sprint with relaxed aggression. She took her time to get to that state. She knew she needed to be explosive, fast, but there was no point in tightening up. Once she was on the sled, peripheral vision became crucial. She detected where she needed to go, locked in all the information and let herself go. She was able to pick out the different shades of ice and even the concrete beneath it. She could see exactly where in a corner she was and navigate through it.

She felt the track starting to slope downwards, at a steady incline, and jumped on the sled just as she saw a pole to the right of the track marking the end of the run. The track then funnelled in up to about thirty metres, and the lever ramp came on the right. She negotiated the first corner with a single steer. Then there was about ten metres until corner two, and then the track started to drop into corner three. Two oscillations in three; she kept it to the right-hand side, brought it onto corner four, and then to five. 'It's a bit like you're laying Lego as you go, so I'm coming out of the corner and I'm thinking, "Okay, what's next?"' Yarnold says. 'I have two corners in my mind at a time.'

Steer, wait, steer, wait, as she goes up and then drops down into corner six. She feels pressure then holds, holds, holds and waits for the exit and across. Wait into corner seven, followed by two oscillations. She shifts her weight, meets corner nine and goes quickly into ten. The sled then drops. Wait for the exit, and fast into eleven. She comes out, onto a straight, gets the early height out up an elevation in the track. There are three corners now, all with two oscillations. She drops and waits out. Last corner, another two oscillations and then she looks up and it's over.

A few weeks before the Winter Olympics, the team psychologist asked Yarnold how she would feel if the race were tomorrow. 'I'm ready,' she replied. On 14 February 2014, Lizzy Yarnold stood at the top of the Sochi ice track, preparing for her last run of the competition. On day one, Yarnold had accumulated a lead of 0.44 seconds over second-placed Noelle Pikus-Pace of the United States. In her third run, on the second day, Pikus-Pace broke the course record. 'She was a very good competitor,' Yarnold says. 'I knew that she could come back and take away that lead quite easily. The third run, I had to put a marker in and make sure everyone knew what I was doing. It was very tight. It was a very concise, tight run. I only moved on the sled when I needed to. It just flowed easily.'

For her final run, Yarnold started out absolutely calm. She negotiated the first corner without a problem. However, on the second she somehow forgot to steer and started skidding down the track uncontrollably. At this point, travelling at speeds exceeding 90mph, she was thinking, 'Who's at the bottom? They're watching me. I'm going to get told off.' If she could just relax and get into corner three, she thought, she would be okay. She just needed to right the sled and relax.

When Amy Williams won, Danny Holdcroft jumped around, beside himself with excitement. In Sochi, when Yarnold finished her race, he didn't celebrate. He was thrilled, of course, but he already knew that this was going to be the outcome. Yarnold had been dominant for the past two years. In the end, she won gold by 0.97 seconds and, as he predicted, it was all down to her start run. Like Williams, Yarnold had followed the training programme to the letter, ticked all the boxes and won the medal. And that certainty, to Holdcroft, was more than just objectivity and methodology. It was about coach's instinct, a belief even. Was that belief unbreakable? Of course not. At some point in every Olympic cycle, Holdcroft always had a moment where he found himself sitting in a café, looking at the data, thinking: 'Shit, this isn't working,' The numbers in the gym had gone up, but the actual performance in the push track had plateaued. 'I would get desperate,' he says. 'Then, eventually, it would come. It never didn't. All of a sudden, they would fly.'

18

UNDER CONSTRAINTS

In 1941, the year when the United States of America entered the Second World War, a researcher from Ohio State University called Paul Fitts was asked to join a team of psychologists that was being assembled at the US Army Air Forces in Washington DC. As part of the war effort, the Aviation Psychology Program was to apply their understanding of human behaviour to the testing of air pilots and the design of military equipment.

Fitts used eye tracking to study pilots' visual scans and how to design flight instrumentation that reduced the probability of human error. (He also dedicated some of this time to analysing interviews with UFO sighters.) After the war, Fitts, who by then had risen to the rank of lieutenant-colonel, submitted a comprehensive report that listed the innumerable challenges humans faced when piloting aircraft that had been designed poorly and without due consideration to the known limitations of human perception. The volume, titled *Psychological Research on Equipment Design*, was one of the first to expound on the psychology of human–machine interaction, a discipline that later became known as human factors.

Fitts broadened the scope of his experimental work when he later returned to academia, using simple motor tasks like mirror drawing, vocalisation exercises and reaction-time tests to continue his investigation of human perception and behaviour. In one experiment, he asked participants to tap a stylus on two rectangular targets a certain distance apart for a period of a few seconds, as quickly and as accurately as possible. He found that the resulting data could be neatly encapsulated by a mathematical formula, showing that the time to move the stylus to the target was a function of the distance and its width. Fitts's equation remains one of the most well-established empirical laws in the study of human–machine interaction.

Like most psychologists at the time, Fitts was influenced in his thinking by the development of computers in the forties and had adopted much of the novel terminology of computer science to describe human cognition and behaviour. In a metaphor still in vogue today, Fitts conceived of the human brain as a computer. In the information-processing analogy, human motion was the result of a linear, deterministic process: sense organs perceived the environment as input data; internal programs, making use of previous mental representations and stored memories, computed a response; and movement was the output.

The computer analogy was so instrumental that Fitts even attempted to write a computer program that could simulate a baseball batter. The virtual batter was equipped with sensors that could register the trajectory of the ball and, using a memory bank of previous experiences, could select the correct stroke to use, in terms of timing and amount of power, given the perceived conditions. 'My own conclusion is that if a digital computer can be programmed to play chess against a human opponent, then it can probably be programmed to hit a baseball thrown by a good human pitcher, a skill not to be dismissed lightly, since in many respects it is much more complex than that involved in playing chess,' Fitts wrote.

Later in his career, Fitts started writing a book that sought to advance a new science of experimental psychology, firmly rooted in information-processing principles, that could explain human skill and how it developed. It was then that, based not only on his work in the military and his laboratory work, but also on extensive survey data from a range of athletes, he proposed his three-stage model for skill acquisition.

Fitts was never able to complete his magnum opus. In May 1965, he suffered a heart attack in his sleep and died. His book was already fully outlined and several chapters finalised, and one of his students, Michael Posner, was asked to finish it. For the title, Fitts used a term he had coined: *Human Performance*.

One day in the summer of 1978, Keith Davids, a physical education graduate travelled to Leeds in the hope of meeting John Whiting. Whiting was one of the pioneers of skill acquisition in the country and the author of the seminal treatise *Acquiring Ball Skill*. When Davids arrived he was informed that Whiting had recently relocated to the Netherlands, where he was now the head of the Human Movement Science group at the Free University of Amsterdam, and was no longer part of the faculty. He was also told that a PhD applicant had just turned down a scholarship, and asked whether he would be interested in taking it up.

Davids was shown to the room that was to be his office. It was small, the walls painted black and the windows covered by dark blinds. The room was also furnished with a tachistoscope and a ramshackle ball-projection machine.

This used to be Whiting's laboratory, where he had conducted multiple visual perception studies. Most of his research had hinged on a simple question: what does it take to catch a ball? More precisely, he had investigated whether the popular dictum of keeping one's eyes on the ball, perpetuated by coaches everywhere, had any actual validity. Whiting, who also subscribed to the theories of information-processing psychology, was interested in understanding why eyes had to be kept on the ball, if at all. And if so, for how long? At what stage of the ball's trajectory?

In one of his experiments, subjects sat at the table in pitch darkness, clenching a bite bar (a restraint device commonly used in visual perception studies to keep the subjects still), throwing and catching balls tied to a pole. Whiting had devised a modified version of table skittles, a game in which players swing a ball attached to the pole by a string, to topple the pins standing on the table. Whiting's contraption involved electronic switches instead of skittles. These would turn lights on and off during specific parts of the ball's flight. This experimental paradigm was called occlusion: by illuminating only parts of the trajectory, Whiting could determine which visual information the participants needed to catch the ball.

The occlusion experiments proved that keeping one's eyes on the ball in order to catch it was altogether unnecessary. Participants only required sight of the ball for a moment, typically one hundred milliseconds (depending on the ball's velocity), to anticipate where it was going to go.

Whiting was also able to demonstrate, using a high-speed camera and the ball-projection machine, the intricate dynamics of ball-catching. As the ball approached, participants would typically first move their hand into the line of flight and then start to close their fingers, even before the ball touched their hand.

In his PhD, Davids pursued similar experiments focusing on the role of peripheral vision. 'I used the original ball-projection machine,' Davids says. 'It was really primitive. One time the spring broke and went flying across the room. I was worried about it hitting a participant, so I had to stop using it.'

In 1985, Davids joined the Department of Sport and Recreation Studies at Liverpool Polytechnic, by then already considered the hub of sports science in the country. The new head of the department, Frank Sanderson, had been a PhD student under Whiting. Davids shared an office with Tom Reilly and befriended a colleague who shared his predilection for beer and curry, Mike Hughes. Davids was invited to be part of the organising committee for the 1987 World Congress of Science and Football, collaborating on two papers on four-a-side football, one measuring the physiological strain, and the other players' anxiety.

'That was the conference when controversy first broke between Mike Hughes and the analysts who followed Charles Reep,' Davids recalls. 'I had not been aware of it at the time.'

In fact, at the time, Davids was rather more preoccupied with a controversy that was brewing in psychology.

It's highly likely that Paul Fitts crossed paths with a psychologist by the name of James Gibson in the early days of the Aviation Psychology Program in Washington, DC. Gibson, who had lectured in psychology at Princeton, was then relocated to Fort Worth, Texas, and, later, Santa Ana Army Air Base in California. He was made director of the Motion Picture Research Unit, where he developed visual aptitude tests for pilots and training films. This experience was formative for Gibson. He would later write: 'It was worrisome, for, as I gradually came to realize, nothing of any practical value was known by psychologists about the perception of motion, or of locomotion in space, or of space itself. The classical cues for depth referred to paintings or parlour stereoscopes, whereas the practical problems of military aviation had to do with takeoff and landing, with navigation and the recognition of landmarks, with pursuit or evasion, and with the aiming of bullets or bombs at targets. What was thought to be known about the retinal image and the physiology of retinal sensations simply had no application to these performances. Birds and bees could do them, and a high proportion of young males could learn to do them, but nobody understood how they could.'

Gibson came to radically reject the mainstream psychology ideas attached to information-processing theory and formulate an alternative that came to be known as ecological psychology. For instance, he hypothesised that perception and action, rather than being separate processes, were irrevocably interconnected: movement is modified by what we perceive and perception is modified by how we move. He called this synergy perception-action coupling.

The implication was that the individual could never really be understood outside the context of the surrounding environment. His argument was that we make sense of the world by interaction with it. Perception, in ecological psychology, was direct, not subordinate to the computer-like brain.

'His research got largely ignored at the time because the CIA had a hunch that the Russians were able to program minds, à la *The Manchurian Candidate*, so a lot of funding went to information-processing psychologists,' Davids says.

By the seventies, however, some psychologists began scrutinising and testing the idea of perception–action coupling. This natural connection was demonstrated, for instance, in experiments by psychologist David Lee at the University of Edinburgh, who showed that visual information could constrain movement. They designed a purpose-built room with walls and ceiling that could be moved imperceptibly. When the walls were moved by a few centimetres, the subjects in the room, unaware of the manipulation, would begin to sway. The more the walls moved, the more they would sway (in some cases, children even fell over). Such was the ease with which they could manipulate them by moving the walls, the researchers called their subjects 'visual puppets'. 'This showed how dependent we are on the surrounding visual information and how we react to it subconsciously,' Keith Davids says. 'For instance, if I ask you to stand on one leg, that shouldn't be a problem for a few seconds, but if I then ask you to do it with your eyes closed, it's a lot harder.'

John Whiting, at the Free University of Amsterdam, had also been converted to Gibson's ecological view, becoming one of its leading proponents and conducting a series of creative experiments that provided empirical ballast to the theory. In one experiment Whiting revisited his ball-catching studies, adding a twist. This time he used three balls: a large ball of 7.5-centimetre radius; a small ball of 5.5-centimetre radius; and a ball that shrank gradually as it approached the subject, imperceptibly changing from a large ball to the small-sized one. This was achieved by encasing a small-sized ball inside a balloon that was mechanically deflated by a vacuum pump. According to information-processing theory, catching a ball required extensive mental calculations involving distance, object size and velocity to estimate a precise time of arrival. If this was the case, subjects would struggle to react in time to the ruse of the deflating ball.

Ecology psychology, on the other hand, maintained that people could perceive and react to environmental information directly and react to it subconsciously, without resorting to laborious background computations. In this case, Whiting hypothesised that the relative rate of expansion of the ball as it moved towards the observer provided such information. During the experiment, the participants reacted as expected to the normal balls. However, with the deflating ball their behaviour changed, with subjects subconsciously closing the aperture of their grasp as they noticed the ball shrinking.

By the eighties, ecological psychologists began integrating Gibson's theory with the theories of Soviet neurophysiologist Nikolai Bernstein. Bernstein had been unknown in the West until his works were translated into English in 1967. He had conducted much of his work in the twenties and thirties at the Central Institute of Labour in Moscow. The remit of the Institute had been to create a new science of labour that increased productivity and eliminated inefficiency. Its director, Aleksei Gastev, was fervently taken with this idea, writing that he dreamt of a future where 'there is no longer any individual face but only regular, uniform steps and faces devoid of expression . . . measured not by a shout or a smile but by . . . a speed gauge'.

Using a high-speed camera that he had invented, capable of tracking human movements with a precision of two hundred frames per second, Bernstein filmed blacksmiths as they hammered metal plates. With light bulbs attached to the workers' arms as markers, Bernstein depicted the sequence of their continuous motions on long-exposure photographic plates, allowing him to study the relative motion of the elbows, joints and muscles.

What Bernstein observed, to his surprise, was that although the outcome of the movement was always the same, the movements of the blacksmith never repeated themselves. This constituted a conundrum to Bernstein. It seemed impossible to him that the brain was able to compute all the necessary commands to coordinate the joints and the muscles.

This was contrary to the tenets of information-processing theorists, where variability in movement was considered to be noise. Acquiring a skill implied reducing that error to a minimum and enacting movements. In other words, practice makes perfect.

Bernstein saw movement variability as something entirely different. To him, variability was a blessing that allowed for a flexible and continuous adaptation of the person to the environment. It's not that all variability was necessarily positive, of course, but its role in the coordination of human movement was nevertheless fundamental. He wrote: 'The process of practice towards the achievement of new motor habits essentially consists in the gradual success of a search for optimal motor solutions to the appropriate problems. Because of this, practice, when properly undertaken, does not consist in repeating the *means of solution* of a motor problem time after time, but in the *process of solving* this problem again and again by techniques which we changed and perfected from repetition to repetition. It is already apparent here that, in many cases, "practice is a particular type of repetition without repetition" and that motor training, if this position is ignored, is merely mechanical repetition by rote, a method which has been discredited in pedagogy for some time.'

As the field of psychology gradually split into two seemingly disparate, incompatible camps, Keith Davids stood firmly on the side of the emergent theory of ecological dynamics. He was particularly inspired by the theory of a psychologist called Karl Newell, an experimentalist who studied the problem of movement coordination in children, elderly adults and people with disabilities. Newell had shown that individuals developed higher levels of coordination as they interacted with what he called constraints. He divided constraints into three general categories: organismic (pertaining to the individual – genetics, brain synaptic structure, emotions, memories); environmental (such as gravity, light, sound, temperature, social norms); and the rules and goals of the task at hand. 'This was an "aha" moment for me,' Davids says. 'I could immediately see the implications for sports research.'

In 1991, when Keith Davids moved to Manchester Metropolitan University and resumed his studies of visual perception with one of his PhD students, Mark Williams, he attempted to inject ecological psychology concepts into his work. The typical experiment set up to study visual perception in sports, for instance, involved a static image projected on the screen – for instance, the image of a football player dribbling a ball – and the participant would then be asked to anticipate where the attacker was going to go, either by using a joystick or verbalising his actions. That's not what a player does, Davids would think. A player doesn't press buttons or verbalise actions. Instead of static images, they projected life-size video clips of a player dribbling a ball towards the camera and used pressure mats to track the participant's reaction.

Still, Davids felt frustrated and isolated. Ecological psychology didn't have many proponents in sports science at the time. His colleagues were sceptical and journal reviewers didn't have a clue what he was talking about. Even his collaborators at the Free University of Amsterdam, who were more focused on studying human behaviour, were sceptical of Davids's focus on sports performance. 'They felt they needed more lab experiments, under rigorous lab conditions,' Davids recalls.

In 1999, Davids met a young Portuguese scholar by the name of Duarte Araújo. Araújo was studying sports psychology at the Technical University of Lisbon and, attracted by the new ideas in ecological psychology, had decided to spend a semester at the Free University of Amsterdam. Like Davids, he had never been persuaded by the idea that traditional laboratory protocols of behaviour research could explain the elaborate feats of athletic coordination.

One of Araújo's colleagues was Luis Rocha, a sailing coach (Rocha would later work with the Portuguese and Italian Olympic teams) and the two students would often accompany sailors to observe first hand how they made decisions at sea. In one of their early studies, they asked the sailors to play a computer game, in which they controlled a boat with a joystick, that realistically simulated wind conditions and sea states. Although many of the decisions made in the game were similar to how they performed in real life, the sailors would also make several tactical-technical moves, particularly near other boats, that were completely different. 'This emphasised the idea that we think with the body, we think with our own actions, in a much more effective way,' Araújo says. 'It was not a belief, it was evidence. If we wanted to study cognition in sport, we had to do it in situ.'

Araújo considered Davids's early papers, applying Newell's constraints-led approach to sport, seminal references in this new field of study. However, he was willing to go even further. 'If these principles make sense,' he said to Davids, 'they can't be studied in a laboratory at all. I don't want to drag athletes to a laboratory to record passive perception and passive action. I want to study them as they play.' Davids was emboldened by the idea of moving out of the lab and the two began sketching out Araújo's PhD studies over dinner and wine. 'Our best insights would come after we shared a few glasses,' Davids recalls. 'We would have to write them down in case we forgot them in the morning.'

Their first study took place at the picturesque Cascais marina in Lisbon. They recruited a group of competitive sailors, attached fluorescent markers to the masts of their boats, and simply told them to race. In match-sailing regattas, the boats first enter an area from opposite ends of the start line. They are then given four minutes to jockey for position and put themselves in an advantageous position to cross the start line first. Araújo and Davids wanted to study how sailors behaved depending on different race conditions. Araújo filmed more than twenty races, at various points from the quay, and then digitised the footage using bespoke software that he had written. 'Their behaviour had nothing to do with what the coaches had instructed them before,' Araújo says. 'Instead, it was highly dependent on the behaviour of their opponents.'

In another study, the two researchers filmed one-on-one situations in basketball. The attacker and the defender initiated their move from the 3-point line, while the rest of their teammates were scattered in positions near the paint. The two would play mano-a-mano for five seconds and then proceed as normal by involving the other players. Again, they noticed how the two players obeyed clear patterns of coordination. As the attacker attempted to dribble the ball past the defender and towards the basket, he would subconsciously try to lead the defender to mirror his actions, sometimes only for a few seconds, and would then suddenly try to break that coordination with an abrupt change of direction and speed. The defender, on the other hand, would try to maintain that coordination at all costs by trying to anticipate the attacker's next move and staying between the basket and the attacker.

These patterns of coordination, although obvious, were not at all intentional. They emerged naturally and subconsciously as the result of the players' interaction. 'They falsified this notion that players did whatever they were instructed to do by the coach,' Araújo says. 'This notion of pre-programming, whereby the players first had to program the solution in their minds, was nonsense.' Araújo would sometimes ask players to explain what they had just done on court, and he frequently realised their explanations either simply didn't add up or were very different from what had just happened on court. 'They were very obviously just parroting what the coach had told them,' Araújo says. 'But what they were doing from game to game was completely different, and it depended on the various states of the game.'

The key point about these experiments was that none of the athletes had been instructed to behave in a specific way. The behaviour just emerged as athletes interacted with the constraints imposed on them. This became increasingly obvious as Araújo, Davids and colleagues continued their in situ experiments. For instance, in a study of one-on-one situations in football, they found that a player's behaviour naturally changed when they were near the goal: defenders closed the distance to the attacker, while attackers near their own goal played more conservatively. 'What we showed was that to conduct any valid study in sport you need to understand the context,' Araújo says. 'The moment you exclude the environment, or when you detach perception from the action, behaviour becomes artificial. You might as well be playing a computer game with a joystick.'

These experiments had a second, perhaps deeper, implication, as they realised that the constraints-led approach wasn't just relevant to the study of individual coordination. They could use it to study the coordination and the interactions that emerged between players. They could use it to study football.

The Faculty of Human Kinetics at the Technical University of Lisbon was founded in 1975. The institution has been innovative since its foundation, awarding not only physical education degrees but also coaching certificates.

One of its first students was Carlos Queiroz. He was an eager student of sport, devouring the literature and conducting his own experiments. He not only filmed training sessions at professional football clubs, but also kids playing with ragged balls in the street. He was soon publishing articles explaining his conceptualisation of the game, which he increasingly saw as complex and dynamic. As such, it required a new approach to training, in which all exercises had to integrate all the aspects of competition, from the emotional to the cognitive. The game should be taught by playing it, Queiroz argued. He eschewed repetitive drills in favour of small-sided games that retained the complex essence of the sport. He called that principle 'simplification of the complex structure of the game'. 'We can't use information to guide our behaviour that won't be available during competition,' Araújo explains. 'The best information to calibrate my action is the information I have available to me during competition. It's the position of the ball, the displacement of my teammate. Those guys couldn't conceive of a different way of coaching. All training was done on the basis of competition. Anything that detracted from that was considered a step backwards.'

In 1985, Queiroz was invited by the Portuguese Football Federation to take the helm of the national youth team, where he was able to put his theories into practice. 'If I had any doubts when I started training the youth team on the basis of my methods, I lost them all,' Queiroz said in 2017 to the Portuguese weekly *Expresso*. 'The progression of the players was exponential and the results spectacular in a short period of time.' Under Queiroz, Portugal would go on to win two World Youth Championships back to back, in 1989 and in 1991. That group of talented players, who became known as the Golden Generation, would later form the basis for a senior team who, led by players like Luis Figo and

Rui Costa, reached the semi-finals of the 2000 European Championships, were runners-up in 2004, and World Cup semi-finalists in 2006. Queiroz himself would later coach at some of the best clubs in the world, from Manchester United, as Alex Ferguson's assistant, to Real Madrid, and take three different countries – South Africa, Iran and Portugal – to the World Cup on four occasions.

The impact of Queiroz's methodology extended beyond the talent on the pitch. As a lecturer, he taught a generation of coaches who, in recent years, have been champions in Russia, France, Greece and England. Even after his departure, the Faculty of Human Kinetics remained faithful to its philosophy. Training centres were established, ensuring that sports science students, while pursuing research projects, also learned on the job by coaching actual teams rather than just analysing video footage.

'They are like scientists,' Davids recalls. 'They have this experiential knowledge from just trying this out in the field day in, day out, experimenting. They didn't use the language of ecological dynamics. They weren't aware of the theoretical ideas of Gibson. They were just intuitively applying them.'

Like Queiroz, Davids bemoans the traditional approach to training that he frequently witnesses at professional clubs and youth academies, often based around isolated, repetitive drills. One of the problems of such methods is what Davids calls task decomposition. For instance, when teaching kids how to dribble, coaches frequently teach them to first control the ball, often dribbling around and through static cones on the pitch; they only later try to dribble the ball past other players. 'The information present in both environments are very different and the actions that emerge are consequently different,' Davids says.

Davids studied task decomposition in terms of the

volleyball serve, in which a player throws the ball in the air and then volleys it over the net to the opposite side of the court. Typically, coaches would instruct the players to first practise tossing the ball, and only after mastering that particular movement could they then combine it with hitting the ball in the air. 'We understand why coaches were doing it. The learners would get overwhelmed by all that they had to do if we just tell them to play the game,' Davids says. What he found, however, was that when simply asked to toss the ball in the air the players would throw it a lot higher, whereas when they were asked to serve, they would throw it to a lower height and with less variability. According to Davids, the volleyball serve requires a coordination between the hip, the back and the striking arm, all of which are controlled by the sight of the ball at the zenith of its trajectory. 'By decomposing the task, the coaches effectively were teaching two different tasks,' he says. 'The idea was that you practise the first part of the action and become good at it, then you practise the second and then you fit it all together. It doesn't really work that way. It's a whole, continuous action and what you do at the beginning can shape what happens in the next phase and then the next phase.'

With another one of his students, Ross Pinder, Davids investigated the use of bowling machines in cricket. Pinder played cricket and remarked to Davids that some of the fastest bowlers could bowl at a speed of 150 kilometres per hour, which would give batsmen about seven milliseconds to react. Earlier studies by Mark Williams had shown that a skilled player used visual cues such as the bowler's run-up, their body orientation, and their grip on the ball. 'That's a lot of information in a bowler's action that a bowling machine simply doesn't give you. All you see is a ball coming out of a hole,' Davids says. When Davids and Pinder compared the movement coordination of a player batting during a game and practising against a machine, they found that the player acted very differently, both in terms of hand and feet coordination and timing. In other words, they weren't really simulating what happens in the game.

The constraints-led approach rejects the role of the coach as an instructor, constantly barking orders or prescribing repetitive drills. Instead, it argues that the coach should be a designer, constantly creating learning environments that simulate aspects of competition within certain constraints. The design needs to be achieved through simplification rather than omission, by building scaled-down versions of what happens during competition, rather than by simplistically decomposing them. This is what Davids and Araújo call representative learning design.

For instance, a tennis player who persists in using a two-handed backhand can be forced to play a one-handed shot by having to hold a tennis ball with his non-dominant hand. Coaches can also bend the rules of games during training, perhaps by disallowing shooting from areas very close to the goal to hone the player's long-range scoring ability; or by reducing the area of the pitch when they want to force players to interact more with the ball to improve their technique. 'The constraints you impose on athletes during training need to represent what happens in competition, otherwise you're just practising in an artificial way,' Araújo says. Athletes should learn through exploration and self-discovery; or, in Bernstein's words, through 'repetition without repetition'.

In recent years, Davids and Araújo began proposing an idea that initially wasn't too popular among sports analysts. 'Our criticism was that performance analysis was a relevant science

but it was just a methodology,' Davids says. 'It had no theory.'
Their suggestion was that ecological dynamics could be such
a theory.

Consider, for example, football. Football is a game built on
the occurrence of goals, and goals are rare.

In *The Numbers Game*, Chris Anderson and David Sally
argue that football is as much a matter of luck as it is a question
of skill. Studies show that 44 per cent of goals are fortuitous.
In any match, the favourite team wins only 55 per cent of
the time. Football, they conclude, is a game dominated by
randomness. That doesn't, however, mean that nothing can
be done to influence its outcome. Football's inherent randomness makes analysis even more impactful.

Performance analysts used to believe that the distance run
by a player was a good indicator of individual performance,
and that a team's possession had a positive correlation with
winning.

Those numbers turned out to be meaningless. Analysts
now know that it is the distance run by a player when sprinting that indicates good performance, and that it is possession
within the last third of the pitch that correlates with success. Better metrics imply a more refined understanding of
the game. 'Sometimes we look only at the individuals and
forget the context,' says Blake Wooster, a former director at
Prozone who now runs a sports start-up called 21st Club.
'For instance, Barcelona's [Lionel] Messi is one of the best
players ever, but what would happen if you took him out of
that context and put him in another team? You can't assess
talent in a vacuum.'

Some of the most important elements of football remain
very hard to quantify, and it's difficult to understand what
we can't measure.

Consider defence. Using data from ten seasons of the

Premier League, Anderson and Sally compared the value of a goal scored and the value of a goal conceded. They found that scoring a goal, on average, is worth slightly more than one point, whereas not conceding produces, on average, 2.5 points per match. 'Goals that don't happen are more valuable than goals that do happen,' Anderson says. 'It's counterintuitive. The question is: how do we measure something that doesn't happen? The challenge is to see the unseen.'

Evaluating an attack traditionally consists of measuring what happens with the ball: shots, passes, crosses, sprints. As for defence, actions such as tackles, clearances and saves give a measure of defensive performance. However, the essence of the game arguably lies in collective behaviour, which mostly happens off the ball.

In 2008, Araújo began developing statistical methods to understand collective team behaviour that could not be captured by individual metrics. One such metric, for instance, is the surface area: essentially the area covered by all the on-field players, calculated as the area of a polygon drawn by linking all the players at the periphery of the team on the field.

Another quantity, called centroid, a kind of centre of gravity of a team that's derived from the mean position of all the players, can be used to measure how two opposing teams are synchronised in their collective motion during a match and can potentially indicate what might cause a break from that equilibrium – for instance, a goal-scoring opportunity. Some results indicate that if the centroid of the attacking team is closer to the goal than the defending team's centre, the probability of a goal-scoring opportunity is much higher.

Another geometric measure, stretch index, quantifies how the players are dispersed around the field. Both measures neatly track how teams naturally expand and contract as they oscillate between attack and defence. When teams attack, their stretch index is higher, meaning that the players tend to occupy wider spaces. When defending, players tend to populate the area around the ball carrier, and this is indicated by a lower stretch index. Furthermore, they also show how the shapes of opposing teams coordinate, one expanding as the other contracts.

Around 2011, Araújo contacted a former student called Pedro Marques. Marques had studied high-performance training at the Faculty of Human Kinetics. During his degree, Marques did work experience at Sporting Club Portugal as an academy coach and later became part of its department of analysis. In 2010, he joined Manchester City as a performance analyst.

Araújo had not yet been able to analyse data from a competitive match. Prozone had not been willing to share data with the researchers, claiming copyright protection, but Marques, as a Manchester City analyst, had access to raw positional data related to City's Premier League matches.

With the Prozone data, they were able to validate their previous findings, observing how the collective patterns changed when, for instance, goals were scored, or just before game breaks. 'This showed exactly what we mean by how constraints shape behaviour,' Keith Davids says. 'The state of the game is a constraint. The score is a constraint. It was real evidence of what we had been saying all along.'

In another study, the football scientists tried to measure player synchronisation. Players are said to be highly synchronised when they move in the same direction and at the same velocity. Synchronisation is, in a sense, a measure of how well players are working as a tactical unit, rather than as a band of individuals. Some studies indicated that teams with lower synchronisation tended to lose games.

Specifically, Marques and his colleagues wanted to study

how a team's synchronisation was affected during a congested fixture period. A busy schedule was a common problem for the top teams, who were sometimes obliged to play more than a match per week, leaving players with less than the recommended seventy-two hours of recovery. However, there was still no study proving that players' individual performance metrics actually suffered during these periods.

In this study, they used data from two different periods: one when City played three matches, each three days apart; and another when they played three or more matches every six days. They not only tracked the movement synchronisation of the players, but also measured their individual performance indices using standard metrics like distance covered and distance covered at different speeds. As expected, the latter measures were indistinguishable for the two periods. They had also had a similar number of passes, number of duels won and number of touches per possession.

However, the tactical statistics painted a very different picture: the team was much more synchronised during the quieter period.

'It meant that although they were physiologically recovered, mentally they weren't as sharp,' Marques says. 'The decrease in performance is not physiological, but in terms of coordination and decision-making. The players are no longer in the right place at the right time.'

This study showed that focusing purely on physical recovery strategies for regaining a players' fitness might not be enough. Coaches should also design exercises that continuously enforce coordination and stimulate decision-making. This was an idea that Duarte Araújo and colleagues put to the test with two regional-level teams. He first profiled the team, using standard metrics like centroids. He also tracked how long it took teammates to react and reposition themselves in relation to the player who carried the ball. One of the teams was then put through the paces for fifteen weeks, using small-sided games and constraints-led exercises. 'Their evolution was astonishing,' Araújo says. 'The players were now reacting a lot quicker, and not just the closest ones to the ball. The whole team seemed to reposition itself almost spontaneously when one of the players received the ball.'

This conclusion reinforced what Davids always believed. The study of the complexity in a game like football wasn't just an academic divagation. It was a science that should be at the core of the coach's understanding of the game. Davids likes to compare the ideal relationship of coach and athlete to two species who have to co-evolve on an evolutionary times-cale, each adapting to the other. It's a concept that biologists call co-adaptation. For instance, in predator–prey relations, when a predator develops acute vision to detect his prey, the prey might consequently evolve a more effective camouflage. Similarly, according to Davids, a coach cannot allow the athlete to remain in his comfort zone. The athlete needs to be constantly adapting new ways of dealing with the game, with opponents. It's uncomfortable, but that's how we learn.

19

THINKING THURSDAYS

In October 2014, during an emergency meeting between the players, coaches and chief executive of England Hockey at Bisham Abbey, captain Kate Walsh remembers thinking 'What the hell has happened to this team?'

A few months before, their World Cup campaign in the Hague had been an unmitigated disaster. The team was then coached by Jason Lee, the former men's hockey coach; Danny Kerry had been appointed performance director of England Hockey after the London Games. England lost their opening game against the United States, a team ranked eleventh in the world. They then lost to China 3–0, followed by a 4–1 loss to South Africa. With morale low and their confidence shattered, the team was structureless on the field.

There had been signs that all was not well with the team leading up to the World Cup. Lee was the polar opposite of Danny Kerry in terms of his coaching philosophy. While Kerry had empowered his athletes to take ownership of the programme, Lee had a more laissez-faire approach. 'When he first spoke of his vision, Jason drew a hill with a tree and him holding his children's hands on top of his hill,' Walsh says. 'He was more about making sure everyone was having a good time holistically. I can be quite stubborn and was very conscious of my go-to reaction when it comes to changes. I tried to be open to change, to welcome it, but we felt that the programme we had worked and fought for so long was being picked apart.'

Lee had tried to flatten the hierarchy in the team, an initiative that only left the younger athletes feeling directionless and experienced leaders like Kate Walsh and Helen Richardson feeling disenfranchised. Richardson, for instance, had just spent almost a year in the Intensive Rehabilitation Unit at Bisham Abbey following the rupture of a prolapsed disc and was still recovering from a back operation. She had not been selected for the World Cup and was now unsure whether she would ever be selected again. Lee didn't know Richardson well. He had never seen her in training, despite the fact that she had been vice-captain at the London Olympics. 'I was coming towards the end of my career with a new coach who knew nothing about me,' Richardson says. 'He didn't know what I could offer to the team. It wasn't just about the World Cup. It was feeling that that was how my career was going to end. With Jason, I didn't really know. I had to prove myself again, and with the injury that made it even harder.'

Kerry had been aware of the conflicts festering in the background. Although he supported Lee's long-term view, he also realised that the culture was beginning to verge upon the dysfunctional. His former players would come to see him privately and complain that standards were slipping. 'The World Cup was just the culmination of all those things,' Kerry says. 'All the small cracks that appeared during training became massive under the pressure of a big tournament. Pressure makes people do erratic things.'

On returning to England after the World Cup, Jason

Lee resigned. To replace him, the England Hockey board interviewed coaches at home and abroad. In the end, they reinstated Kerry. He had been beginning to grow impatient and frustrated with the endless number of meetings he had to attend as performance director. He missed the performance side of things. In short, he missed being a coach.

Kerry knew that the problems he inherited from Lee were straightforward, but difficult to fix. He knew he could reinstate the quality of the training environment and staunch the marked decline in standards. That was his bread and butter. But the simmering, fractious dissent among the players? He had no idea how to address that. It was clear that the team lacked mutual understanding and respect, and a clear agreement on a common vision, values and behaviours like they had in London. What he didn't know was the extent of some of the ill feeling, how long it would go on for and how much conflict resolution he would have to do. 'We were the most dysfunctional team at that point,' Walsh says.

When Danny Kerry decided to coach the women's hockey team again, he settled on a new training method called the constraints-led approach.

Kerry had first heard about this theory from psychologist Mark Williams, who at one point in 2010 came to observe a training session at Bisham Abbey. At the time, Williams was collaborating with Stafford Murray. One of their projects involved the Great Britain archery team, applying a constraints-led approach to their training. In late 2009, Oliver Logan, a bio-mechanist with the archery team, had come to Murray with a problem. Their new coach, an American named Lloyd Brown, had noticed that some of his athletes had inefficient technique when drawing the bow. They were less than a year away from the Commonwealth Games, and

Logan wondered if there was any way they could accelerate the learning of better technique.

When Murray mentioned Oliver Logan's approach to Williams, he saw the archery team as an opportunity to test out the constraints-led approach in full. Even though the coach had a very specific technique in mind, Williams designed a programme that would use task constraints to allow the archers to learn by exploring the movement by themselves and minimise explicit instructions from the coach, except when absolutely necessary.

They first asked the archers to try the new technique in the easiest possible way, using a stretch band rather than a bow. There were cameras overhead as the archers practised drawing and releasing the band, emulating the movement that they would make with an actual bow, using live video feedback to watch themselves from above. Later, they delayed the feedback by ten seconds, allowing the archers to cross-reference what they thought they had done with the visual feedback from the video. Sometimes, unless the session had been particularly bad, they wouldn't receive any feedback at all.

After a couple of months, the archers were practising with targets, with background noise to mimic real crowds and in direct competition with one another. Brown would call their names out and commentate live. He would also give the archers small financial incentives based on their score, or have them drink a pint of water so that they would have to shoot while needing urgently to urinate.

Within six months, Lloyd Brown's archers had not only learned how to draw the bow differently, but had also improved their scores by an average of ten points. Three archers won silver medals at the 2010 Commonwealth Games. Through accelerated learning they had reached unconscious competence. 'It's fundamental that athletes get feedback to learn, but what's the best method for coaches to provide feedback and promote accelerated learning?' Williams asks. Sports coaches had assumed that the best way to run a training session was to provide lots of instructions and hands-on demonstrations. It seemed that this was not, in fact, the best way to accelerate learning. Williams compares learning to a Darwinian process, because expertise arises from adaptation to constraints: 'Athletes have to find solutions to problems they will encounter in competition. They fail, repeatedly, and it's by trying that they will eventually solve the problem and register the solution. The result is adaptation.'

The idea of a constraints-led approach was a revelation to Kerry. Like most coaches, he tended to prescribe isolated, repetitive drills, never considering the context of performance. 'In many ways, I was very much the classical coach: a lot of repetitive drills, a lot of telling people what to do and when to do it,' he says. This new approach piqued Kerry's curiosity and he started reading up on the subject, coming across the research of Duarte Araújo and Keith Davids.

In 2013, when Kerry was asked by the English Institute of Sport to formalise his What it Takes to Win programme, he patiently explained that, while in some sports there's an ability to objectify a linear view of what you need to produce in a period of time to achieve a performance, that was definitely not the case with hockey. 'I felt that it was ridiculous to expect us to write a What it Takes to Win model along a uniformity of approach that UK Sport could understand,' Kerry says. 'It's absurd.' Hockey is a sport that involves twenty-two bodies on the pitch at any point in time, in eight matches over perhaps thirteen days with varying tactics. It is complex and dynamic and chaotic. If, on the one hand, they could quantify the performance indicators that corresponded to robust and resilient athletes, on the other Kerry couldn't provide a neat, clear model for success that also included tactics, player dynamics and opposition. 'It wasn't like "produce X goal shots out of X possessions",' Kerry says. 'That's great in some cases, but it's not a recipe for success. There are many ways to win in hockey. It's absurd to try and break it down.' Tactics change depending on whether the opposition plays with a deep defence or an open and expansive game. Performance indicators mean different things depending on your game model.

Kerry also conveyed that their goal was to develop athletes who were able to score goals under the pressure of a playoff match, creative and adaptable to the unpredictability of an Olympic final. To achieve that, they were no longer engaged in traditional approaches to training that separated technique from the context of competition. Instead, they would be designing training programmes that coupled perception and action, and employing exercises that retained the complexity of competition. 'Some athletes felt anxious about that,' Kerry recalls. 'Hitting a hundred balls makes athletes feel good but they didn't practise in a contextually rich situation, with teammates and defenders flying around. They think they're ready but the reality is that they are not.'

When Ben Rosenblatt replaced David Hamilton as the team's strength and conditioning coach in 2013, he was excited by the challenge of transforming a team of bronze medallists into contenders for gold. At the 2012 Games, they had been known as one of the fittest and fastest teams. Rosenblatt was aware of their methods: managing training loads according to the menstrual cycle and individualising training based on hormonal status. 'I was expecting them to blow my balls off with science,' Rosenblatt says.

Instead, he found players who couldn't do a single-leg squat and who lacked endurance. The players who had competed in London were only just returning from their post-Olympic break, while nearly half the squad was new to the programme. Instead of cutting-edge sports science, Rosenblatt first had to make sure the players were conditioned properly.

Rosenblatt, a jovial man with infectious enthusiasm, had been at Bisham Abbey's IRU since 2009, having previously worked at Birmingham City FC and as a strength and conditioning coach for the BOA. He was also completing a PhD in perception–action coupling, researching how gym-based physical exercise translated into specific performance outcomes in rugby. This involved looking at the biomechanics behind the exercises and the movements required during a game, and what exercises should be selected to facilitate that transfer.

When Kerry returned to the role of head coach he made it clear to Rosenblatt that he had to make do with less time with the athletes. With less than two years to prepare the team for the Rio Games, Kerry was going to need as long as possible with the players on the pitch, working on technique and tactics. Rosenblatt's job would be to ensure not only that the players turned up on the pitch properly conditioned to train and able to absorb the training load, but also that they would be able to develop physically while running across the pitch with a stick in their hands, rather than in the gym.

By January 2015, after months of conflict resolution, the players finally reached an agreement regarding their common vision and values for the Rio Olympic Games. The visions: 'Be the difference. Create History. Inspire the future.' The values: 'We are Winners. Be Alive. We are one team.' The conversations had been difficult and took several months. 'They were like pulling teeth,' Kerry says. He would seldom be present, to allow players the space to vent and to reach their own conclusions.

Once the women had settled on the mantra that was going to define their new cycle Rosenblatt sat down with them and asked one question: 'How do you want to be defined physically?' After a lengthy deliberation they came up with a list:

Fast.
Strong.
Intimidating.
Agile.
Relentless.
Robust.
Look the part.

They agreed on a set of habits: professionalism, individual responsibility, consistency, quality, determination, pushing themselves, pushing each other, recovery and punctuality. 'Punctuality was important,' Rosenblatt says. 'If they didn't turn up on time they weren't allowed in the gym. Social exclusion is really big for female athletes.'

Rosenblatt compiled a list of the specific match components that were central to the way the team wanted to play. Each factor was dissected according to its physical needs, training interventions and measure of success. The list had six categories: warrior mentality; tough in possession; winning the ball; defending high-speed changes of direction; elimination; and tournament durability. Warrior mentality, for example, was described as follows:

Definition: to execute winning-orientated actions and decisions under extreme physical, cognitive and emotional stress, regardless of the environment.

Physical requirements: development of capability to repeat and sustain high-intensity work under climatic duress.

Training tactics: mismatched expectations, group and competitive running, shared data feedback, running before/ during/after hockey.

Measure of success: execution of game plan and individual technical elements at major international tournaments.

Of course, this was Rosenblatt's understanding of what it took to win in hockey, as pertaining to its physical requirements. And part of that process involved getting inside Kerry's head, trying to understand the coach's thinking about the game and what mattered to him, and then suggesting which drills and training constraints could be used to develop the players accordingly.

Rosenblatt devised a hierarchy of priorities. The first was training durability: he had to guarantee that his players could be out on the pitch training every day. The hockey team had a set of GPS units that Hamilton had used intermittently – mostly during tournaments, to analyse the physical demands of international matches. Rosenblatt decided to use them every day, in order to understand the physical demands of training itself.

His second priority was tournament durability: the ability to last a whole Olympic tournament – eight matches in thirteen days – without fatigue. Using GPS data in training and matches, as well as a daily fitness test consisting of a countermovement jump and heart-rate readings from a timed run, Rosenblatt looked for correlations between how hard a match had been and the fitness test results.

'What I expected to see from the data was that classic kind of thing: you have a match, you get tired and then as you have another match you get more and more and more tired.

As a result, the jumps will go down and the heart rates will increase,' Rosenblatt explains. 'I didn't see that. What I saw was a massive muddle of data everywhere.'

Puzzled by the lack of a clear pattern, Rosenblatt looked at the problem the other way around. Based on the training data, he categorised the players according to their fitness, strength and diet. Then he looked at the match data. What he was able to demonstrate was that when the fittest, strongest players, on high carbohydrate diets, had to do more work during a game than they normally did, they not only didn't become fatigued, but actually got stronger and more powerful throughout the tournament.

This gave Rosenblatt a clear direction for how he could train his players. He devised a system of diagnostics and profiling for each player, using GPS information to calibrate the workload daily.

Rosenblatt's final priority was a concept he called game impact. This was a direct application of much of his PhD work in perception-action coupling. He had noticed that, often, even after intensive speed training players wouldn't necessarily become faster on the pitch. 'I was asking myself, what did that mean? It was an important lesson. The only place that matters is on the pitch, not in the testing results.'

Something that Rosenblatt had regularly heard from coaches when a player wasn't fit enough was that they had to make them run. Rosenblatt would ask how, exactly, that was going to make a difference on the pitch. He would ask them to find video footage of the situations in the game where the player was struggling. Was it that when the ball broke she just couldn't get to it? Or that she got there in time but then struggled to get back to position? Was it that she began to tail off towards the end of the game?

To Rosenblatt, these were all very different problems,

each requiring a specific training programme. For instance, if coaches questioned how fit the players were and how much they ran in a game, Rosenblatt broke that down, not only into discrete performance components but also by evaluating players on a case-by-case basis. There were players who were fit but were making the wrong decisions, so they would work on their decision-making. Others, who were fast at running forward but struggled tracking back, would work on the movements and muscles involved in that.

He wanted their training to have an actual impact on their game, for their fitness to reflect the actual skills they needed while playing. He didn't want to train them unnecessarily, and neither did he want to train them in aspects of the game they had no use for. What Rosenblatt didn't want to hear were generic requests like 'I need to get faster' or 'I need to get more agile'. What he wanted was to show the players exactly where they needed to change and improve. They had to learn how to measure performance on the pitch, not in the gym.

In 2015, the final year of the Olympic cycle, Kerry wanted to put his players under pressure, mimicking, as much as possible, the specific demands of the Olympic tournament. He wanted to create the smartest team in the world, one that could self-organise around the problems they faced in real time. That was going to be their super-strength.

The training week was divided up into segments, and each day a different aspect would be tackled. Tactical Tuesdays would be spent working on tactics, and on video analysis. Warrior Wednesdays, with Rosenblatt leading the sessions, would take the players through a set of different exercises like wrestling and flipping tyres. ('It was carnage,' Rosenblatt recalls.)

And then there were Thinking Thursdays. These were the perfect exemplar of the constraints-led approach. They manipulated all three components: the individual, the environment and the task. The overarching goal was to win, but to win by doing certain things very well. Every Thursday, the squad was split into four teams to play a tournament, with the coaches refereeing. The day before, each athlete would have received an email from Kerry, informing them of the rules of the tournament and which team they had been assigned to. Each team would be responsible for their own warm-up and preparation.

The idea was to recreate unexpected situations that players might face during a game, and then pile on the pressure, both physically and mentally, to force them to make decisions on the fly. As long as the situations were relevant to technical and tactical changes, the crazier the rules, the better.

For instance, a hockey game has four quarters of fifteen minutes, and the team's analysts had noticed that their attacking momentum was markedly sub-par during the first two minutes and the last two. To improve their ability to perform at the start and at the end of each quarter, Kerry made a rule that any goal scored in the initial period of the game was worth two points. In another instance, when Kerry wanted to hone their high pressing, he invented a rule stating that two points would be awarded if the ball was won back within three seconds of a turnover.

They would play tournaments that varied the size and geometry of the pitch. Sometimes they would change how scoring worked midway through a game. Or they would have rules that players could only pass the ball forwards or could only keep the ball on the left-hand side of the pitch. 'They would just throw in variations to try and recreate the pressured environment of, say, suddenly losing your captain,'

Walsh says. 'Now you're a woman down, and you were 2–1 up and now the other team is coming at you. You have to just make a plan.'

Thinking Thursdays recreated the volatility of an Olympic environment, forcing the players to think on their feet, to self-organise as a group, to learn and adapt under pressure. Crucial to this exercise was the fact that they weren't receiving instructions from the coach; they were learning through the training environment that had been created by the rules. Thinking Thursdays had the added incentive that the winners would get their photograph on the Team GB Instagram feed. 'It would be war the moment we arrived,' Crista Cullen remembers. 'All that mattered was to get our photo on that Instagram. That was our medal.'

20

SIXTY-SEVEN MEDALS

In the afternoon of 16 August 2016, Andrea Wooles stood in the stands at the Rio Olympic Velodrome. It was Day 11 of the Games, the final day of the track cycling competition, and Wooles, who was now the sport science, medicine and innovation manager for the Canadian team, was paying close attention to the races.

She was standing on the long metal platform crowded with performance analysts from the various competing countries, working side by side, opposite the home straight. Some of the analysts were hunched over their laptops, while others filmed the ongoing action on the track, perched on foldable plastic chairs.

'When I started there was no dedicated space for the analysts, so we would be scattered all around the stands,' Wooles said as she observed this, while remaining attentive to what was happening on the track as she spoke. 'The stewards would chase us out, but we would just relocate somewhere else in the arena. As more teams started adopting performance analysis, they just realised they had to give us a space to work.' Wooles was referring to the period when she worked at British

Cycling, in the early days of the English Institute of Sport. 'I remember when Stafford Murray first came in to help us out. They showed us the video analysis work they were doing with squash and we started to think laterally about how we could apply those techniques to cycling. We used to film before, but we weren't analysing anything. With Stafford, we actually began to use video properly.'

A short distance from Wooles were the two British analysts, William Forbes and Deborah Sides. They were filming the last event, the men's keirin final. This was an eight-lap race in which six riders initially rode in the slipstream of a motorbike pacer – the derny – for five and a half laps, at which point the derny pulled off the track, leaving the cyclists to sprint it out. Competing that day was the British cyclist Jason Kenny, chasing his sixth Olympic gold medal. During the sixth lap of the final, as the derny peeled away, the commissaire fired a pistol to signal a false start. Two of the riders – Azizulhasni Awang, from Malaysia, and Kenny – seemed to have passed the back wheel of the derny before it had left the track, which meant automatic disqualification.

At that precise moment, Stafford Murray was at Team GB HQ on the other side of town. Sitting alongside him were analysts Paul Worsfold, Julia Wells and Chris White.

When they saw what was happening at the velodrome, Chris White rang Forbes and Sides straight away and asked them what they needed. They had footage of the incident taken from a straight-on point of view, but would need video taken from a different angle to make a case for Kenny to be reinstated. Murray texted a group of analysts stationed in Manchester, asking them to send over every single piece of video footage they had captured, and then forwarded these to Forbes and Sides.

Kenny's coach, Ian Dyer, went up to the commissaire,

iPad in hand. Forbes and Sides streamed the video clips to Dyer's iPad, showing the moment when the derny started moving away from the race. The coach showed it to the commissaire. They talked for ten minutes. Few people at the velodrome knew what was being discussed. The commissaire, who had made his decision using the naked eye, eventually conceded that it was impossible to say that Kenny had definitely passed the wheel. 'There was an element of doubt proven by the video, which was the key to overturning the decision,' Murray says. 'Without it, he would have been disqualified.'

The commissaire revoked his decision and the race was restarted. In the following race, another false start; this time German cyclist Joachim Eilers had skipped the derny. Again, the judges couldn't reach a conclusive verdict. The third race was the final, won by Jason Kenny by a margin of 0.040 seconds. With that gold, British Cycling's final medal tally added up to six gold, four silver, one bronze and first place in the track cycling rankings. In second place were the Netherlands, with one gold and one silver. When asked if she still rooted for the British team, Wooles retorted, 'No. I prefer it when other teams win. They are so dominating that it's getting boring.'

The hockey team had arrived ten days before the start of the Games. They had opted to set up their holding camp at the Olympic Village, instead of the official Team GB camp in Minas Gerais, one hour's flight north of Rio. 'The Olympic Village is a very exciting place to be,' Walsh says. 'Everything is free, and you can go get your nails done and you can get your hair done and you can go play in the games room. There's the distraction of a lot of other athletes and if it's your first time, it's really special. Even if it's not your first time it's always special – but we needed to get that out of our system.'

On the last day of their camp, they went up Sugarloaf Mountain, the peak that overlooks Rio de Janeiro. As agreed, the moment they left the mountain, the holding camp was officially over. 'From that point on, we had our game faces on,' Richardson says.

Before the Games, Kerry, the coaches and the team captains had sat down to make plans. They planned the timing of meals, travel periods, downtimes and physiotherapy sessions. The variation from the schedule was minimal and their routine heavily scripted. As a group, they were a fairly superstitious bunch. Every member had their own little routines that they didn't deviate from: where they sat on the bus, where they sat in the changing room, who listened to music, who didn't.

As before, the focus was on eight matches in fourteen days. 'If you want to win, you have to be as good on the last day as you are on the first,' Rosenblatt says. 'You can see sport as a traumatic event, particularly when they lose. How do you help them recover? There's social anxiety, there's ability work, there is priming to flip the switch and stop them being in a high-cortisol state.'

Rosenblatt had collated a spreadsheet detailing the threats to tournament durability for each individual player. These were divided into five categories – mental, robustness, nutrition, medical and other – and each came with an action plan. The list of individual problems ranged from 'willpower' to 'first Olympics and confidence in own ability', from 'pelvic strength' to 'clash of personalities'.

As with all the other aspects of their training, recovery was periodised. An intensive recovery strategy can undo training adaptation by sabotaging the underlying physiological mechanics at work, so these would seldom be used during training blocks. But when it came to tournaments, they were applied aggressively.

Rosenblatt stopped referring to recovery sessions, and instead used 'preparation sessions'. He wanted the players to set their minds to the next game. This could include yoga sessions in the stairwells of hotels, cool-down sessions in car parks and, of course, pool sessions.

Rosenblatt, like Hamilton before him, was the sunshine-yellow personality type. He believed in fun as a crucial ingredient for recovery and performance. So, as the designated fun-guy in the group, Rosenblatt's manner – of being a barrel of laughs, the guy taking the piss – had to remain constant, regardless of whether they won or lost. The players expected it; they benefited from it.

They decided not to march at the opening ceremony – the procession meant they would spend too long on their feet and the festivities would affect their fitness and hydration levels for their first game, against Australia, the following day.

At half-time, they were winning comfortably. When the referee blew her whistle they ran into the changing room, while the Australians straggled behind. This detail was something they had planned: they were always going to run to the changing room to show that, regardless of the result, they remained a united team, still physically fresh. 'As I ran past the Aussies I got this real buzz, this tingly feeling,' Richardson remembers. 'Other players felt the same. I honestly felt like I could run for ever.'

Before the tournament, they had agreed to abide by the principle of focusing on one game at a time, on only the next moment, so when they won that first game they didn't celebrate. Instead, they began planning the next one. 'Whether we were warming up, whether we were on the changing room, whether we were on the pitch, whether we were in our apartments, whether we were doing our recovery, it just felt like we were so in the moment,' Walsh says. 'We weren't looking ahead, and we weren't looking back. We were just very in the moment.'

Great Britain won their group, beating eternal rivals Argentina in the process. They then beat Spain in the quarter-finals and qualified for the semi-finals against New Zealand. On 17 August, Danny Kerry looked relaxed as he presented the game plan to his players on the morning of the match. Inside, he had never felt so ill, so nauseous and so anxious that he couldn't bring himself to eat. He had ominous recollections of the semi-final loss against Argentina four years before. A psychologist had told him about the air-steward effect: 'When you're inside an aeroplane and there's a lot of turbulence, passengers will look at you,' Kerry says. 'You need to look like all is normal, all is good. If the steward is flapping, people are going to flap. This is what you're going to control. You can have that effect.' During the game, he sat in the stands, where he usually went to get the big picture of the game and communicate clearly to his assistant on the bench. 'I nailed it, but it took a gargantuan effort to look calm,' Kerry says. To the players, it was just another game, regardless of what was at stake: qualification for their first-ever Olympic final.

The match was a bloodbath. In the first half, Crista Cullen got elbowed in the head. Blood was pouring from her face. The goalkeeper, Maddie Hinch, ran over and said, 'Quick, answer these questions: what venue are we at today? Which half is it now? Who scored last in this match? What did you play last week? Did your team win the last game?'

'I was worried that I was going to get done for concussion, so I answered the questions before the doctor came,' Cullen recalls. 'I had to play in the final.' She received eight stitches in her forehead. Five minutes later she was on the sidelines, shouting to get back in the match.

After the final whistle, they congratulated each other and gathered around the semi-circle:

'One more game.'

'We're going for gold. Let's not forget that.'

The morning before the final, Rosenblatt ran what was to be his final training session with the hockey team. A month earlier, he had accepted a job at the Football Association, working under Dave Reddin. At the end of the workout he gathered the players together and showed them PowerPoint slides listing the attributes they had chosen to define them physically – strong, robust, intimidating, looking the part. 'Look around, look at yourselves,' he said. 'You've demonstrated all of this in the most extreme of circumstances. You've done it all and you can get out there and win.'

Against the Netherlands, the British were clearly the underdogs. During the game, they were the second-best team on the pitch. The Dutch were coming at them in waves and they were being completely outplayed.

Kerry sat in the crowd, thinking that they were fine. His team had been in this position before, hundreds of times, on Thinking Thursdays at Bisham Abbey. He knew they would get back into the game. He knew they would go to penalty shuttles. He knew that they had the best keeper when it came to penalty shuttles and how that would play on the Dutch's minds.

'There's stuff that goes on that we just don't comprehend,' Kerry says. 'It's stuff that goes on in human existence and that science just doesn't have the tools to comprehend. It's a bit like when we used to believe that the world was flat.' Unlike the semi-final, he now felt calm, collected and absolutely convinced they were going to win, even when they were facing an offensive onslaught from the Dutch. He still can't explain why he felt that way. This was Danny Kerry, the cool-blue, hyper-analytical individual who, eight years ago, had been lambasted for being too disconnected from his players, now describing a feeling he had picked up on a subconscious level from his players. 'I just knew were going to win,' he says. 'I knew, I knew, I knew.'

When the hockey team arrived at the British School after their medal win, Stafford Murray made a point of congratulating them personally. 'They were the most polite and thankful people,' he says. 'Zero ego, zero arrogance, no one-upmanship. I thanked them for being so British about the whole thing.'

The school had a 25-metre swimming pool and had been equipped with a boxing ring, a dojo for judo and taekwondo, and a gym. Most of that equipment had been shipped directly from the UK so that the athletes could train under the same conditions as they were used to back at home.

Murray, Julia Wells and Chris White worked from the school's IT classroom. A large Union flag was draped across one of the walls, and in the centre of the room was a long table with fourteen laptops and nine flatscreen TVs. 'When we arrived there, it was just an old IT room with computers from the nineties,' Murray says. 'The air conditioning didn't work. In fact, it made it hotter.'

The preparation for the Rio performance analysis project had started two years before. At first, they had considered replicating what they had done in London, with twelve analysts on site, working from a centralised system, but later they opted for two locations: the Team GB headquarters at the British School in Rio's affluent neighbourhood of Barra da Tijuca, and Manchester.

Julia Wells had been at UWIC under Mike Hughes at around the same time as Murray. Chris White, another UWIC alumnus, had been one of Murray's first hires to the EIS analysis team. During the two years of planning and preparation for Rio, they fell out a few times. Wells accused Murray of being old-fashioned, stubborn and wanting to do things as they had in London. Murray was adamant that they were over-complicating the process with new technology.

Before the Games, the three had agreed on a ground rule. Even though they had the utmost love and respect for each other, if it got to a point where they needed some respite, they could be totally honest about it. For instance, if White had had enough of Murray he was free to tell him so, with full transparency: 'Right, I'm not going to see you today because you're getting fed up with me. I'm getting fed up with you. Let's not see each other today. It's not because I don't love you, but we need some space.'

'When you're in that environment, it becomes like a soap opera,' Murray says. 'When you're in that moment and you're tired, and the pressure is on, and you've got athletes and coaches asking you for stuff, the smallest things become irritating and aggravate you.'

Besides, Murray acknowledged he was the most annoying person to share a space with. He was compulsive about tidiness and planning every minute. He was also obsessive about finding beer at the end of a shift, even when it was three in the morning and nothing was open. That really irritated his colleagues at times, and they would tell him to 'stop worrying about beer, for fuck's sake'.

Murray's team spent a few days prior to the start of the Games getting the room ready for the operation, and testing the systems to death. They drove around the city to estimate how long it would take to deliver hard drives at night and during rush hour, and whether it was safe. 'I drive slower than my nan, whereas Chris and Julia really got into the Rio culture of driving as fast as you can,' Murray says. In the evening, it wasn't safe for anyone to travel alone, so two analysts would make the delivery. They mapped out the internet speed at venues and hotels across Rio. In some places it was so slow that jumping in a car and delivering a USB stick was quicker than downloading two minutes of footage. Unlike London, they only had access to the Olympic Broadcasting Services feed over Wi-Fi, which kept crashing. As a contingency, the team of analysts in Manchester would capture footage from the BBC iPlayer. All the performance analysts were in constant communication via WhatsApp, where they could request a specific clip ASAP.

'The power went out on the first day, but this time we were ready,' Murray says. 'We really prepared this time. Actually, I think we over-prepared.'

On the final day, Team GB was on the verge of making history and Murray was in a pensive mood. These were going to be his last Games as part of Team GB. He had been at the EIS for twenty years, the longest-serving sports scientist to date. A few months earlier, he had made the decision to leave.'It's a bittersweet feeling. I know it's time to go and part of me doesn't want to let go,' Murray said. 'But Chris and Julia are better than me in a lot of aspects. I'm leaving this in perfect hands.'

Just a few years ago, when first asked whether surpassing the 2012 medal haul – Team GB's official goal at the time – was a realistic target for Rio, Murray had said: 'To be honest with you, I don't think we have any chance. Officially, I have to say it's a stretch target and it's going to be hard. If I was talking to you in the pub after about three pints I'd say, "We've got no bleeding chance."'

At two o'clock that afternoon, while the analysts chatted animatedly about how many gigabytes of video had been transferred and analysed throughout the Games, they had to be reminded that Nicola Adams was about to fight in the women's flyweight final. Olympic boxing bouts are brief and intense, and this one was no exception. The final was over in less than twenty minutes. Adams won on points and Britain had now won more medals than it had in London 2012. Second place in the medals table, above China, was guaranteed.

When he got the news, Murray went into the toilets and cried for five minutes. He kept thinking about his grandfather, who had died five months before. He wished he could speak to him now, to tell him that they had surpassed London.

21

THE FLYING BOAT

On 6 August 2011, Ben Ainslie took a break from training for the Olympics to watch TV. He wanted to see the first race of the America's Cup World Series.

Ainslie had been obsessed with the America's Cup since the age of twelve, when he first saw the British yacht that was competing in the tournament moored at Falmouth port, near his home in Cornwall. The America's Cup is the oldest trophy in the world, first awarded in 1851 by the Royal Yacht Squadron in Cowes, when it was won by the US schooner *America* against a fleet of fifteen British yachts.

However, by 2011, the competition had changed almost beyond recognition. The rules allowed the winner to dictate the format of the next competition. Larry Ellison, the world's fifth-richest man and owner of BMW Oracle Racing, the winners of the thirty-third edition, had ditched traditional yachts for 22-metre catamarans with rigid wingsails, which could reach speeds of more than 90kph.

That decision had been broadly criticised by sailors and designers: the former had little experience piloting these boats, and the latter had little experience designing them.

The new class of catamaran, the AC72, was considered an unstable, fragile and complicated structure, which was difficult to sail.

Ainslie was among the critics. 'Believe it or not, I'm a bit of a traditionalist at heart,' he explains. 'I had spent my life developing my skills in classic mono-hull boats.'

He changed his mind only five minutes into the broadcast. 'I was just impressed by these boats and their speed,' he recalls. 'It dawned on me that this was the future of sailing.' The following day, Ainslie phoned Russell Coutts, CEO of the Oracle team and a three-time America's Cup winning skipper.

'I want to start a team,' Ainslie told him. 'How do I do it?'

'I was just about to call you,' Coutts replied. 'I want you to come and join us.'

Ainslie agreed to join Oracle and helm its second boat, training as a sparring partner for its main vessel, skippered by the Australian Jimmy Spithill, in the run-up to the 2013 America's Cup, which would take place in San Francisco Bay.

Ainslie joined the team in August 2012, two weeks after competing for Team GB in the London Olympic Games, when he won gold in the Finn class. This was his fourth consecutive Olympic gold, which, added to his silver from Atlanta, made him the most successful Olympic sailor of all time.

'I was on a high from the Olympic Games and then, straight away, I was racing in a completely different sport,' Ainslie recalls. 'I had never raced in those boats before. I was really on the back foot against the other people I was racing.'

Later that month, the sport mutated once again. On 29 August 2012, photos were posted on an obscure sailing website of Team New Zealand's AC72 training in the Hauraki Gulf, on the North Island, which showed the boat sailing with both hulls out of the water. When the images first came to light, Team New Zealand offered no official comment. The pictures went viral, and many considered them to be a Photoshopped hoax. Less than a week later, the Kiwis invited a group of journalists to see a flying catamaran with their own eyes.

Team New Zealand had been experimenting with one of the boat's components: the hydrofoil-retractable blades designed to provide stability. The breakthrough happened when they discovered that at wind speeds of 22.2kph, an L-shaped hydrofoil could lift the boat out of the water, which reduced drag and allowed it to accelerate to speeds of up to 92.6kph.

Flying a catamaran – or, in sailing parlance, foiling – added an extra dimension to sailing. Suddenly, sailors had to contend with a sport that seemed to obey completely different physical laws. Even to experienced America's Cup sailors, this was akin to relearning how to sail. Team New Zealand's skipper Dean Barker equated it with 'sailing a monster'. 'Most of us associate sailing with getting wet and with waves coming over the boat,' Ainslie says. 'When you lift up out of the water, you don't feel that sensation. It's about the wind blowing over your face, the noise in your ears from the airflow.'

On 7 September 2013, Oracle Team USA and Team New Zealand lined up for the inaugural race of the 34th America's Cup, in a first-to-nine final. The Americans were the favourites: they were defending champions, sailing in front of a home crowd, and they had a technologically superior boat – the product of Ellison's millions and Oracle's top engineers.

On the first day of competition, however, Team New Zealand won race one by a margin of thirty-six seconds and race two by fifty-two seconds. After race five, on

10 September, the Kiwis were 4–1 ahead. They were sailing faster; their foiling prowess was superior.

Team New Zealand were running away with the competition. Before race six, Spithill informed his tactician John Kostecki that he was going to be replaced. Then he walked into the office of a sailor with no experience in the role and asked him whether he was ready to step up. Ainslie said yes.

'Some people close to me suggested it was a bad idea,' Ainslie recalls. 'They were saying that the team was going to lose and that I was just being set up to be the fall guy. To me, there was no question whether or not I should go on that boat. I was asked to do a job and the team needed positivity.'

With Ainslie on board, and with the design team making incremental improvements to the AC72 and the crew honing their boat-handling and tactics, Oracle gradually began to match the Kiwis in speed and technique. On day ten, with the score at 8–3 – and match point to New Zealand – Ainslie decided to ignore their opponents' strategy and focus on directing Spithill to areas where he believed the wind was strongest. 'It was the first time these boats were being raced like that,' Ainslie explains. 'The tactical playbook was pretty much thrown out of the window and I started playing around with different ideas.'

With flawless decision-making and an uncanny ability to 'see' wind, Ainslie's tactical daring propelled Oracle to a comeback. On 24 September, with the score sitting at 8–6, Ellison cancelled his keynote speech at Oracle's annual convention – his own event – so that he could watch his sailing team win two races and tie at 8–8. It was the third instance in America's Cup history that a final would be decided after seventeen races. Regardless of the result, the winner-takes-all final race would be the culmination of one of the most compelling sporting finals in history. In the race, Oracle moved into the lead during the upwind leg and, on the downwind leg, stretched it, foiling at more than 72.4kph. 'This is it! This is it,' Ainslie shouted. 'Work your arses off!'

As the boat crossed the finish line, spectators who had gathered on the pier erupted in cheers, having witnessed one of the most extraordinary comebacks in sporting history. Ainslie had triumphed in the sailing competition that had obsessed him since childhood. However, there was still something left to be done. Now he wanted to win it with a British team.

One cloudy morning in January 2017, Martin Whitmarsh sat in his office in a six-storey building positioned prominently in Portsmouth Harbour. Having left McLaren, he was now the CEO of Land Rover Ben Ainslie Racing (BAR), launched in 2014 to compete in the next America's Cup.

Whitmarsh's office was one of the few rooms on the open-plan top floor, sparsely populated by engineers and designers tapping away on computers. On the ground floor was the 12-metre-high workshop, where the shore crew assembled and maintained boats. That day, a catamaran dominated a section of the workshop. It was a stunning carbon-fibre machine, with narrow 13.7-metre hulls joined by two 9-metre-wide crossbeams. The space between the crossbeams was covered with a netting trampoline. In the middle of the forward beam was a tennis ball-sized titanium sphere, into which the 38-metre rigid wing was to be inserted.

Whitmarsh spoke excitedly about the America's Cup trophy, an ornate silver ewer created by the jewellers Garrard & Co. in 1848. 'I got to touch it yesterday,' he said. 'They had flown it from one of Larry Ellison's lairs in California to London. It travelled in business class with a bodyguard. I asked the guard if he would take a bullet for it. He was taking himself very seriously. When he unwrapped it, I just wanted to touch it with my bare hands. You're not allowed to do that.'

When Whitmarsh met Ainslie, the sailor had been searching for a CEO for his new team for months. The America's Cup trophy had been won thirty times by the Americans, twice by the Kiwis and the landlocked Swiss, and once by the Australians, but never by the country who had designed it in the first place. That is what Ainslie hoped to rectify with a UK team capable of bringing the trophy home; a team that, as he put it, would be doing it 'for Queen and country'.

Whitmarsh was the CEO he needed for his team. 'I'd met several people, but it was hard to find someone with the right mix of experience and personality,' Ainslie says. 'With Martin, we just clicked.'

Just across the corridor from Whitmarsh's office was mission control, a room furnished with a bank of monitors displaying video streams and live sensor data from a black box attached to the wingsail of one of BAR's boats. This data-intensive treatment was part of the reason that Whitmarsh called the sport Formula One on water. Each boat was fitted with more than four hundred sensors. These included GoPro cameras, six-axis motion sensors and fibre-optic cables. The intricacies of analysing data from a high-performance catamaran, however, were in danger of making Formula One's data analysis look like basic algebra. 'In motorsports, most variables are understood,' says Mauricio Muñoz, a Land Rover engineer embedded at BAR. 'With these boats, dynamics change depending on the set-up and the wind.'

Muñoz recalls spending months grasping the dynamics of foiling catamarans. First, there is the rigid wing that acts as the boat's sail. According to simple, but counterintuitive, physics, the wing is capable of propelling the boat forward at three times the speed of the wind. Then there are the hydro-foils, the two L-shaped carbon-fibre appendages encased in the middle of each hull. Their cross-sectional shape is the same as an aeroplane wing — full at the front and tapering into a thin trailing edge – and they function exactly like one, with the difference that they are immersed in water, not air.

With an 11kph breeze, the difference in pressure between the upper and the lower surface of the foil creates an upward force that elevates the windward hull out of the water, cutting drag in half. At around 22kph, it generates enough force to lift the entire weight of the catamaran and crew out of the water. While flying, the slim windward hydrofoil and two thin rudders are the only components that make contact with the water.

'When you are sailing at speeds of forty-five knots, as the pressure changes, the water begins to boil around the surface of the foil,' Muñoz says. 'It is that crazy.'

By the time of the Sochi Winter Olympics in 2014, James Roche already knew he was leaving British Skeleton. That decision was partly made because of a conflict of interest: he and Lizzy Yarnold had been dating since 2013. Immediately after their first date, they told everyone in the team about their relationship. 'It was a hard thing to do because it was so early in the relationship,' Roche says.

Roche had read that Ben Ainslie was assembling his own British team to compete in the America's Cup. 'I studied ship science at Southampton precisely because of the America's Cup,' Roche says. 'Pretty much everyone on that course wanted to be an America's Cup designer.' Ainslie, however, wasn't necessarily looking for a boat designer. Rather, he was looking for someone to build them a sailing simulator.

For six months, Roche and a computer graphics designer sequestered themselves in their workshop and got to work.

No one had really built a sailing simulator with a high degree of fidelity before, and certainly not something that resembled the new AC72 class of catamarans. Part of the rationale for building a simulator was to be able to sail this new, potentially dangerous and very unstable class of boats at zero risk and minimal cost, gauging what level of stability was required and understanding what happened when things went wrong. The simulator would also be used by the design team to iterate and test different boat configurations and aerodynamic upgrades. 'Everything is a compromise when it comes to designing a boat,' Richard Hopkirk, BAR's engineering manager, explains. 'With the hydrofoils, it is a compromise between stability and speed. We could design the ideal hydrofoil that would be the fastest. However, it would also be so unstable that a human would find it impossible to control.'

Building a simulator for a particular task, like sailing or motor racing, requires a thorough understanding of the environmental cues necessary to perform that task in the real world. A simulator must be constructed at a level of resolution and complexity that is indistinguishable from the perceptual reality of the test subject in the real world. This means understanding exactly which environmental cues matter to the test subject. For a sailor on the water helming a catamaran, those environmental cues range from the creaking of the boat to the wave patterns created in the sea by wind and weather. Everything else was incidental.

Roche's simulator consisted of an interactive motion platform, complete with a cockpit equipped with a steering wheel and virtual reality headsets. It allowed the sailors to configure different cockpit layouts, along with the human–machine interface displays used by the helmsman and the sea patterns. The noises made by the boat were captured by microphones attached to the different components of the real test boat and then randomised by the algorithm. Real wind data and other atmospheric models were used to simulate conditions, and recorded wind noise was used to provide realistic audio cues.

One of the most challenging aspects of the simulator was replicating the motion of a foiling catamaran. In the case of motor-racing or flight simulators, pilots are strapped into the seat and their perception of motion is mainly dependent on their vestibular system, located in the inner ear. 'As soon as you have people standing, with limbs flailing and your centre of gravity moving all over the place, motion perception becomes more complex,' Roche says.

Roche would be the first test pilot whenever new elements were introduced to the algorithm. When Ben Ainslie and wing-trimmer Paul 'CJ' Campbell-Jones first tested the simulator, their feedback was, as Roche puts it, 'polite'. Early versions of the motion algorithm were erratic and would occasionally cause motion sickness. Also, the virtual hull didn't actually float. 'Which is quite hard to explain to someone who's expecting to float,' Roche says. 'They sort of saw the potential. At least they never told me to stop the project.'

On 6 October 2015, Land Rover BAR launched the second iteration of their racing boat, the T2. Ainslie had been sailing the T2 on the simulator for a few months by then, and after testing the boat on the water he told Roche that it was the same as the simulator. 'Which is not necessarily what I wanted to hear,' Roche says, 'because that boat was very unstable.'

Ben Ainslie is slim and tanned, with an elegant manner. Face-to-face, he is personable and almost introverted. He is described by friends as unfailingly polite, a gentleman who will remember the name of a person he hasn't seen for ten years. His demeanour on the boat, however, elicits very different descriptions.

Of course, all sailors have their idiosyncrasies. Paul Campbell-Jones likes to be the first on board, to make sure everything is exactly as he wants it: every lashing done up properly, every line tensioned correctly. 'The lads take the piss out of me because they think I'm very nervous to get on board. I just want things done right,' he says. David 'Freddie' Carr, BAR's bowman, likes to bring a piece of wood on board, which he touches before the race: 'I am very superstitious. I believe all boats should have wood on them.' On the other hand, Nick Hutton, who is also a trimmer, does not have any particular routine: 'I'm from Devon. We just get on with it.'

What happens when Ainslie steps on the boat is not so much an idiosyncrasy as a metamorphosis. His countenance becomes intense with concentration. His crew calls it his Terminator face. According to Campbell-Jones, once the boat is on the water, a switch is flicked: 'There's no downtime or humour when we are in the water, even in training.'

'When he's done with all the noise and the management, there's a moment where you see Ben just changing,' Carr adds. 'It's pretty impressive to witness.' Hutton agrees: 'We all see it. Fortunately for me, I'm facing forward on the boat.'

These sailors were very much aware of this reputation when they accepted Ainslie's offer to join BAR. They knew about his aggressive tactics and uncompromising competitiveness. They knew he was the sort of relentless competitor who, during a regatta, is capable of jumping onto one of the TV boats to furiously accost a cameraman who has inadvertently interfered with his course – something Ainslie did at the world championships in 2011, a move that got him disqualified.

'In the first few months it was full on,' Hutton recalls. 'Then I learned that is part of what makes him so good. He gets five per cent more out of everyone because of it.' In short, they knew that Ainslie was the sort of skipper they wanted to sail with.

Of course, persistent focus and an extra 5 per cent in performance might be what it takes simply to sail these boats, which all sailors compare to flying a plane – albeit one without computer-assisted navigation and with unstable dynamics. For instance, as the boat pops out of the water, it begins to sequentially lift and drop as the lifting force oscillates around an equilibrium point. Ainslie needed to orchestrate this movement with deft precision, controlling the angle of the hydrofoil with a two-button switch. Add inclement weather and choppy seas, and things can easily spiral out of control. A sharp angle can shoot the bows skyward. A narrow angle will plunge them into the sea, which was exactly what happened during a training session in June 2015. Ainslie, positioned at the stern of the boat, was thrown forward, flipping mid-air and colliding with the front crossbeam of the boat. 'We are learning that these boats are fast and crazy,' Ainslie says, 'and it's easy for everyone on board to get hyped up. It's like driving a racing car around a corner at high speed.'

On 25 July 2015, the new America's Cup season began in Portsmouth. It was a sunny day, with winds blowing at 27.8kph across the Solent. These were favourable conditions for the first regatta of the World Series, the initial stage of the America's Cup.

In the World Series rounds, all teams sail the same type of boat, with the overall winner earning two points towards the final competition, to be held in Bermuda two years later. BAR, sailing in front of a home crowd, did not enjoy the most auspicious start. They reached the end of the first

upwind leg in third place, behind leaders Oracle Team USA.
As they entered the first downwind leg, two tactical options
were available, depending on where their strategist, Giles
Scott, could detect stronger winds: towards the shore or further out to sea. 'Wind tends to oscillate back and forward,'
Scott explains. 'You're looking for darker, glossier patches of
water. These are signs that tell you what the breeze is going
to do in the next few minutes. It's a bit of a dark art.'

It's also an imprecise one, especially when it relies on
split-second decisions. Scott directed them towards the shore
and Ainslie's boat found itself lagging behind the rest of the
fleet. 'This team is very good at digging deep when they're
experiencing adversity,' says Rob Wilson, BAR's coach. 'If
they're pushed, they'll push back harder.' By leg six, going
downwind, BAR was in first place, with Team New Zealand
trailing 351 metres behind. At that point, Ainslie's boat
popped out of the water and accelerated to 44kph. Their lead
was now unassailable. 'We thought we sailed a bit scrappy,'
Hutton said. 'I guess our scrappiness was a little less scrappy
than everyone else's.'

Throughout the World Series, Land Rover BAR gradually evolved from an inexperienced outfit to one of the
most accomplished teams, especially when it came to boat-
handling. By the time they returned to Portsmouth for the
seventh fixture, on 23 July 2016, they were just behind leaders
Team New Zealand on the points board. 'In the final race,
we were chasing them downwind,' Carr recalls. 'If we kept
that position, we would move to the top of the ranking.' The
Kiwis did a foiling gybe, a difficult manoeuvre that made
the boat change direction while foiling, and BAR matched
them. 'The rest of the fleet just crashed. We have a saying in
the team: when we need to deliver, we don't raise our game
at all, but we just sink to your highest level of training. That's

why we've put in so many hours on the boat, because these manoeuvres are really hard to get right.'

When Ainslie's team is performing well, the internal comms system is mostly silent, apart from occasional dialogue between the helmsman and the strategist, while the crew move in synchrony. 'They need to accomplish an extraordinary choreography to manoeuvre that boat,' Whitmarsh says. 'You have the helmsman steering the boat, and the guy in front controlling the throttle. Imagine driving a car when you do the steering and someone else is doing the throttle. It's bizarre. Then you have sailors in control of other systems that all need to be activated at the right time, while flying at 80kph. You have a neural network of six brains looking for wind, checking the boat's performance, deciding how to keep it flying.'

When the team is struggling, on the other hand, voices are raised, the sailors frantic and distracted by the fact that nothing is going well. That was the case in Toulon, the regatta after Portsmouth, on 10 September 2016, when Giles Scott made a return to competition after winning a gold medal at the Olympic Games. 'It was a disaster,' Ainslie remembers. 'I was waiting for him to make decisions, he was waiting for me to decide, and no decision was being made.' At one point, Ainslie asked Scott if he could turn the boat without hitting any boat in the vicinity. 'We ended up T-boning the Kiwis,' Paul Campbell-Jones laughs. 'Giles had been sailing on a tiny dinghy for so long that he thought he could fit a catamaran into that space.'

Then there are moments of brilliance capable of turning a mediocre performance into a victorious one. One such moment occurred in 2016, in the penultimate race of the final World Series regatta, in Fukuoka, Japan.

BAR needed only to finish one place behind Team New

Zealand to clinch the title. Going into the final downwind leg of the course, however, they were behind the fleet, with the Kiwis in the lead. It was a light-wind day and the boats were plodding along at just a few knots, making every change of direction a laborious manoeuvre. 'Ben made an off-the-cuff tactical call and asked for a gybe, then another,' Campbell-Jones says. 'It was a big risk. But once we did the second gybe, we realised what was happening.' The boat accelerated, overtaking other teams at twice their speed, and zipped through the final gate.

'All the boats almost stopped,' Campbell-Jones recalls. 'We shot around the outside.' BAR had won the World Series with a race to spare. The sailors started celebrating, but after a few minutes Ainslie interrupted: 'Okay, let's refocus. What do we need to do to win the next race?'

'I name this boat *Rita*. May God bless her and all who sail on her,' Georgie Ainslie, Ben's television presenter wife, said as she activated a contraption designed to swing a bottle of Nyetimber sparkling wine to smash on the bows.

It was 6 February 2017, under leaden skies at the Royal Naval Dockyard in Bermuda. The bottle remained intact on the first and second attempts, so the situation was swiftly resolved with a hammer. A mixed crowd of sailors, reporters and local dignitaries applauded.

The boat was then slowly hoisted by a crane and placed in the Great Sound, the ocean inlet where the America's Cup was to take place. *Rita* was the fourth in the evolutionary line that began with T1 (the boat donated to Ainslie by Oracle), T2 ('Over-ambitious and initially unreliable,' according to Richard Hopkirk) and T3, which the team referred to as a training boat. 'With the World Series, every team was sailing with the same equipment – and our team won. Which shows that we have the best sailing team,' Hopkirk said. 'Now it's our job to give Ben and his team a boat that's as fast as the competition.'

With a length of 15 metres and a wingsail of 23.5 metres, *Rita* was a bigger, faster boat than the AC45Fs sailed in the World Series, but was also operated differently, making the America's Cup not only a sailing competition and a technological race, but also a physical contest of brawn and endurance. Gone were the ropes and winches used to control the sails and the hydrofoils. These had been replaced by a hydraulic system comprising 130 metres of pipes and powered by pedestal-mounted cranks fixed to the hollow hulls of the catamaran.

'With these new boats, we're no longer moving rope, we're moving hydraulic fluid,' Ben Williams, BAR's strength and conditioning coach, and a former member of the SAS, explained. In other words, every boat manoeuvre would require a supply of human-generated hydraulic power from the crew's four grinders. These sailors must constantly revolve the cranks, and must be as strong as possible. 'I lost four kilos over Christmas,' Campbell-Jones explained. 'Ben weighs less than eighty kilos, [about] as much as he did when he was eighteen. Because there is a weight restriction for the crew, for every four kilos I lose, that is a kilo of muscle that every grinder can put on.'

The physicality of the competition meant that every decision had an added cost. 'We might want to make a manoeuvre, but I can't because the guys don't have the energy,' Ainslie said. The most effective position in which to grind is on one's knees. A tell-tale sign of exhaustion is when the grinders need to stand up. That's when Ainslie knows that his crew is working flat out. 'That will dictate whether we call a manoeuvre or not. If I steer the boat in the wrong direction, we have wasted energy and it's demoralising. It is really physical.'

On 26 May 2017, the opening day of the Louis Vuitton Challenger's Trophy – the qualification rounds for the 2017 America's Cup – no boat sailed the waters of the Great Sound. The winds were blowing at over 30 knots, outside the safety range allowed for the competition, so racing was postponed until the following day. Between 27 May and 3 June, teams competed in two round-robin stages, which were then followed by semi-finals and a final. The winner of the final – and the Louis Vuitton Challenger's Trophy – would then face the defending champions, Oracle Team USA, in the America's Cup final between 17 and 26 June.

The British team were widely considered to be the under-dogs. In the pre-race practice, it had become clear that *Rita* was lagging behind the competition, as the boat struggled with light winds and straight-line speed. Even though Land Rover BAR had proven to be the best sailors during the World Series, when all teams handled the same type of boat, in the technological race of the America's Cup it was becoming obvious that the young British upstarts were still in a race to catch up with their more established competitors.

A case in point was Team New Zealand. According to Land Rover's CTO Andy Claughton, the Kiwis, just like they did in 2010 when they foiled a catamaran, 'would again come up here with something completely different. They have a can-do attitude and are not afraid of experimenting. It will be something odd and it will surprise everybody.'

The Kiwis had been the last team to arrive in Bermuda, the better to stay out of sight of their competition. When they showed up, they didn't fail to surprise. They had, for instance, instead of arm grinders, opted for a bicycle system to power their boats. Their hydrofoils were also much longer than those of the other teams, with a kinked shape instead of a smooth blade. 'They were consistently pushing for a lot longer and a less stable foil,' James Roche says. 'When we got to Bermuda, we started to realise that's where we had to go. In fact, the simulations consistently showed that less stable was faster, but then we weren't able to push that further. I think we believed that we would iterate the boats on the water, whereas we could have been smarter earlier and made those leaps based on the simulator.'

During the qualifiers, every morning at six, Roche would meet the team meteorologist to go over the forecast for the day and review computer simulations of boat performance in the expected weather conditions. Using this information, they would decide on the configuration of the boat and choose the hydrofoils, the rudders and the elevators optimised for the conditions. During the races, Roche would sit at mission control, looking at various screens and data streams.

Land Rover BAR started the competition by beating the Swedish Artemis Racing team with a confident and dominating performance by Ainslie and crew. They were to race SoftBank Team Japan later that day. In the final line-up towards the start, as the boats manoeuvred for position, SoftBank's skipper moved dangerously close to the British catamaran. Land Rover's boat slipped sideways, its hull emerged from the water and came crashing down on their opponent's hull. No one was hurt, but Land Rover's boat was left with a six-foot hole in the hull. After the race, the boat was ferried back to the dockyard. As soon as they docked it, it started to sink, and the sailors had to start bailing water.

The shore team pulled an all-nighter to try to repair the boat in time for racing the following day. No one had any idea whether they would accomplish it. 'I left last night thinking we had a twenty per cent chance of going sailing today,' Carr said at the time. 'We're all on the WhatsApp group, where we fire each other up. These messages were pinging in overnight, all the lads drinking their Red Bull with their cheesy dance music. That fired them through the night, and they got the boat out on the water. I've been doing this for fifteen years, and I've never seen such a massive hole in a boat and then it go sailing the next day.'

During the qualifiers, Ainslie's aggressive tactics made them one of the best starters in the competition, but their performance around the course was frustratingly erratic. With the winds at the lower end of the legal range – around 6 knots – they struggled to manoeuvre the boat. In a race against Team New Zealand, a mechanical failure affected the control of the hydrofoils. Against Oracle Team USA, they were leading comfortably when the bow dipped and the boat crashed off the foils. Still, when Land Rover BAR went through to the semi-finals, the feeling in the camp was one of optimism.

Their semi-final opponents would be decided by Team New Zealand, who had won the qualifiers on points. Roche was by then frantically testing new hardware parts in the simulator at least three times a week. They would then manufacture, waterproof and ruggedise those and add them to the boat, which the sailors would test forty-five minutes before a race. 'Every day, they were effectively sailing a different, faster boat, but one that the sailing team had to keep adapting to,' Roche says. Looking at their development plan, he felt that they had a good chance of beating the Swedes or the Japanese, but they would struggle to develop a boat that would be competitive against the Kiwis, who had so far displayed impeccable boat-handling and flawless navigation. Team New Zealand chose Land Rover BAR.

In race one, Land Rover BAR were leading comfortably when, as they rounded the first gate, the wingsail cracked, forcing the team to retire. They immediately returned to base to install a new wing, but ran out of time and were forced to concede the second race of the day. They also lost the third race. On the fourth race, Ainslie's crew made another great start and bore away towards the start line. New Zealand were forced to make an abrupt turn. The sudden acceleration caused the bows to splash on the water and the boat capsized. Unable to right their boat without help from the support boat, they were disqualified.

After losing the fifth race, Land Rover BAR finally managed to win a race. 'That showed us that we were able, on our day, to be competitive with them, to keep them behind us,' Roche says. 'We knew we weren't faster, but we were close enough that we could hold them.' Land Rover lost the semi-finals 5–2 to the Kiwis, who then went on to beat Artemis in the final, and, in the Cup match, avenge the 2013 loss, by beating Team USA. 'I think we were probably a week away from being able to make it through to that final at the rate we were developing,' Roche says. He believes that perhaps they could have made faster progress with the boat development had they trusted the simulator a lot more. In the next America's Cup, they will. Next time, he says, they have to win.

22

THE COMPLEX GAME

On 9 August 2005, Southampton Football Club analyst Simon Wilson gave a pre-match briefing to the team. Southampton had been relegated from the Premier League the previous season and they were about to play their first away game in the Championship, against Luton Town. A tactical briefing was supposed to take around ten minutes: three on team tactics, three on the opposition, three on set pieces. Wilson went on for twenty. A few minutes were wasted at the start when his laptop refused to boot up, then crashed. He had created a fairly sophisticated presentation – he had just discovered the joys of PowerPoint – recreating an aerial-view animation of the team's tactics, with little dots sprinting across a pitch and the reaction of the opposition. He emphasised that 40 per cent of matches in the new league were decided by one goal, which, in high-scoring matches, was often the result of a set piece. Cue more animations with moving dots. A few assistant coaches interrupted with pertinent questions. Harry Redknapp, the manager, was beginning to get impatient. 'Harry was more intuitive than analytical,' says Wilson. 'He was nervous about overloading the players with information.'

Southampton lost 3–2. They had been ahead 2–1, before Luton equalised – from a free kick routine. On the team bus after the match, Redknapp turned to Wilson and said, 'I'll tell you what: next week, why don't we get your computer to play against their computer and see who wins?' Wilson felt hurt and embarrassed.

Simon Wilson had joined Prozone in 2001. At the time, the company had just three customers – Derby County, Manchester United and Aston Villa – but demand for its proprietary pixel-tracking software within the Premier League was about to explode. Wilson had been part of the first group of students on the science and football degree course at Liverpool John Moores University, launched by Tom Reilly in 1998. He was interviewed at Prozone by Marvyn Dickinson and Danny Northey, and the two men were impressed by the young graduate. He fitted the profile they were looking for: Wilson, a slender, wiry man with a whispery delivery, played football on a semi-professional basis. After the interview, he flew to Finland for a three-week trial with AP-Seinäjoki, in the Veikkausliiga, the Finnish premier division, and was offered a contract. A week later, he received a job offer from Prozone. 'I think that the fact that I had a background in professional football looked like gold dust to them,' Wilson says. He was offered eighteen thousand pounds, two grand more than anyone else recruited at the time. 'They told me to keep quiet about it,' Wilson says. 'I guess I took the sensible option.'

His first club was Preston North End, whose coach at the time was David Moyes. Preston had only one club room at Deepdale, where players ate, met with their agents and gathered for tactical meetings. The room had no curtains, so if Wilson wanted to use a slide projector to give a presentation, they would hang towels over the windows.

'At the time, match analysis wasn't recognised, so that first group of guys created a standard for how analysts worked in football clubs,' Wilson says. 'Before, clubs weren't taking on any analysts. If you went to a coach and just talked about data and sports science, they would switch off. They didn't have the bandwidth. Video analysis sessions were a joke. Players would sit in dark rooms and the coach would be trying to fast-forward to minute fifty-seven, and he'd go to minute fifty-eight and then minute fifty-six. The players would just sit there laughing and nudging each other. By the time he got there they wouldn't be listening any more. Just the fact that Prozone allowed them to select any minute of the game instantly transformed everything. It changed how analysis began to be perceived.'

In 2002, Wilson was transferred to Southampton. The club was an up-and-coming prospect, having achieved their highest-ever place – eighth – in the previous season.

Two years later, they had been relegated from the Premiership. Wilson, as a young analyst full of ideas, was struggling to make an impact: 'I was naive, but I couldn't understand why they didn't want this kind of information.' Some coaches, however, did get it – and Wilson had an ally within the Southampton coaching staff: Clive Woodward. In 2005, two years after the victorious Rugby World Cup campaign as England coach, Woodward had been offered a one-year contract to serve as Southampton's performance director. His remit was to bring the sort of innovative 'critical non-essentials' elements that had made him so successful in rugby. In the world of football, however, some people just called them non-essentials.

'Clive would challenge me at every level,' says Wilson. 'He would ask questions about every aspect of the game: why do we spend so much time working out how to score goals and not how to stop them? Or why wasn't the goalkeeper part of sessions with the ball? I would try to explain to him what they're doing and he'd just keep asking why. At the end of it, I usually realised he was absolutely right.'

Woodward and Wilson tried things such as filming players striking the ball, to study technique from a biomechanical perspective. Those initiatives, however, never had much impact, or would be blocked.

Redknapp left the club before the end of the year. Woodward left at the end of his contract and was appointed director of elite performance at the British Olympic Association. Of his relationship with Woodward, Redknapp writes in his autobiography *Always Managing*, 'There wasn't a clash of personalities, more a clash of cultures. Clive was feeling his way in football and thinking long term, meanwhile we had Saturday, Wednesday, Saturday, Wednesday matches to win. He might have had a good idea, but we didn't have the time to implement it.' Wilson left the club shortly before Woodward, convinced that there was a better way of running a football club. 'Woodward believed that evidence, be it video, or statistics, or any kind of data, was fundamental to how you prepare a team,' says Wilson. Woodward remains his biggest influence. 'He taught me that we didn't have to do things just because they had always been done a certain way.'

Wilson was very much aware that was the reality of Premier League clubs: by nature reactive, by necessity conservative. There was, of course, one exception: Bolton Wanderers.

Bolton was the first professional football club ever to employ full-time performance analysts. The club had been using Prozone since 2000, the first non-Premier League club to subscribe to the software. Bolton's manager was Sam Allardyce, also known as 'Big Sam'. When Allardyce had first called Ram Mylvaganam, the other Prozone clients were Premier League clubs paying large retainers. A lower-division team such as Bolton, Mylvaganam told Allardyce, couldn't afford Prozone.

'Ram, I'll tell you whether we can afford it – just send a man over,' Allardyce had insisted, and so Mylvaganam sent a consultant. On his return, Mylvaganam asked him how the presentation went.

'That was a strange one, Ram,' Danny Northey said. 'I went and sat down to do a presentation to Sam. Sam arrived, he had just had a shower, came and sat with the towel around his waist. He was seated in the cafeteria, which looked like something out of the Dark Ages, and I did this presentation to him and all I could see was all his private parts hanging out.'

Mylvaganam assigned them one of his best analysts, Gavin Fleig. Bolton became the first lower-division team to use the system. That season, they beat Preston North End 3–0 in the Championship playoffs and were promoted to the Premier League. The playoff took place on a Monday. The following day, Mylvaganam received a phone call from a highly pissed off David Moyes. 'I hear Sam's using your system,' Moyes said. Mylvaganam confirmed this was the case. Moyes demanded a presentation. 'David, you haven't got any money,' Mylvaganam said, to which Moyes replied, 'I'll fucking decide whether I've got money or not, you just come and see me!'

At Bolton, Sam Allardyce had assembled not only a team of inexpensive players but a team of analysts as well. He was the first manager to buy out a consultant from Prozone to work full time at the club, an exceptional analyst called Dave Fallows, whom Allardyce nicknamed Fingers. Later, when most Premier League teams still employed only one performance analyst, Allardyce had hired three: Gavin Fleig, David Fallows and Ed Sulley.

Between them they concocted a model they called the Fantastic Four, referring to the four statistics that dictated success: 1) Out of the thirty-eight matches in a season, a team had to prevent the opposition scoring in at least sixteen games to avoid relegation; 2) If they scored first, they knew they would have a 70 per cent chance of winning the game; 3) They also knew that set pieces accounted for nearly a third of all the goals scored, and that in-swinging crosses (when the ball curves towards the goal) were more successful than out-swinging; 4) They had an 80 per cent chance of not losing if their players outworked their opposition, by covering more distance at speeds above 5.5 metres per second.

Allardyce also insisted on his players using long throw-ins, deep into the opposition's area, and if a player failed to follow that simple command he'd go crazy because he knew that the odds of scoring had been reduced. Moreover, Bolton's performance analysts reassessed one of the concepts that had been emphasised by Charles Reep: POMOs (positions of maximum opportunity). POMOs were supposedly areas of the pitch where the majority of the goals were scored from. Fleig and his team studied a large number of throw-ins, and they worked out the locations on the pitch where the ball had the highest probability of landing. 'POMOs weren't just relevant to throw-ins. In training, [Allardyce] would shout to the players to attack their POMOs when trying to score,' Ed Sulley says. 'He used a microphone connected to speakers all around the pitch to make sure that the players could hear him.'

And the results were impressive. Between 2003 and 2007, Bolton recorded consecutive top-eight finishes in the Premier League, a record only bettered by the top four teams in the league. They qualified for the UEFA Cup for the first time in 2005 and again in 2006. Sam Allardyce left Bolton the following season, dissatisfied with the club owner's unwillingness to invest, in order to work for more ambitious teams and his backroom staff disbanded.

'I don't think Sam would ever pretend to have been great around a computer, but he was brilliant at not having an ego and getting the right people around him,' Marvyn Dickinson says. 'I remember people at other clubs looking down their nose at them and being dismissive about the number of analysts they had. They were like, "What are they even doing there?" I just thought, "You have no idea."'

When Wilson joined Manchester City in 2006 to start a new department of football analytics, Bolton was one of the models that inspired him. So when he set out to hire the best analysts he knew, he poached Gavin Fleig and Ed Sulley. Manchester City was a very different football club then. City's glory days were long past – the club had won the First Division championship in 1968, clinching the title in the last game of the season. However, by the late seventies and through the eighties, the team was in steep decline. By 1999, they were down in Division Two. In 2006, they were the type of mid-table Premiership club that struggled to win away games.

At City, Wilson initially found himself fighting the same old fights. For instance, his analysts would spend a week scouting the opposition but were only delivering their pre-match analysis a few hours before the game, when there was already a game plan in place. 'Whatever intelligence we had to offer them had no effect. The players all nod their heads and then just go and play the game, and there wasn't really a relationship between what happened and what you'd asked them to do.' Even more problematic was the lack of post-match briefings. 'After a game there wasn't any kind of analysis,' Wilson says. 'Emotionally, the manager and the coaching staff would just draw a line and move on. It was part of the culture. They wouldn't ask themselves if the game plan had been right or even well-executed. My team of analysts had to fight that habit and create a continuous loop between what happened in games, why it happened and what we are going to do next time.'

Wilson, however, persisted in establishing his new department, even when the club faced turbulent times. City was a run-of-the-mill club, privately owned, built on a budget, and poorly managed and in a constant state of turmoil. On 15 May 2007, the manager, Stuart Pearce, was sacked. That same day, Thaksin Shinawatra, the former prime minister of Thailand and a wealthy businessman, was given a tour of the City of Manchester Stadium. In June, he made a successful £81.6 million bid for the club and shortly after brought in the club's first international manager, Sven-Göran Eriksson, on a three-year contract. Eriksson left after ten months, despite a decent campaign in the Premier League, and was replaced by Mark Hughes. Two months later, Shinawatra faced fraud and corruption charges in his home country, and £800 million of the businessman's assets were frozen.

In September 2008, the club was acquired by the Abu Dhabi United Group for Development and Investment, a private equity outfit owned by Sheikh Mansour, a member of the Abu Dhabi royal family, and the team suddenly found itself with the resources to mount a challenge for the Premier League. The same day, the transfer of Brazilian superstar Robinho, for a club record £32.5 million, was announced with bombast. Robinho had been expected to join Chelsea after protracted negotiations with his previous club, Real Madrid. 'On the last day, Chelsea made a great proposal and

I accepted,' Robinho said at the press conference, before correcting himself: 'Manchester – sorry!' Pele, who had once heralded the twenty-four-year-old as his heir apparent, lambasted him for joining a nouveau riche club with no football ambitions. 'The boy needs counselling,' he said.

In December 2009, Roberto Mancini arrived, the club's third manager in three years. 'Each time a new manager came in we were starting at zero again and had to build trust in the way that we were working,' Wilson says. Wilson, in the meantime, had been promoted to a senior strategy role overseeing five departments, which together comprised what they called the House of Football. It was based on five pillars: scouting and recruitment, player care, coaching and development, medicine and sports science, and performance analysis, each with its own head of department. The House of Football departments were staffed by full-time employees that serviced the first team, but were independent of the current manager. 'What happens in football is that managers have an eighteen-month tenure on average, and so every eighteen months, as has been my experience, the manager usually gets blown up, and where he goes some of his support staff follow,' Wilson says. 'All that goes out the club: that information, all the lessons that they've learnt, their IP.'

But under the stability and prosperity of the new regime, Wilson had more resources and more time.

With Gavin Fleig as head of the performance analysis group, they undertook a vastly ambitious project of analysing every single goal scored in Europe. They rang data providers to request footage of the goals. They also had to manually rename every video file to include the home team, the away team, goal scorer and assisting player. 'We ended up with these real long filenames, but that was the only way to make it searchable in the computer,' Wilson says.

Wilson recalls one particular period when Manchester City hadn't scored from corners in twenty-two games, so his team decided to analyse more than four hundred goals that had been scored from corners. They noticed that about 75 per cent resulted from in-swinging corners, so in training the players were drilled in those types of corners. 'In the first twelve games of the next season we scored nine goals from corners,' Wilson says. 'You usually get six coaches and they'll have different experiences and they'll throw their opinions in, whereas we had objective evidence to suggest that this was a pattern.'

They also started benchmarking themselves against the top clubs in England and in Europe, and a few trends became obvious: the best teams dominated possession of the ball in the last third of the pitch; 70 per cent of possession happened in the final third of the pitch; and they had very high pass-completion rates, particularly forward passing. Players who fitted that profile – like the Brazilian superstar Robinho – became the target for Manchester City.

But if Robinho had been a coup, the reality was that the club, even though many now called it the richest in the world, still struggled to attract the world's best footballers – some of the richest athletes on the planet. They still weren't in a position to compete with, say, Paris Saint-Germain, who not only had a new billionaire owner, but a prestigious foot-balling history, not to mention their neighbours Manchester United.

Wilson had assembled a team of twenty scouts who would log reports based on five to ten matches for each player. For every player they signed, they would compile a fifty-five-page report, with details like regular appearances, how they responded to busy fixture periods, how well they recovered after an international match, how they reacted to a referee who was having a bad day, or if there were any behavioural issues off the pitch that they should be aware of, as in the case of the Italian striker Mario Balotelli.

Wilson had created a player care team that could proactively manage the players, not only to deal with problems, but also to welcome foreign players and ensure that they settled in. For instance, when they realised that the Argentinian striker Sergio Agüero, who had come from Real Madrid, didn't speak a great deal of English they changed his satnav to Spanish, created a map of Manchester highlighting Spanish bars and restaurants, and found him a house similar to the one he had lived in in Spain. The player care team dealt with everything on behalf of the players: flights, schools for their children, transportation. They would also feed pertinent intelligence back to Wilson: on the player's state of mind, whether his kids were doing well at school, if he was going out partying a bit too much.

A club that had spent a paltry £2 million in transfer fees in 2006 could now afford astronomical sums: £128 million in 2008, £125 million in 2009, £155 million in 2010 and £76 million in 2011. In the 2011–12 season, City had an enviable roster that included names like Carlos Tevez and David Silva, and it was part of Simon Wilson's remit to ensure the talent on the pitch was fine-tuned and prepared. After each match, City's analysts compiled exhaustive reports about the team's performance, including statistics like the number of line breaks – a term borrowed from rugby for a forward pass that goes through the opposition's line of defenders – and detailed analysis of what happened in the twenty seconds after the team won or lost the ball.

Every week during that season, Manchester City's captain, Vincent Kompany, would sit down with the other defenders and a performance analyst, and examine their performance.

'They would look at videos and statistics and ask questions,' Wilson says. 'Was the pressure effective? How many forced errors did they commit? What would happen in the ten seconds after losing the ball? On the basis of that analysis they would design their own defensive tactics for the game. You can have a fantastic analytics team but you can never win a game with data if you're not influencing the behaviour of the players.'

On 23 October 2011, Manchester City played reigning champions Manchester United at Old Trafford. The night before the match, Balotelli had invited friends over to his house. During the party, someone began playing with fireworks, then the bathroom caught fire. The player care team intervened immediately, transferring Balotelli to a hotel.

Balotelli redeemed himself the following day. In the twelfth minute, James Milner, the City and England left-back, scampered down the left wing and hopped a low cross to the edge of the area, finding Balotelli, who slotted the ball in the lower right-hand corner with a neat one-touch shot. He then proceeded to lift up his shirt, unveiling a T-shirt with the words 'Why always me?' – and received a yellow card.

Manchester City thrashed the champions 6–1 and went five points clear at the top of the table. 'It was a freak game,' Wilson recalls. 'If you compared the performance data from that game with a one-all draw at Swansea you wouldn't be looking at massive differences.' After the game, Manchester City's dressing room was quiet. Roberto Mancini said to his team: we haven't achieved anything yet, so we walk out of the dressing rom and we keep quiet. They had just beaten the champions. There was no gloating, no celebrations.

Wilson missed the last game of the season, on 13 May 2012. City were now level on points with Manchester United, but had a superior goal difference. All they needed was a win against Queens Park Rangers, a club fighting relegation, or a better result than Manchester United, who were playing Sunderland away. Twenty minutes in, Wayne Rooney scored, sending Manchester United two points clear of their rivals. Nineteen minutes later the Etihad Stadium erupted as Pablo Zabaleta put City at 1–0. 'I had a flight, but it was delayed, so I ended up only watching the first half on TV,' recalls Wilson. 'By then we were winning one-nil, so I was confident.' Wilson boarded the plane.

At forty-eight minutes, QPR equalised, and, eighteen minutes later, scored again. United were now three points clear, with twenty-four minutes left to play. The players started betraying the anxiety typical of anyone who's about to lose the championship at the very last minute. They were unnerved, and making rash decisions in their eagerness to salvage the game.

Two minutes into stoppage time, with dejected City fans already leaving the stadium in tears, Edin Džeko equalised. Two minutes later, Sergio Agüero received the ball on the edge of the box, in a position to shoot. According to a statistic called goal-expectation, which assigns a probability of success depending on the position of the shot, Agüero had a 12 per cent chance of scoring from that location. Instead, he went around a defender to a corner of the penalty area and, from a spot where he had a 19 per cent chance of scoring, slotted the ball past the keeper. By the time Wilson landed at Gatwick, the news ticker running across the TV screens said that Manchester City were the new champions. He saw replays of Agüero's goal, the explosion of relief in the stands, a frantic Mancini racing onto the pitch. He had missed the most dramatic finale in Premier League history. It was City's first league title in forty-four years. Manchester City had conceded the fewest number of goals in the Premier League and had scored the highest number of goals and yet had won the championship on goal difference.

In the summer of 2011, City's CEO, Gary Cook, who had been hired by Thaksin Shinawatra, resigned after allegedly sending an insensitive email to a player's mother. His replacement arrived in September 2012, a man called Ferran Soriano, who had been an executive at Barcelona between 2003 and 2008. He recruited Txiki Begiristain, a former Spanish international who had been Barcelona's technical director under Soriano. In 2008, the two men had been instrumental in promoting Pep Guardiola, then in charge of the youth team, to replace Frank Rijkaard as Barcelona's senior manager. Under Guardiola, Barça became an indomitable force, conquering the Champions League twice in four years. They became known for their brand of football – tiki-taka, a roaming style of possession football that deprived the opposition of the ball. Tiki-taka had its greatest practitioners in plyers like Lionel Messi, Xavi Hernandez and Andres Iniesta, all players made in Barcelona's youth academy, La Masaia.

Tiki-taka itself was an evolutionary mutation of a prior exemplar, the *totaalvoetbal* (total football) style concocted by Dutch coach Rinus Michels in the Ajax youth academy. To Michels, the game was about the control of space and the positional flexibility of its players. The maximum expression of total football was on full display when the Netherlands team played in the 1974 World Cup. The Dutch team, led by the dazzling Johan Cruyff, pulsated to the rhythm of the game, expanding when they had the ball – in football parlance, making the pitch big – by opening lines of pass and contracting when they lost it, by smothering opponents with pressure. The ball was the priority and keeping it was of the essence.

By then, the game model of total football had already been

implanted in Barcelona, during Michels's three-year stint as the manager of the Catalan club, before he took the Dutch national team to the World Cup. But it was Cruyff, who played for the club between 1973 and 1978, and a decade later returned as manager, who cemented it as the team's identity. It had been his suggestion for the club to copy the Ajax system and establish a youth academy that taught a game model which was unique to the club. La Massia's methodology was the mirror of Cruyff's idea of the game: no two training sessions were the same, all exercises involved the ball, physical drills were unheard of. Its epitome was the rondo, an exercise that involved players passing the ball in a small circle while two players in the middle tried to intercept it. It was a pure reflection of Barcelona's game model: lots of passes, infinite ball possession, playing with the ball rather than running after it. This was the aesthetic expressed by the team who became known as the 'Dream Team' of European football, after conquering Barcelona's first-ever European Cup in 1992. They were a stellar combination of football artists, combining global stars like Romário, Ronald Koeman and Hristo Stoichkov with such Spanish talent as Txiki Begiristain and the La Massia graduate Pep Guardiola.

Soriano and Begiristain wanted to emulate at City what had been accomplished at the Catalan club: build a team that could win the Champions League with a group replete with home-grown talent forged by a unique style of football.

But which style, exactly? A year after he arrived, Soriano started asking Wilson: 'What's the football idea here?' Wilson replied that they had a project under development.

The project of developing a style of football unique to City was indeed in development. In 2009, as part of the challenge of transforming a club built to finish fourteenth into a Champions League regular, Simon Wilson had been asked to review the City academy. The academy had been successful at turning out players who would end up playing in the Premier League at minor clubs, but no graduates had yet played a Champions League game.

Once Soriano expressed an interest, creating a game model became something that had to be done as a matter of priority. To help him coordinate the project, Wilson recruited the services of one of the first team analysts, Pedro Marques.

The pair had first met in 2007, when Marques, then an analyst at Sporting Club Portugal, cold-called Wilson. Prozone had pitched their services to the Portuguese club and Marques wanted an independent opinion. Sporting ended up not purchasing the technology but Wilson and Marques stayed in touch. That same year, Marques welcomed Wilson to Sporting's youth academy, one of the most prestigious footballing schools in the world. 'I guess he was positively surprised that we had no way of tracking data but we were still capable of analysing the game in a very qualitative, methodical way,' Marques says. An invitation to join Manchester City's growing squad of analysts followed in 2010. For Marques, who had by then been at Sporting for six years, it was an offer he could not refuse.

Marques arrived in Manchester in July 2010, and was given the task of opposition analysis, working under the head of department, Gavin Fleig.

At first, Marques struggled to adapt to the new culture, particularly to an approach to performance analysis that was different from what he had been used to. In England, the starting point for analysis would usually be extensive Prozone reports detailing everything from work rates to all the sprints that a player had made during the game.

'I just couldn't see the game from that perspective. It was too granular: passes forward, number of sprints. None of that gave me a qualitative, behavioural view of the game.'

As an opposition analyst, Marques was supposed to watch

only other teams' matches, but he was eager to absorb as much of the Premier League as possible, so he spent a year watching games day and night, in the stadium and on television. 'I had no life,' he recalls. Marques still wasn't familiar with most Premier League players. Teams would change manager, or a player was injured, and Marques had to ask his colleagues how that would change the team's dynamics. 'Some teams were more predictable,' Marques says. 'For instance, with Stoke, you knew their goalkeeper was going to flick to the tall guys in the front and wait for the second ball. After three matches, you're like, okay, I'm comfortable they are not going to divert from this.'

After his first year, Marques had started busying himself with understanding what was the underlying game model at Manchester City's youth academy, when Wilson asked him to help with the new project.

The concept of the game model was also ingrained in the footballing approach in Portugal. It was a methodology that Carlos Queiroz had pioneered after taking charge of the national youth team. For years, Queiroz travelled to France, Italy, the Netherlands, Spain, visiting youth academies and national training centres for ideas that could inform what would be Portugal's game model, one that would be specific to the talent he had at his disposal. He conceptualised a game model as a hierarchical structure of general principles of play objectives, which applied to any situation in the game, and sub-principles, which were rules of action pertaining to specific moments. He identified five different moments in the game: attack, defence, transition attack–defence, transition defence–attack, and set pieces. These moments were not siloed. They were fluid, interdependent and constantly interchanging. 'With the ball you attack and you defend. Without it, you attack and defend as well,' Queiroz said.

To Queiroz, the game model should be ever-evolving and reflect the coach's philosophy, the culture of the club, the characteristics of the players. It formed the identity of the club, the guiding principle; the players coordinated their actions as a collective. There are many ways to win a game. The game model reflected how you believe you should win. And, as such, it reflected how the team should train. 'I was aware of the idea of the game model but meeting Pedro was influential,' Wilson says. 'He was able to go into much greater depth.'

Formulating a game model for Manchester City didn't involve inventing a new style of football. Rather, it was about finding one that was congruent with the identity of the club. 'We used to talk about it all the time,' Wilson says. 'When you close your eyes and think about Manchester United or Barcelona, you are immediately able to visualise their style of football.' Of course, that style had been forged and honed over decades of tradition. Manchester City was not a new club – it had been founded in 1880 by Anna Connell, a vicar's daughter, as a working men's club, originally called St Mark's West Gordon FC, to keep men away from drink and gang brawling – but it was a club without a storied past of glory. 'Of course, we had a deep history into which we could tap into,' Wilson says. 'It was very much a research project.'

Manchester had been the birthplace of the Industrial Revolution, so City's football had to reflect hard work and an entrepreneurial spirit. It had also been the city of Madchester and the Gallagher brothers, so City's football had to reflect that braggadocio and swagger. 'We wanted a winning, innovating club that played beautiful football that excited people beyond the ninety minutes,' Wilson says. 'Our game philosophy had to reflect that. City could not be reactive, long-ball, slow football. It had to be inventive.'

Wilson gave them eight weeks to get a first draft done.

Their first meeting took place in March 2013, in the changing room at the Etihad Stadium. Present were the academy manager, the head of coaching, the head of physical performance and coaches from the academy, as well as the first-team head of recruitment and Marques and Wilson.

Marques put up a diagram of a football pitch on the screen with superimposed captions. They read:

- What are the strategies to construct and set up the game?
- What are the strategies to create space and imbalance?
- What are the strategies to create chances and finish?
- What is our reaction to winning the ball?
- What is our reaction to losing the ball?
- How do we set up to protect the goal?
- How do we set up to defend as a block?
- How do we set up to defend from the front?

Wilson knew that for the coaches present at those meetings this was a new language of football, a different dimension of analysis: 'I had worked with many British managers and none had ever been exposed to this way of thinking about the game,' Wilson says. 'The coaching education system here was so outdated. We were miles behind and we didn't understand the game in the right way.' British coaches, he says, typically understood attack and defence as very linear, discrete aspects of the game. For instance, moments of transition were typically ignored. In the Iberian school, transitions were seen as probably the most crucial moments of the game, when equilibrium between opponents could be swiftly broken and exploited. 'In England, I felt that only attack and defence were acknowledged, and transitions were almost seen as turnover,' Marques says. 'The way I saw it, transitions might be the shortest moments in time, but are the most crucial moments of the game. It's then when you break the equilibrium and when you're at your most vulnerable.'

Marques used to tell Wilson that football was a product of culture and society. The British have a preference for organisation and order. Latin countries have a propensity for chaos and unpredictability. Football was organised chaos, so finding the right balance was of the essence.

Every week, Marques and Wilson would meet with the club's coaching staff – from academy coaches to sports scientists – and gradually map out each of the phases of the game. For each they would write down a series of hierarchical principles that were to dictate the behaviour of the team, a sort of algorithm for game style. They would start by playing a few clips of the City teams. Wilson would ask: 'All right, what do you believe in? What are your main principles here?' The coaches would talk through what they were and they would write them down. They would debate the merits of their approach. They would play clips of teams they wanted to emulate. They would then devise exercises to train those principles. 'For a phase, say, build up from the back, we would start with about eighty variations of a training session,' Wilson says. 'Far too many. We had to analyse each one in depth.' They would iterate until they found exercises that preserved the complexity of the game. 'We train as we play,' Marques says.

When the eight weeks were up, they had completed the first draft of City's game model. They called it the City methodology.

The team wants to have the ball. When attacking, they build up from the back, luring the opposition into their own defensive third, creating more spaces and opportunities to attack in the opposition half.

Although the goalkeeper's main task is to defend the goal,

the player also acts as an outfield player, and is very involved with the build-up of play.

Passes are preferably short with an adjusted tempo, aiming at moving the opposition to create spaces to attack. The frequent passing also allows the team to move up the pitch as a unit, so when they lose possession they are close and able to press immediately to regain or avoid progression of the opposition.

In defence, the intention is make the pitch small. Pressing from the front with a high block, and creating a high density of players around the ball. The objective is to get the ball back as soon as possible, higher up the pitch if possible so that they are closer to attack the goal straight away.

By that point, Wilson was no longer working just for Manchester City. He was now with City Football Group, overseeing football performance, human performance and talent management across a network of clubs that included New York City FC, Melbourne City, Yokohama City and, of course, Manchester City. 'I used Pedro as the "guardian" of the football knowledge in the group and put him in charge of spreading it to the other clubs,' Wilson says. 'Once we had shared and educated we had to sit back and assess if it was being deployed in the teams.' They built an interactive app, encapsulating the City principles and methodologies, that anyone who was part of the City Group could consult. 'What we had at Barcelona was only five pages,' Begiristain told him. 'You created an encyclopaedia!' If you asked anyone at City what their game style was, they could recite it:

We want to dominate the ball; create lots of chances; score many goals; when we have the ball the pitch is big, when we don't have the ball the pitch is small; we want the ball.

Of course, a game style could never be considered a finished product, but rather a continuous work in progress that coexisted with and adapted to the views of the current manager.

Under Roberto Mancini, there were some differences between the first team's style of football and the City game model. When Manuel Pellegrini was hired in 2013, the Chilean manager was well aligned with City's game style and fluent in the terminology.

But it was only in 2016, when Pep Guardiola arrived, that coaching philosophy and the City way were in perfect alignment. After all, Guardiola's Barcelona had been the obvious inspiration for the new City way. Even so, City's first season under Guardiola was inconsistent, as the players were still assimilating his philosophy. His second season, on the other hand, was historic. In 2017–18, City not only demolished the opposition, but also smashed records: most consecutive wins (18), most goals scored in a season (108), most wins in the season (32), biggest goal difference (+79), most passes completed in a game (904). But, more than that, they dazzled, playing with élan and flair. Infinite possession, frequent passes, the fluidity of the transitions. Pundits debated in earnest whether Guardiola's City was the best team in the history of the Premier League. 'At City people had doubts that I would be able to win that way,' Guardiola said in an interview. 'Even myself.'

CONCLUSION

One of the most renowned scholars of expert performance is Anders Ericsson, a Swedish psychologist at Florida State University. Ericsson has spent more than thirty years studying the outliers at the far end of the performance spectrum: musical prodigies, sport stars, memory champions. He considers expertise as a whole, finding and correlating the common dynamics that lead extraordinary people to excel in fields as disparate as music and chess, athletics and mnemonics. Ericsson's overarching assertion is that experts are made, not born. They are made from years of dedicated effort and specialised training. They are made in the rollercoaster of failure and success, carved from the incessant practice that culminates in mastery.

Ericsson's theory first gained wider attention when he was profiled in *Outliers*, the 2008 book by Malcolm Gladwell. In it, Gladwell emphasised one of Ericsson's seminal papers, a study that he had conducted with violinists at the Berlin Academy of Arts to dissect how these musicians practised their craft. After extensive interviews, Ericsson estimated that, on average, the very best violinists reached the age of twenty with ten thousand hours of solitary practice under their belts. What was particularly interesting was that this number was in stark contrast to those of their less-than-stellar colleagues, who by the same age had clocked up significantly less time practising. According to Ericsson, there was a direct correlation between the number of hours spent in practice and the level of expertise, independent of the musicians' prior level of 'natural talent'. In conclusion: experts were made, not born.

It was on the basis of that finding that Gladwell coined his popular 'ten thousand hour rule', claiming that ten thousand hours of practice was what it took to become a master *in any field of expertise*. Ericsson would later disavow Gladwell's generalisation, taking particular exception to the fact that the writer had failed to grasp the distinction between general practice and what he calls 'deliberate practice': a type of practice that requires focus, motivation, feedback and the adoption of effective, proven techniques. It is an often painful process, aiming towards an overarching goal in an incremental and deliberate approach. 'Deliberate practice is the gold standard,' Ericsson writes in *Peak*, his 2015 book, 'It's the ideal to which anyone learning a skill should aspire.'

A few years ago, Keith Davids and Duarte Araújo published a study that explained why Brazil was the birthplace of some of the most talented footballers in the world. The South American country is a five-time world champion and the birthplace of players like Garrincha, Pele, Socrates, Romário, Ronaldinho and Neymar. In Brazil, Araújo and Davids noticed, young players receive little, if any, structured coaching. Instead, they play *pelada* (which can be literally translated as 'naked'). *Pelada* can be played anytime and anywhere: in the streets, on the beach, in dirt fields. Balls are often made from socks; goal posts are made from rocks; and the rules are made up: three corners equals a penalty; the last player can use his hands to protect the goal.

In the absence of coaches, kids improvise without fear of being admonished for their mistakes; faced with the constraints of their environment, they are forced to adapt. Socrates, the Brazilian striker and World Cup winner in 1983 and 1986, frequently played with an avocado seed in an orchard. Garrincha, the Brazilian winger who won the World Cup in 1958 and 1962 and is often considered one of the best dribblers in history, once described how he used to play on the border of a slope: not allowing the ball to drop down that slope was crucial – he hated having to retrieve it.

Street play is also common in Portugal, Spain and the Netherlands. Portuguese coach José Mourinho once said, 'In England you teach your kids how to win, in Spain and Portugal they teach their kids how to play.' Dutch coach Rinus Michels believed that playing on the streets, unencumbered by rules and coaches, was the most natural learning environment.

Davids and Araújo consider *pelada* the kind of environment that's naturally replete with the sort of constraints that engender creativity and enforce adaptability. It's the antithesis of deliberate practice: unrestrained, chaotic, joyful, improvised.

In 2000, Keith Davids published a paper openly criticising Ericsson's deliberate practice theory. 'I was ignored because the theory was so popular,' he says. Davids took particular exception to the culture of relentless repetitive training that it encouraged. This was problematic, Davids argued, especially when it encouraged children to start focusing on one sport from a very young age. Recent research indicates that early specialisation is associated with burnout and repetitive stress injuries. 'China recently announced a national plan to become a football superpower,' Davids says. 'They basically want to train babies to play football.'

When he visited elite academies in the UK, he would

regularly find 'mollycoddled' young players, playing with proper equipment in manicured football fields, who had everything done for them. 'We wasted years in the wilderness chasing the benefits of the deliberate practice approach,' he says. Davids is adamant that this approach explains why the last time England featured in the semi-final of a major tournament was in 1996.

The national team needs to be more streetwise, captain Wayne Rooney said in the aftermath of the 2014 World Cup, where England had suffered the ignominy of another early exit. 'You see a lot of the great teams over the years, international teams and club teams, and they all have that,' he said. In December that year, Dan Ashworth, the FA's director of elite development, announced a manifesto called England DNA, which aimed to cement a footballing identity, common to all England teams. The initiative was very clearly designed to emulate the success of similar ones in other countries: 2010 World Cup winners Spain launched theirs in 1995; 2014 champions Germany in 2000. Of course, their game identity would be faithful to the English lineage.

England DNA was steeped in the principles of constraint-based coaching. Official documents detail a new approach to coaching, focusing on aspects like 'developing practices that enable the players to make lots of decisions'; 'deliver realistic game-related practices'; 'aim for a minimum of 70 per cent ball rolling time in all sessions'. Principles for the different game phases – in possession, out of possession and transitions – highlight aspects such as 'intelligently dominating the ball'; 'recovering the ball as soon as possible'; 'the goalkeeper is no longer viewed apart from the outfield players'. These are obvious attempts to modernise the English game and eradicate the vestiges of the footballing mentality – the long ball, the direct play, sheer physicality – that had originated in

Charles Hughes's *Winning Formula*, while remaining faithful to a distinctive English way of playing that privileges high tempo and forward momentum. 'We're finding a consensus emerging. We don't pluck something out of the air and say, "Ah, let's play like this." We've taken into account what we're good at in this country,' Ashworth said.

Davids considers the *annus mirabilis* of the English youth teams in 2017 to be a direct consequence of this new philosophy. They were under-21 European semi-finalists, under-20 world champions, under-19 European champions and under-17 world champions.

One of the clubs that contributed the most players to these teams was Manchester City. One City player in particular stole the show: Phil Foden, scorer of two goals in the 5–2 demolition of Spain in the under-17 final and the tournament's best player.

Later that year, when City played Shakhtar Donetsk on 6 December, Foden would become the youngest English player to start a Champions League match. Unexpectedly, Guardiola tried the midfielder at left back.

The player had been brought to Pep Guardiola's attention by Txiki Begiristain. 'He's looks skinny, not that strong, or tall,' Guardiola said. 'But he's a special player.'

Foden likely reminded him of a former Barcelona player who had been discovered by Johan Cruyff. The Dutch manager saw the boy in La Masia and was impressed by his sublime skill and sharp intelligence. When he enquired why the player hadn't already been promoted to the senior reserves team, Cruyff was told that the boy, called Pep Guardiola, was too weak. Cruyff ignored the concerns and gave him a chance. Guardiola thrived: first as the midfield maestro in Cruyff's magnificent Barcelona team and later as a manager, as the guardian of Cruyff's legacy. 'I was a skinny player,'

Cruyff once said. 'The weak have to develop a special intelligence, an ability to find alternatives.' A capacity to learn not just with their brains, but with their bodies.

One afternoon in September 2017, Stafford Murray addressed an audience at the Middlesex University campus in north-west London. The event, organised by the International Society of Performance Analysis of Sport, was leisurely and friendly, and Murray was introduced with a certain degree of reverence by his own PhD supervisor. After all, most of the analysts in the audience had probably called him boss at one point or another.

Three weeks after Rio, Murray had received a call from High Performance Sport New Zealand. They wanted to offer him the post of innovation manager, a job similar to Scott Drawer's previous position at UK Sport. At that point, Murray believed he was going to end his career where he had started it: at the EIS. But the offer on the table was appealing enough for him to fly out to Auckland to continue the conversation. He arrived in New Zealand jet-lagged and exhausted, and fell asleep during dinner. 'I realised when the guy asked the end of the question, that I'd missed about the first ten seconds of it,' Murray says. 'Honestly, what an idiot.'

Still, he was impressed by the team, and further enticed by the fact that his brother, Warwick, had been living out there for some time. When he finally made the decision to leave the English Institute of Sport, he was the longest-serving sports scientist in its history. He still attended his final annual EIS conference in December 2017. Nigel Walker, the national director of the EIS, thanked him in his speech. 'I was crying, of course,' Murray says. 'I'm such a bloody emotional flower.'

At the Middlesex workshop, Murray paced across the stage, cracking bad jokes. He began by showing pictures from his early days. ('This is me at Trent Bridge, working for the South African cricket team. Back then we still called ourselves notational analysts. They we got all clever and cocky and called ourselves performance analysts.') He then vaguely described the projects he had been supervising: an automated tracking system for pole vault; a vertical eccentric loading machine that captured real-time data for athletes; a GPS system with real-time kinematic processing and accuracy down to a few millimetres ('GPS on speed'). He concluded by sharing a few thoughts about his experiences so far of New Zealand. ('They're all bloody good bastards, as they call each other. So if they call you a "good bastard" you are doing okay. If they call you just a "bastard" then you aren't.')

When asked how he reconciled his national pride with working for another country, he was hesitant. 'It's strange, and it was a bloody hard decision to make. I worked here twenty years, have been to five Commonwealth Games and to four Olympics.' He paused. 'But it got to a stage I realised it's not just about countries. It's about the people. I still give my bloody hundred per cent for them.'

The discussion then extended into the future of analytics in sports. Beyond current projects to improve tracking and processing capabilities, such as those he had been overseeing himself, Murray listed new developments like neuromorphic computing and artificial intelligence. But technology, he said, was ultimately not the point. It was the human element, and the application, that mattered. There was no purpose in even the most advanced technology if the data was being extracted just for data's sake, without the ability to have an impact on the athlete, or to persuade a coach.

After the talk, we walked out together. Murray was wearing a black polo shirt emblazoned with a silver fern and was his usual cheerful self. He had taken some time during his visit to finish a chapter of his PhD thesis, he told me, but he was still concerned with the slow progress of his research, which he had started more than ten years ago. 'Ten bloody years, mate,' he said, with some exasperation. 'A lot got in the way.'

His research concerned a topic called perturbations. They were first discovered in squash in 2003, by Ian Franks and Tim McGarry, who had studied with Mike Hughes.

On a squash court, the most strategic area is at its centre, where the middle line meets the line that divides the back half of the court, colloquially known as the T. A player located at the T is in prime position to respond to any shot from their opponent. David Pearson always instructed his players to return to the T after each shot. Dominating the T means controlling the flow of the game, keeping the opponent in the back corners of the court and under pressure.

When Franks and McGarry tracked the movement of squash players in terms of their proximity to the T, they noticed that the players seemed to be engaged in a coordinated choreography between the T and the moving ball: as one player moved towards the T, the other would move away.

At some points in the game, this back-and-forth oscillation, punctuated by a metronomic exchange of shots, would be suddenly perturbed. This perturbation could be, for instance, an accurate shot that left the other player scrambling to respond, or a very clumsy one that left the player exposed. As result, one of the players momentarily held the upper hand, while the other lost control, chasing the ball in the outer confines of the court, away from the safety of the T. Sometimes the player under pressure recovered their rhythm and the match returned to its coordinated dance. More often than not, however, these perturbations would set in motion a cascade of exchanges that terminated the rally with a winner or an error.

This discovery confirmed something that squash coaches intuitively know: it's not the last shot that is the most important, but what leads to it. And although these perturbations were hard to define objectively, they were relatively easy to spot. When Franks and McGarry played footage of a series of matches to a group of coaches, most seemed to be able to independently agree on the exact moment a perturbation occurred. 'In Canada, there was a Scottish TV commentator and whenever something happened in the game, like a breakaway, he would go "oh oh". And, sure enough, a few moments later you'd get a goal or a dangerous strike,' Franks says. 'I went back to all the games that he'd been commentating on and, sure enough, he just appeared to know when something was going to happen.'

Perturbations reflect the deeper dynamics of the sport and yield insight into the natural principles that rule it. 'We can't just keep counting actions all the time,' says Mike Hughes, who afterwards found perturbations in rugby and football. 'We have to rate them.'

Perturbations are the cause, not the effect. They reflect how players put others under pressure, how players respond when under pressure. 'With Nick Matthew, it was the forehand volley. Very explosive,' Murray says. 'Peter Nicol was totally different. He would accumulate pressure gradually, by taking the ball early, with a series of minor perturbations.' As such, perturbations could also provide analysts with a much more accurate and reliable profiling tool. 'It was Mike Hughes junior who first noticed that the way teams played changed when they played against a different team, it changed if they were winning or losing,' Murray recalls. 'We went back to our profiles and thought, shit. These are bad, man. Not all bad, but we definitely had to change how we profiled players.' By the 2010 Commonwealth Games, England squash players were briefed with opponent-specific profiles that included perturbation analysis.

During his research, Murray had intended to define perturbations not in terms of subjective opinions, but precise quantifiable parameters: biomechanical movement, distances, speeds, what types of shots caused them, what tactics created or mitigated them. 'I don't think I'm anywhere near,' he says. 'We keep adding more and more stuff. At some point we might just implode. Paralysis by analysis. We'll revert back to good old video!' We still don't know what the best in the world do differently, he mused. We still don't know what their magic is; we still don't know what makes them great.

ACKNOWLEDGEMENTS

When I started writing this book in 2012, I had no idea what it took to write a book. I'm grateful to the many people who have assisted and taught me how along the way.

My heartfelt gratitude to my agent Patrick Walsh, who read my incipient book proposal and told me I had something worth publishing. His decision to take me on as his client changed my life. Without his unfailing encouragement, belief and dedication this book would not exist. Thank you also to Carrie Plitt and John Ash. At Conville & Walsh, thanks to Jake Smith-Bosanquet and Alexander Cochran.

At Little, Brown, I had the pleasure of working with a team of extraordinary professionals. I owe a great deal to Zoe Gullen for her meticulous and thorough editing. She caught many style faults and factual errors. The mistakes that remain are all mine. Thank you also to Marie Hrynczak, Duncan Spilling and Grace Vincent. And most of all, my deepest thanks to my editor Richard Beswick, for his patience and editorial insight, and for the enthusiastic support for this project since our first meeting.

Thank you to my colleagues at *WIRED*, where parts of *Game Changers* first appeared in the form of feature stories. I would like to specially thank my editor-in-chief, Greg

Williams. I doubt I would be writing about sports – or writing at all – without his encouragement and mentorship.

The primary source material for this book emerged from nearly 350 interviews conducted since the London 2012 Games with athletes, coaches and scientists, who have generously shared their stories and insights. Many of the names are quoted in the story, but those that are not have still contributed vitally to the text. In the text, those interviews by the author are in the present tense. Quotations drawn from supplementary material are in the past tense.

Some generously made a lot time for this reporter and were constantly available for another phone call, an extra meeting, one more question. Stafford Murray, whenever I met him – be it in Manchester or in Rio de Janeiro – always made sure he had time for me. Scott Drawer was a constant source of insight from day one, opening many doors and expanding my horizons. I owe a great deal to scientists like Christian Cook, Keith Davids, Mark Williams, Al Smith and Duarte Araújo for changing my worldview in ways that go beyond sport. Thank you to pioneers of sports science for sharing their war stories: Mike Hughes, Ian Franks, Vaughan Lancaster-Thomas and Frank Sanderson delighted me with their stories. Thank you to the football analysts and disruptors: Pedro Marques, Simon Wilson, Blake Wooster, Barry McNeill, Omar Chaudhuri, Ram Mylvaganam, Neil Ramsay, Ben Dickinson, Marvyn Dickinson, Danny Northey, Jean-Marc Giorgi, Barry McNeill, Paul Boanas, Chris Anderson, Ed Sulley and Pedro Sampaio.

It was a privilege speaking to athletes like Peter Nicol, Nick Matthew, Rebecca Romero, Sarah Storey, Amy Williams, Lizzy Yarnold, Christa Cullen, Helen Richardson-Walsh, Kate Richardson-Walsh, Ben Ainslie, Paul Campbell-Jones, Freddie Carr, Giles Scott and Nick Hutton. Their stories were moving and insightful.

My deepest gratitude to the coaches who've shared the secrets of their competitive advantage: Clive Woodward, David Pearson, Simon Jones, Peter Keen, Dave Brailsford, Dan Hunt, Danny Holdcroft and Danny Kerry. To the team behind the team: thank you to Andrea Wooles, Mandy deBeer, Mike Hughes, Chris White, Julia Wells, Dave Reddin, Sherylle Calder, Marco Cardinale, Oliver Logan, Naomi Stenhouse, Tony Biscombe, Chris Gaviglio, Will Forbes, Mike Jarvis, Ben Rosenblatt, Dave Hamilton, Pete Lindsay and Mike Loosemore. At McLaren, my thanks to Geoff McGrath, Caroline Hargrove, Mike Philips, Andy Latham, Duncan Bradley and Caleb Sawade for welcoming me into the secretive world of Formula One. At Land Rover BAR, thank you to James Roche, Rob Wilson, Andy Claughton, Martin Whitmarsh, Richard Hopkirk, Maurizio Muñoz and Sarah Alexander. Thank you also to the engineers designing the future of sport: Rachel Blackburn, Stephen Turnock, Victor Bergonzoli, Paul Hurrion and Dimitri Katsanis. At the EIS, my thanks to Mark Jarvis and Nigel Walker. And few people who don't feature in this book: Lachlan Penfold, Andy Walshe, John Coates and Michael Merzenich.

Shout-outs to Olly Figg and Katherine Hirst, who have generously read early drafts and remained honest. Thank you also to Abigail Beall and Ríona Judge-McCormack for their assistance. And finally, for their support, kindness, and for not giving up on me: thank you Jack Kreindler, Marje Kreindler, Hope Lawrie, Victoria Pattinson and my parents. You're my team.

BIBLIOGRAPHY

Ainslie, B., *Ben Ainslie: Close to the Wind: Britain's Greatest Olympic Sailor* (London: Random House, 2009)

Allardyce, S., *Big Sam: My Autobiography* (London: Headline, 2015)

Anderson, C. and D. Sally, *The Numbers Game: Why Everything You Know About Football is Wrong* (London: Penguin Books, 2013)

Anson, G., D. Elliott and K. Davids, 'Information processing and constraints-based views of skill acquisition: divergent or complementary?', *Motor Control*, 9 (2005)

Araújo, D., K. Davids and R. Hristovski, 'The ecological dynamics of decision making in sport', *Psychology of Sport and Exercise*, 7 (2006)

Araújo, D., C. Fonseca, K. Davids, J. Garganta, A. Volossovitch, R. Brandão and R. Krebs, 'The role of ecological constraints in expertise development', *Talent Development & Excellence*, 2 (2010)

Araújo, D., P. Passos and P. Tiago Esteves, *Manual de Psicologia do Desporto para Treinadores* (Portugal: Omniserviços, 2011)

Araújo, D., A. Diniz, P. Passos and K. Davids, 'Decision making in social neurobiological systems modeled as transitions in dynamic pattern formation', *Adaptive Behavior*, 22 (2013)

Bacon, E., *Great British Cycling: The History of British Bike Racing* (London: Transworld, 2014)

Bangsbo, J. and T. Reilly, *Science and Football III: Proceedings of the Third World Congress of Science and Football* (Wales: Cardiff Institute, 1996)

Beaven, C. M., C. Cook, D. Gray, P. Downes, I. Murphy, S. Drawer, J. R. Ingram, L. P. Kilduff and N. Gill, 'Electrostimulation enhances recovery during a rugby pre-season', *International Journal of Sports Physiology and Performance*, 8 (2013)

Bent, I., *Football Confidential* (London: BBC Books, 2000)

Bevan, H. R., P. J. Bunce, N. J. Owen, M. A. Bennett, C. J. Cook, D. J. Cunningham, R. U. Newton and L. P. Kilduff, 'Optimal loading for the development of peak power output in professional rugby players', *Journal of Strength and Conditioning Research*, 24 (2010)

Bloomfield, J., *Australia's Sporting Success: The Inside Story* (Sydney: UNSW Press, 2004)

Boardman, C., *Triumphs and Turbulence: My Autobiography* (London: Ebury, 2016)

Bompa, T. O., *Periodization: Theory and Methodology of Training* (Leeds: Human Kinetics, 1999)

Bongaardt, R. and O. G. Meijer, 'Bernstein's theory of movement behavior: historical development and contemporary relevance', *Journal of Motor Behavior*, 32 (2000)

Bourne, N. D., 'Fast Science: A History of Training Theory and Methods for Elite Runners Through 1975', doctoral thesis (2008)

Burns, P., *White Gold: England's Journey to Rugby World Cup Glory* (Edinburgh: Birlinn, 2013)

Cabral, M., 'Treinadores portugueses – Porque são especiais?', *Expresso*, 23 September 2017

Cardinale, M., R. Newton and K. Nosaka, *Strength and Conditioning: Biological Principles and Practical Applications* (Hoboken: Wiley-Blackwell, 2010)

Carling, C., M. Williams and T. Reilly, 'Handbook of soccer match analysis: a systematic approach to improving performance', *Journal of Sports Science and Medicine*, 5 (2006)

Coates, J. M., M. Gurnell and Z. Sarnyai, 'From molecule to market: steroid hormones and financial risk-taking', *Philosophical Transactions of the Royal Society B*, 365 (2010)

Coates, J., *The Hour Between Dog and Wolf: Risk-taking, Gut Feelings and the Biology of Boom and Bust* (Toronto: Random House, 2012)

Colyer, S. L., 'Enhancing Start Performance in the Sport of Skeleton', doctoral thesis (2015)

Cook, C. J. and C. M. Beaven, 'Salivary testosterone is related to self-selected training load in elite female athletes', *Physiology & Behavior*, 116–117 (2013)

Cook, C. J. and B. T. Crewther, 'Changes in salivary testosterone concentrations and subsequent voluntary squat performance following the presentation of short video clips', *Hormones and Behavior*, 61 (2012)

Cook, C. J. and B. T. Crewther, 'Effects of different post-match recovery interventions on subsequent athlete hormonal state and game performance', *Physiology & Behavior*, 106 (2012)

Cook, C. J. and B. T. Crewther, 'The effects of different pre-game motivational interventions on athlete

free hormonal state and subsequent performance
in professional rugby union matches', *Physiology &
Behavior*, 106 (2012)

Cook, C. J. and B. T. Crewther, 'The social environment
during a post-match video presentation affects the
hormonal responses and playing performance in
professional male athletes', *Physiology & Behavior*, 130
(2014)

Cook, C. J., B. T. Crewther and A. A. Smith,
'Comparison of baseline free testosterone and cortisol
concentrations between elite and non-elite female
athletes', *American Journal of Human Biology*, 24 (2012)

Cook, C. J., C. M. Beaven and L. P. Kilduff, 'Three
weeks of eccentric training combined with over-
speed exercises enhances power and running speed
performance gains in trained athletes', *Journal of
Strength and Conditioning Research*, 27 (2013)

Cook, C., D. Holdcroft, S. Drawer and L. P Kilduff,
'Designing a warm-up protocol for elite bob-skeleton
athletes', *International Journal of Sports Physiology and
Performance*, 2 (2013)

Cooper, M., T. Goodenough, R. Herbert and M. Hall,
In the Zone: With South Africa's Sports Heroes (Cape
Town: New Holland, 2007)

Corbett, J., *Everton: The School of Science* (London:
Macmillan, 2003)

Crewther, B. T., J. W. L. Keogh, J. Cronin and C. J. Cook,
'Possible stimuli for strength and power adaptation:
acute hormonal responses', *Journal of Strength and
Conditioning Research*, 22 (2008)

Crewther B. T., L. P. Kilduff, C. J. Cook, M. K.
Middleton, P. J. Bunce and G. Z. Yang, 'The
acute potentiating effects of back squats on athlete

performance', *Journal of Strength and Conditioning Research*, 25 (2011)

Crewther, B. T., C. E. Sanctuary, L. P. Kilduff, J. Carruthers, C. M. Gaviglio and C. J. Cook, 'The workout responses of salivary free testosterone and cortisol concentrations and their association with the subsequent competition outcomes in professional rugby league', *Journal of Strength and Conditioning Research*, 25 (2011)

Crewther, B. T., C. J. Cook, T. E. Lowe, R. P. Weatherby and N. Gill, 'The effects of short-cycle sprints on power, strength, and salivary hormones in elite rugby players', *Journal of Strength and Conditioning Research*, 25 (2011)

Crewther, B. T., C. E. Sanctuary, L. P. Kilduff, J. S. Carruthers, C. M. Gaviglio and C. J. Cook, 'The workout responses of salivary-free testosterone and cortisol concentrations and their association with the subsequent competition outcomes in professional rugby league', *Journal of Strength and Conditioning Research*, 27 (2013)

Crewther, B. T., K. Shetty, D. Jarchi, S. Selvadurai, C. J. Cook, D. R. Leff, A. Darzi and G-Z. Yang 'Skill acquisition and stress adaptations following laparoscopic surgery training and detraining in novice surgeons', *Surgical Endoscopy*, 30 (2015)

Crewther, B., C. Cook, L. Kilduff and J. Manning, 'Digit ratio (2D:4D) and salivary testosterone, oestradiol and cortisol levels under challenge: Evidence for prenatal effects on adult endocrine responses', *Early Human Development*, 91 (2015)

Crewther, B. T., D. Hamilton, K. Casto, L. P. Kilduff and C. J. Cook, 'Effects of oral contraceptive use on the salivary testosterone and cortisol responses to training sessions and competitions in elite women athletes', *Physiology & Behaviour*, 147 (2015)

Davids, K., C. Button and S. J. Bennett, *Dynamics of Skill Acquisition* (Leeds: Human Kinetics, 2008)

Davids, K., *Visual Perception and Action in Sport* (London: Routledge, 1999)

Davids, K., R. Hristovski, D. Araújo, N. Balague Serre, C. Button and P. Passos, *Complex Systems in Sport* (London: Routledge, 2013)

Davids, K. and R. Stratford, 'Peripheral vision and simple catching: the screen paradigm revisited', *Journal of Sports Sciences*, 7 (1989)

Davids, K., C. Handford and M. Williams, 'The natural physical alternative to cognitive theories of motor behaviour: an invitation for interdisciplinary research in sports science?', *Journal of Sports Sciences*, 12 (1994)

Davids, K., S. Bennett, D. Kingsbury, L. Jolley and T. Brain, 'Effects of postural constraints on children's catching behavior', *Research Quarterly for Exercise and Sport*, 71 (2000)

Davids, K., D. Kingsbury, S. Bennett and C. Handford, 'Information-movement coupling: implications for the organization of research and practice during acquisition of self-paced extrinsic timing skills', *Journal of Sports Sciences*, 19 (2001)

Davids, K., R. Shuttleworth, D. Araújo and I. Renshaw, 'Understanding constraints on physical activity: implications for motor learning theory', in R. Arellano and A. Oria (eds), *Proceedings of Second World Congress on Science of Physical Activity and Sports* (Granada: University of Granada Press, 2003)

Davids, K., D. Araújo and R. Shuttleworth, 'Applications

of dynamical systems theory to football', in J. Cabri, T. Reilly and D. Araújo (eds), *Science and Football V* (London: Routledge, 2005)

Davids, Keith, Duarte Araújo, Vanda Correia and Luis Vilar, 'How small-sided and conditioned games enhance acquisition of movement and decision-making skills', *Exercise and Sport Sciences Review*, 41 (2013)

Davies, G., A. Fuller, M. T. Hughes, S. Murray, M. D. Hughes and N. James, 'Momentum of perturbations in elite squash', in A. Hoekelmann and M. Brummond (eds) *Performance Analysis of Sport VIII* (Magdeburg: School of Sport, Otto von Guericke Universität, 2008)

Dawson, M., *Matt Dawson: Nine Lives* (London: Harper Willow, 2004)

Dick, F. W., P. Werthner, S. Drawer, V. Gambetta, C. Mallett, D. Jenkins and T. Noakes, *Sports Training Principles: An Introduction to Sports Science* (London: Bloomsbury, 2016)

Di Salvo, V., A. Collins, B. McNeill and M. Cardinale, 'Validation of Prozone®: a new video-based performance analysis system', *International Journal of Performance Analysis in Sport*, 6 (2017)

Duarte, R., D. Araújo, H. Folgado, P. Esteves, P. Marques and K. Davids, 'Capturing complex, non-linear team behaviours during competitive football performance', *Journal of Systems Science and Complexity*, 26 (2013)

Duarte, R., D. Araújo, V. Correia, K. Davids, P. Marques and M. J. Richardson, 'Competing together: assessing the dynamics of team–team and player–team synchrony in professional association football', *Human Movement Science*, 32 (2013)

Duarte, R., D. Araújo, M. Richardson, V. Correia, P. Marques and K. Davids, 'Competing together: assessing the dynamics of team-team and player-team synchrony in professional football', *Human Movement Science*, 32 (2013)

Ellingworth, R., *Project Rainbow: How British Cycling Reached the Top of the World* (London: Faber & Faber, 2014)

Elliott, D., S. Carr and D. Orme, 'The effect of motivational music on sub-maximal exercise', *European Journal of Sport Science*, 5 (2005)

Ericsson, K. A., R. Th. Krampe and C. Tesch-Romer, 'The role of deliberate practice in the acquisition of expert performance', *Psychological Review*, 100 (1993)

Ericsson, K. A., M. J. Prietula and E. T. Cokely, 'The making of an expert', *Harvard Business Review*, July 2007

Fisher, B., *Sailing on the Edge: America's Cup* (London: Insight Editions, 2013)

Fitts, P. M. 'Perceptual-motor skill learning', in Arthur W. Melton (ed.), *Categories of Human Learning* (New York: Academic Press, 1964)

Fitts, P. M. and M. I. Posner, *Human Performance* (Belmont: Brooks/Cole, 1967)

Folgadoad, H., R. Duarte, P. Marques and J. Sampaio, 'The effects of congested fixtures period on tactical and physical performance in elite football', *Journal of Sports Sciences*, 33 (2015)

Franks, I. and M. Hughes, *Soccer Analytics: Successful Coaching Through Match Analysis* (Oxford: Meyer & Meyer Sport, 2016)

Gaviglio, C. M., B. T. Crewther, L. P. Kilduff, K. A. Stokes and C. J. Cook, 'Relationship between pregame concentrations of free testosterone and outcome in rugby union', *International Journal of Sports Physiology and Performance*, 9 (2014)

Gibson, J. J., *A History of Psychology in Autobiography*, vol. 5 (Worcester, MA: Clark University Press, 1930)

Gilmour, R., *Trading Secrets: Squash Greats Recall Their Toughest Duels* (Brighton: Pitch, 2015)

Greenwood, W., *Will: The Autobiography of Will Greenwood* (London: Random House, 2004)

Guadagnoli, M. A. and T. D. Lee, 'Challenge point: a framework for conceptualizing the effects of various practice conditions in motor learning', *Journal of Motor Behavior*, 36 (2004)

Guthrie, J., *The Billionaire and the Mechanic: How Larry Ellison and a Car Mechanic Teamed Up to Win Sailing's Greatest Race, the America's Cup* (New York: Grove, 2013)

Hamilton, L., *Lewis Hamilton: My Story* (London: HarperSport, 2007)

Handford, C., K. Davids, S. Bennett and C. Button, 'Skill acquisition in sport: some applications of an evolving practice ecology', *Journal of Sports Sciences*, 15 (1997)

Headrick, J., K. Davids, I. Renshaw, D. Araújo, P. Passos and O. Fernandes, 'Proximity-to-goal as a constraint on patterns of behaviour in attacker–defender dyads in team games', *Journal of Sports Sciences*, 30 (2012)

Hodges, N. J. and A. M. Williams. *Skill Acquisition in Sport: Research, Theory and Practice* (London: Taylor & Francis, 2004)

Hopker, J., *Performance Cycling: The Science of Success* (London: Bloomsbury, 2012)

Hughes, M. and Ian Franks, *The Essentials of Performance Analysis: An Introduction* (Leeds: Human Kinetics, 1995)

Hughes, Mike and Ian Franks, *Notational Analysis of Sport: Systems for Better Coaching and Performance in Sport* (London: Routledge, 2004)

Hughes, M. and S. Murray, 'Performance profiling in squash and other individual sports', www.uksi.com, 2002

Hughes, M., R. Ponting, S. Murray and N. James, N 'Some example of computerised systems for feedback in performance analysis', www.uksi.com, 2002

Hughes, M., B. Fenwick and S. Murray, 'Expanding normative profiles of elite squash players using momentum of winners and errors', *International Journal of Performance Analysis in Sport*, 6 (2006)

Hughes, M., M. T. Hughes and H. Behan, 'The evolution of computerised notational analysis through the example of racket sports', *International Journal of Sports Science and Engineering*, 1 (2007)

Hughes M. D., M. T. Hughes, S. Murray, D. Reed, M. Howells, L. Hurst, G. Davies, A. Fuller and N. James, 'The enhancement of performance profiles using perturbations and momentum', Keynote paper presented at the 8th World Congress of Performance Analysis of Sport, Magdeburg, September 2008

Hughes, M., T. Caudrelier, N. James, A. Redwood-Brown, I. Donnelly, A. Kirkbride and C. Duschesne, 'Moneyball and soccer – an analysis of the key performance indicators of elite male soccer players by position', *Journal of Human Sport & Exercise*, 7 (2012)

Hughes, M., P. Bürger, M. T. Hughes, S. Murray and N. James, 'Profiling in sport using momentum and perturbations', *Journal of Human Sport & Exercise*, 8 (2013)

Hughes, M. T., M. Howells, M. Hughes and S. Murray, 'Using perturbations in elite men's squash to generate performance profiles', in *Science and Racket Sports IV* (London: E & F. N. Spon, 2006)

James, N., T. Caudrelier and S. Murray, 'The use of anticipation by elite squash players' *Journal of Sports Sciences*, 23 (2005)

Juggins, S., *The History Makers: How Team GB Stormed to a First Ever Gold in Women's Hockey* (Brighton: Pitch, 2017)

Kademian, S. M. E., A. E. Bignante, P. Lardone, B. S. McEwen and M. Volosin, 'Biphasic effects of adrenal steroids on learned helplessness behavior induced by inescapable shock', *Neuropsychopharmacology*, 30 (2005)

Kiely, J., 'Periodization paradigms in the 21st century: evidence-led or tradition-driven?', *International Journal of Sports Physiology and Performance*, 7 (2012)

Kiely, J., 'Periodization theory: confronting an inconvenient truth', *Sports Med*, 48 (2018)

Kilduff, L. P., C. J. Cook and J. T. Manning, 'Digit ratio (2D:4D) and performance in male surfers', *Journal of Strength and Conditioning Research*, 25 (2011)

Kilduff, L. P., C. V. Finn, J. S. Baker, C. J. Cook and D. J. West, 'Preconditioning strategies to enhance physical performance on the day of competition', *International Journal of Sports Physiology and Performance*, 8 (2013)

Knecht, G. B., *The Comeback: How Larry Ellison's Team Won the America's Cup* (n.p.: CreateSpace Independent Publishing Platform, 2016)

Kuper, S. and S. Szymanski, *Why England Lose: And Other Curious Phenomena Explained* (London: HarperCollins, 2010)

Kyndt, T. and S. Rowell, *Achieving Excellence in High Performance Sport: Experiences and Skills Behind the Medals* (London: A. & C. Black, 2013)

Lavallee, D., *Sport Psychology: Contemporary Themes* (London: Macmillan Education, 2012)

Lees, A., *Science and Racket Sports II* (London: E. & F. N. Spon, 1998)

Lewindon, D., *High-Performance Training for Sports* (Leeds: Human Kinetics, 1976)

Lyons, Keith, *Using Video in Sport* (Huddersfield: Springfield Books, 1988)

Mallo, J., *Complex Football: From Seirul-lo's Structured Training to Frade's Tactical Periodisation* (n.p.: n.p., 2015)

Manning, J., L. Kilduff, C. Cook, B. Crewther and B. Fink, 'Digit ratio (2D:4D): a biomarker for prenatal sex steroids and adult sex steroids in challenge situations', *Frontiers in Endocrinology*, 5 (2014)

Matthew, N., *Sweating Blood: My Life in Squash* (Cheadle: internationalSPORTgroup, 2014)

McEwen, B. S., 'Allostasis and allostatic load: implications for neuropsychopharmacology', *Neuropsychopharmacology*, 22 (2000)

McGarry, T., P. O'Donoghue and J. Sampaio, *Routledge Handbook of Sports Performance Analysis* (London: Routledge, 2015)

McGuigan, M., *Monitoring Training and Performance in Athletes* (Leeds: Human Kinetics, 2017)

Mehta, P. H. and R. A. Josephs, 'Testosterone and cortisol jointly regulate dominance: evidence for a dual-hormone hypothesis', *Hormones and Behavior*, 58 (2010)

Meijer, O. G. and K. Roth, *Complex Movement Behaviour: The Motor-Action Controversy* (Amsterdam: North-Holland, 1988)

Meijer, O. G. and S. M. Brujin, 'The loyal dissident: N. A. Bernstein and the double-edged sword of Stalinism', *Journal of the History of the Neurosciences*, 16 (2007)

Milho, J. and P. Passos, 'An exploratory approach to
    capture interpersonal synergies between defenders
    in football', 5th International Congress Complex
    Systems in Sports, 2017
Moore, R., *Heroes, Villains and Velodromes: Chris Hoy
    and Britain's Track Cycling Revolution* (London:
    HarperCollins, 2008)
Murray, S. and M. Hughes, *Science of Sport: Squash*
    (Marlborough: Crowood, 2016)
Murray, S. and M. Hughes, 'Tactical performance profiling
    in elite level senior squash', in M. Hughes and I. M.
    Franks (eds), *pass.com* (Cardiff: CPA, UWIC, 2001)
Murray, S. and D. Pearson, 'The picture game', in C.
    McQuillan, C. (ed.), Skills of the Game: Squash
    (Marlborough: Crowood, 2001)
Murray, S., M. T. Hughes, C. White and D. Locke,
    'Performance profiling in track sprint cycling', in
    G. Whyte (ed.) *Proceedings of EIS Research Conference,
    June, Bisham Abbey* (2005)
Murray, S., A. Harrison, M. Parker, M. T. Hughes and
    K. Thompson, 'Replicating ghosting in squash –
    an investigation into the validity of simulating
    real match-play using visual and audio cues and its
    potential use as a physical and physiological training
    intervention', in *Australian Institute of Sport: Proceedings
    of Commonwealth Games Conference, March, Melbourne*
    (2006)
Murray, S., M. Howells, L. Hurst, M. T. Hughes, M. D.
    Hughes and N. James, 'Using perturbations in elite
    men's squash to generate performance profiles', in A.
    Hoekelmann and M. Brummond (eds), *Performance
    Analysis of Sport VIII* (Magdeburg: School of Sport,
    Otto von Guericke Universität, 2008)

Murray, S., M. T. Hughes, C. White and D. Locke,
    'Fundamentals of preparing for analysis of
    performance', in *A Handbook of Performance Analysis of
    Soccer* (Zagreb: Croatian FA, 2008)

Murray, S., N. James, M. D. Hughes, J. Perš, R. Mandeljc
    and G. Vučković, 'Effects of rule changes on physical
    demands and shot characteristics of elite-standard
    men's squash and implications for training', *Journal of
    Sports Sciences*, 34 (2016)

Neisser, U., 'James J. Gibson, obituary', *American
    Psychologist*, 36 (1981)

Newey, A., *How to Build a Car: The Autobiography of
    the World's Greatest Formula 1 Designer* (London:
    HarperCollins, 2017)

Oakley, B., *Podium: Sporting Champions' Paths to the Top*
    (London: Bloomsbury Sport, 2014)

Okuno, N. M., V. Tricoli, S. B. Silva, R. Bertuzzi, A.
    Moreira and M. A. Kiss, 'Postactivation potentiation
    on repeated-sprint ability in elite handball players',
    Journal of Strength & Conditioning Research, 27 (2013)

Orth, D., K. Davids, D. Araújo, I. Renshaw and P. Passos,
    'Effects of a defender on run-up velocity and ball
    speed when crossing a football, European Journal of
    Sport Science', *European Journal of Sport Science*, 18
    (2012)

Passos, P., D. Araújo, K. Davids, L. Gouveia, S. Serpa
    and J. Milho, 'Interpersonal pattern dynamics and
    adaptive behavior in multi-agent neurobiological
    systems: A model and data', *Journal of Motor Behavior*,
    41 (2009)

Passos, P., D. Araújo and A. Volossovitch, *Performance
    Analysis in Team Sports* (London, Taylor & Francis,
    2016)

Pearson, D., *Squash: The Skills of the Game* (Marlborough: Crowood, 1990)

Pick, A. D., H. L. Pick, Jr., R. K. Jones and E. S. Reed, 'James Jerome Gibson: 1904–1979', *American Journal of Psychology*, 95 (1982)

Ramos, J., R. J. Lopes, P. Marques and D. Araújo, 'Hypernetworks reveal compound variables that capture cooperative and competitive interactions in a soccer match', *Frontiers in Psychology*, 8 (2017)

Rayner, R., *The Story of the America's Cup 1851–2013* (n.p.: Taylor Publishing, 1983)

Reep, C. and B. Benjamin, 'Skill and chance in association football', *Journal of the Royal Statistical Societ, Series A (General)*, 131 (1968)

Reilly, T., 'An Ergonomic Evaluation of Occupational Stress in Professional Football', doctoral thesis (1975)

Reilly, T., 'What research tells the coach about soccer', *British Journal of Sports Medicine*, 109 (1979)

Reilly, T., *Science and Football* (London: Routledge Revivals, 1988)

Reilly, T., *Science and Soccer* (London: Taylor & Francis, 2003)

Reilly, T., *The Science of Training – Soccer* (London: Taylor & Francis, 2006)

Reilly, T., *The Science of Training – Soccer: A Scientific Approach to Developing Strength, Speed and Endurance* (London: Routledge, 2007)

Reilly, T., Mike Hughes and A. Lees, *Science and Racket Sports I* (London: Taylor & Francis, 1995)

Rosenblatt, B. A., 'Biomechanics of Training Principles in Strength and Conditioning for Sprinting', doctoral thesis (2014)

Sanderson, F. H. and K. M. Way, 'The development of

objective methods of game analysis in squash rackets',
British Journal of Sports Medicine, 11 (1977)

Sarmento, H., F. M. Clemente, D. Araújo, K. Davids, A.
McRobert and A. Figueiredo, 'What performance
analysts need to know about research trends in
association football (2012–2016): a systematic review',
Sports Medicine, 48 (2018)

Savelsbergh, G. and K. Davids, '"Keeping the eye on the
ball": the legacy of John Whiting (1929–2001) in
sport science', *Journal of Sports Sciences*, 20 (2002)

Savelsbergh, G. J. P. and H. T. A. Whiting, 'Catching:
a motor learning and developmental perspective',
Handbook of Perception and Action, 2 (1996)

Sawade, C., S. Turnock, A. Forrester and M. Toward,
'Assessment of an empirical bob-skeleton steering
model', *Procedia Engineering*, 72 (2014)

Schmidt, R., *Motor Learning and Performance* (Leeds: Human
Kinetics, 1991)

Silva, P., P. Aguiar, R. Duarte, K. Davids, D. Araújo
and J. Garganta, 'Effects of pitch size and skill
level on tactical behaviours of association football
players during small-sided and conditioned games',
International Journal of Sports Science & Coaching, 9
(2014)

Silva, P., R. Duarte, J. Sampaio, P. Aguiar, K. Davids, D.
Araújo and J. Garganta, 'Field dimension and skill
level constrain team tactical behaviours in small-sided
and conditioned games in football', *Journal of Sports
Sciences*, 32 (2014)

Silva, P., B. Travassos, L. Vilar, P. Aguiar, K. Davids, D.
Araújo and J. Garganta, 'Numerical relations and skill
level constrain co-adaptive behaviors of agents in
sports teams', *PLoS ONE*, 9 (2014)

Silva, P., D. Chung, T. Carvalho, T. Cardoso, K. Davids, D. Araújo and J. Garganta, 'Practice effects on intra-team synergies in football teams', *Human Movement Science*, 46 (2016)

Silva, P., L. Vilar, K. Davids, D. Araújo and J. Garganta, 'Sports teams as complex adaptive systems: manipulating player numbers shapes behaviours during football small-sided games', *SpringerPlus*, 5 (2016)

Slot, O., S. Timson and C. Warr, *The Talent Lab: The secret to finding, creating and sustaining success* (London: Random House, 2017)

Spenkuch, T. B., 'A Bayesian Belief Network Approach for Modelling Tactical Decision-Making in a Multiple Yacht Race Simulator', doctoral thesis (2014)

Stone, J. A, D. Panchuk, K. Davids, J. S. North, I. Fairweather and I. W. Maynard, 'An integrated ball projection technology for the study of dynamic interceptive actions', *Behavior Research Methods*, 46 (2014)

Stone, J. A., D. Panchuk, K. Davids, J. S. North and I. Maynard, 'Integrating advanced visual information with ball projection technology constrains dynamic interceptive actions', *Procedia Engineering*, 72 (2014)

Stone, J. A., I. W. Maynard, J. S. North, D. Panchuk and K. Davids, 'Temporal and spatial occlusion of advanced visual information constrains movement (re)organization in one-handed catching behaviors', *Acta Psychologica*, 174 (2017)

Strudwick, T., *Soccer Science* (Leeds: Human Kinetics, 2016)

Swintal, D., R. S. Tsuchiya and R. Kamins, *Winging It: Oracle Team USA's Incredible Comeback to Defend the America's Cup* (New York: McGraw-Hill Education, 2014)

Thomas, V., *Science and Sport: The Measurement and Improvement of Performance* (London: Faber, 1971)

Travassos, B., R. Duarte, L. Vilar, K. Davids and D. Araújo, 'Practice task design in team sports: representativeness enhanced by increasing opportunities for action', *Journal of Sports Sciences*, 23 (2012)

Turner, A., 'The science and practice of periodization: a brief review', *Strength and Conditioning Journal*, 33 (2001)

Vaeyens, R., M. Lenoir, A. M. Williams, L. Mazyn and R. M. Philippaerts, 'The effects of task constraints on visual search behavior and decision-making skill in youth soccer players', *Journal of Sport & Exercise Psychology*, 29 (2007)

Verchoshanskij, J. V., 'The end of "periodization" of training in top-class sport', *New Studies in Athletics*, 2 (1999)

Vilar, L., D. Araújo, K. Davids and C. Button, 'The role of ecological dynamics in analysing performance in team sports', *Sports Med*, 42 (2012)

Vilar L., D. Araújo, K. Davids and Y. Bar-Yam, 'Science of winning soccer: emergent pattern-forming dynamics in association football', *Journal of Systems Science and Complexity*, 26 (2013)

Ward, P., J. Suss, D. W. Eccles, A. M. Williams and K. R. Harris, 'Skill-based differences in option generation in a complex task: a verbal protocol analysis', *Cognitive Processing*, 12 (2011)

Weinberg, R. S., *Foundations of Sport and Exercise Psychology* (Leeds: Human Kinetics, 1995)

West, D. J., B. M. Dietzig, R. M. Bracken, D. J. Cunningham, B. T. Crewther, C. J. Cook and L. P.

Kilduff, 'Influence of post-warm-up recovery time on swim performance in international swimmers', *Journal of Science and Medicine in Sport*, 16 (2012)

Whiting, H. T. A., *Acquiring Ball Skill* (London: Collins Educational, 1969)

Whiting, H. T. A., *Human Motor Actions: Bernstein Reassessed* (London: Elsevier, 1983)

Whiting, H. T. A., *Motor Development in Children: Aspects of Coordination and Control* (Boston: Martinus Nijhoff, 1986)

Williams, A. M., K. Davids and J. G. Williams, *Visual Perception and Action in Sport* (London: E. & F. N. Spon, 2000)

Williams, A. M., P. R. Ford, D. W. Eccles and P. Ward, 'Perceptual-cognitive expertise in sport and its acquisition: implications for applied cognitive psychology', *Applied Cognitive Psychology*, 10 (2010)

Willstrop, J. and R. Gilmour, *Shot and a Ghost: A Year in the Brutal World of Professional Squash* (self-published, 2012)

Wilmore, J. H. and W. L. Kenney, *Physiology of Sport and Exercise* (Leeds: Human Kinetics, 1993)

Wilson, J., *Inverting the Pyramid: The History of Football Tactics* (London: Orion, 2008)

Wimshurst, Z. L., 'Visual Skills in Elite Athletes', doctoral thesis (2012)

Woodward, C., *Winning!* (London: Hodder & Stoughton, 2015)

INDEX

accelerated learning 284–5
Agüero, Sergio 334, 336
Ainslie, Ben 305, 306, 307, 308, 309–10, 311, 313–15, 316, 317, 318–20, 321, 322
'air-steward effect' 299
All Blacks 69, 70, 80, 82, 83, 174, 175, 177
Allardyce, Sam 327–9, 330
America's Cup 174, 305–10, 311–12, 315–17, 318–23
    Louis Vuitton Challenger's Trophy 320–1
    World Series 305, 315, 317–19, 320
Amisco algorithm 41–2, 43
analysis paralysis 147–8, 355
Anderson, Chris 38–9, 276–7
animal experiments 8–9, 173
anticipation 143
Araújo, Duarte 269–71, 272, 275–6, 277–8, 279–80, 285, 347, 348
archery 283–4
Arsenal FC 34, 50, 72
Artemis Racing 321, 323

artificial intelligence 42, 352
Ashour, Ramy 149
Ashworth, Dan 349, 350
Aston Villa 49, 325
Athens Olympics (2004) x, 100, 110, 230
athletics 219–20, 232, 238–9
Atlanta Olympics (1996) ix
Australian Institute of Sport x
Aviation Psychology Program 259, 263

BAE Systems 161, 231–2
ball-catching, dynamics of 261–3, 265
Balotelli, Mario 334, 335
Barada, Ahmed 55
Barcelona 337–8
Barker, Dean 307
Barrington, Jonah 19
basketball 270–1
Bate, Dick 37
Bath Rugby 177–81
Bath, University of
    Sports Science Department 177
    Sports Training Village 151, 244

Beachill, Lee 67, 106
Beckham, David 53
Beever, Julian 52
Begiristain, Txiki 337, 338, 344,
    350
Beijing Olympics, 2008: x, 111,
    112, 117–19, 196, 207, 225
Benjamin, Bernard 34–5
Bernstein, Nikolai 248, 266, 267,
    275
Bingham, Billy 14–15
biomechanics 91, 139–40, 232,
    237, 287
Biscombe, Tony 71–2, 83, 84
Bisham Abbey 156, 166, 197, 281,
    282, 287
Blackburn, Rachel 158–62, 163,
    164, 165, 168–9
Blanc, Laurent 53–4
BMW Oracle Racing 305
Boardman, Chris 91, 231
bobsleigh 130
body composition analysis 94
Bolton Wanderers 327–30
bowling machines 274–5
boxing 232, 304
Brailsford, Dave 97, 99, 111, 232–3
Brice, Paul 219–20
British Aerospace 125
British Canoeing 232
British Cycling 91–101, 111–19,
    140, 177, 230–1, 232, 237,
    294–5, 296
British Judo Association 240–1
British Olympic Association 191–2
British Skeleton 151, 153, 154, 158,
    161, 163, 169, 177, 245, 246,
    311
Bromley Technologies 163

Bromley, Kristan 163
Brown, Lloyd 283–4
burnout 348

Calder, Sherylle 75–80, 81–2,
    83–5
Campbell-Jones, Paul 313, 314,
    317, 318, 319
canoeing 131, 232
Carlile, Forbes 10
Carr, David 314, 316–17, 320–1
catamaran design 305–6, 307,
    309–12
Cattell's Sixteen Personality
    Factors test 12
Catterick, Harry 1–3, 4, 13, 14
City Football Group 344
Claughton, Andy 320
Coaches
    coach–athlete interaction
        179–80
    cognitive biases 27
    constraints-led coaching 283–5,
        292–3, 267–8, 269, 281,
        275, 349
    feedback 142, 179–80
    performance recollection 27
co-adaptation 248, 280
cognitive biases 27
Commonwealth Games, Delhi
    2010: 185–91, 284, 354–5
Commonwealth Games, Kuala
    Lumpur 1998: 66
Commonwealth Games,
    Manchester 2002: 66–7, 87
Commonwealth Games,
    Melbourne 2006: 105, 106–8,
    148–9, 266
compression socks 209

computational analysis, pioneering 23–7

concept keyboards 30–1, 37, 40

constraints-led coaching 283–5, 292–3, 267–8, 269, 281, 275, 349

Cook, Christian
  collaboration with Victoria Pendleton 177
  hormonal research 171–2, 173–4, 175–6, 177–81, 201–3
  readiness to compete notion 175–6
  works with All Blacks 174, 175
  works with Bath Rugby 177–81
  works with British hockey team 201–3, 204, 209–10, 225
  works with British skeleton team 156, 157, 164, 164, 247–9, 250, 250–1, 252, 253
  works with Team New Zealand 174

Cook, Gary 337

coordination studies 267–8, 270, 274–5

cortisol 172–3, 175–6, 177, 297
  in female athletes 201–2, 203, 249, 250

Coutts, Russell 306

cricket 31–2; bowling machines 274–5

Crickstat software 32

critical non-essentials 69, 326

critical power 92

Cruyff, Johan 337, 338, 350–1

Cullen, Crista 195, 196, 211, 222, 224, 293, 299–300

Cullis, Stan 35–6

cycling 91–101, 109–19, 131, 140–1, 218–19, 236–7
  'Boffins Days' 230–1
  Datarider 131
  fitness index 92–3
  instrumented cranks 232
  laser timing systems 231–2
  London Olympics, 2012: 228, 231–2
  minimum performance standard 92–3
  power meters 94–5, 96, 98, 99, 131
  ramp tests 110–11
  Rio Olympics, 2016: 294–6
  team pursuit 93, 97–8, 100, 101
  World Class Performance Programme 91

Dartfish software 146, 212–13, 214, 218, 236

Datarider 131

David, Antoinc 41, 42 3, 44

Davids, Keith 261, 262–3, 264, 265, 267, 268–71, 273–6, 278, 280, 285, 347, 348–9, 350

Dawson, Matt 84

deBeer, Mandy 219, 222, 235

deliberate practice theory 347, 348, 349

Dennis, Ron 129

Derby County 45–6, 47–9, 50, 325

Dickinson, Ben 40–1, 42, 43–4, 50, 52

Dickinson, Marvyn 49, 50–1, 52–4, 325, 330

'dislocation of expectations' 210–11

dominant eye 75, 79

Donohue, Nigel 240
drag 99–100, 113–14, 307, 311
Drawer, Scott 86, 130, 131, 156,
    157, 158, 162, 176–7, 179–80,
    200–1, 228–31, 233–5, 246
Duncalf, Jenny 186, 187
Dyer, Ian 295–6

ecological psychology 248, 264–6,
    267, 268, 273, 276
elite template 65, 89
Ellison, Larry 305, 307, 308, 309
England Hockey 281, 283
England rugby team 68–70, 71–6,
    80–5
England Squash 64, 185, 186–8,
    191
    see also Squash Rackets
        Association
English Institute of Sport x, xii,
    86–91, 235, 236–7, 351
    see also 'What it Takes to Win'
        programme
Ericsson, Anders 346–7, 348
Eriksson, Sven-Göran 331
Everton Football Club 1–3, 4, 5,
    11–16
experimental psychology 261
EyeGym 80, 85

Falklands War 123, 124
Fallows, Dave 328, 329
Feedback
    as crutch 147
    excessive 142
    extrinsic 141, 142
    intrinsic 141, 142
    testosterone response 179–80
Ferguson, Alex 48–9, 54

Ferrari 120, 133
Feynman, Richard 251
Firefly devices 209
Fitts, Paul 137–8, 259–61, 263
Fleig, Gavin 51, 328, 329, 330,
    332, 339
flow experience 138–9
Foden, Phil 350
football 34–54, 142, 271–3, 276–
    80, 324–45
    collective team behaviour 277–8
    constraints-led coaching 349
    corners 333; defence 276–8, 344
    dribbling 273
    Fantastic Four model 329
    game model 337–8, 339, 340–4,
        345
    goal scoring 35, 38, 40–1,
        276–7, 329
    goal-expectation 336
    long-ball theory 36, 37–9, 40
    passes 34, 35, 36, 40, 41, 344
    pattern recognition 35, 144
    pelada 347, 348
    pioneering performance analysis
        1–4, 11–16, 25–6
    player care teams 334, 335
    player synchronisation 278–9
    POMOs (positions of maximum
        opportunity) 329
    possession football 36, 37, 38,
        276, 333
    randomness 276
    street play 347–8
    throw-ins 329
    tiki-taka 337
    total football 337–8
    transitions 342
    WM system 34

work rate 13–14, 15, 208
zone 14 concept 40–1
Football Association 36, 40, 235–6
England DNA 349–50
Forbes, William 189, 295, 296
Formula One motor racing 120–35
driver-in-the-loop 127
mission control 125
pit stops 120, 122, 133–5, 144–6
race simulators 121–2, 125–6,
127–9
seat-of-the-pants judgement 126
testing events 133
tyre performance 121–2, 123
Franks, Ian 25–7, 37–8, 142, 353,
354
Free University of Amsterdam 261,
265, 268

gait analysis 89
game impact 290
Garrincha 347, 348
Gastev, Aleksei 266
Gautheron, Isabelle 228
Gaviglio, Chris 177
gaze patterns 144–5
general adaptation syndrome 9–10,
70, 172
Gibson, James 263–4, 266, 273
Gill, David 48–9
Giorgi, Jean-Marc 41, 43, 44
Girls4Gold campaign 242–6
Gladwell, Malcolm 346, 347
goal-expectation 336
gorilla in the game (inattention
blindness) 234
GPS systems 223–4, 289, 290, 352
Grünberger, Mickey 159, 160–1,
162, 163

Guardiola, Pep 337, 338, 345, 350

habit pattern interference 139
Hamilton, David 198–200, 201,
207–11, 222, 223, 225–6
Hamilton, Lewis 120, 122–3, 127,
134
Hammond, Matt 56
Hargrove, Caroline 125, 127, 128,
129, 130–1, 132, 161–2
Harvey, Colin 2
heart-rate variability 7, 12, 13, 95,
249
heat pads 156–7
High Performance Sport New
Zealand 351
Hinch, Maddie 299
hockey 76, 77–8, 79–80, 195–211,
281–93
centralised programme 196–7
conditioning tests 199
constraints-led coaching 283–5,
292–3
London Olympics (2012) 222–6
periodisation training 200
physical performance indicators
199–200
recovery sessions 209, 225–6,
297–8
Rio Olympics (2016) 296–301
strength and conditioning
286–91
work rate 207–8
Hodges, Nicola 142
Holdcroft, Daniel 153–6, 157–8,
160, 167, 177, 201, 244, 246,
247–8, 249–50, 251, 252–3,
258
home advantage 171

Hopkirk, Richard 312, 318–19
hormones 170–6, 177–81
    hormonal tracking 177–81
    priming 209–10, 297
    see also cortisol; testosterone
hot hand 171
Houllier, Gérard 42
Houvenaghel, Wendy 115, 116, 118
Hoy, Chris 87, 88, 131, 185
Hughes, Charles 36, 37, 40,
    349–50
Hughes, Mark 331
Hughes, Michael
    English Institute of Sport analyst
        86, 87, 88–90, 91, 96, 354
    works with British Cycling
        96–7, 98–99, 100, 107,
        112–14
Hughes, Mike 21–7, 36, 37–8,
    38–9, 51, 58, 60, 65, 87
    at Liverpool Polytechnic 26,
        37–8, 263
    at UWIC 28–9, 30, 31, 33, 182,
        302
    pioneering computational
        analysis 23–5
human–machine interaction
    259–60
Hunt, Dan 109–13, 114, 115, 116–
    19, 231
Hutton, Nick 314, 315, 316

iBoxer software 232
ice baths 209
inattention blindness 234
information-processing psychology
    260, 261, 262, 264, 265
Insight Profiling test 204–5,
    215–16

International Bobsleigh and
    Toboggan Federation 168
International Society of
    Performance Analysis of Sport
    351

Jackman, Cassie 59, 105
Jacquet, Aimé 42
Jarvis, Mark 236, 237, 238, 239,
    240
Johnson, Martin 185
Johnson, Paul 55, 60
Jones, Charlie 34
Jones, Emma 110
Jones, Simon 91–3, 98, 99, 100–1,
    231
judo 240–1
Jung, Carl 204, 205

Keen, Peter x–xi, 91–3, 94, 95, 97,
    101
Kenny, Jason 295–6
Kerry, Danny 195–6, 197–9,
    200–1, 203, 204, 205–6,
    207, 208, 210, 211, 222, 223,
    224–5, 281, 282, 283, 285–6,
    287–8, 289, 291, 292, 297,
    299, 300–1
Khan, Jansher 62
Kompany, Vincent 334–5
Kostecki, John 308
Kumaritashvili, Nodar 165–6

Lancaster-Thomas, Vaughan 3–4,
    5–8, 11, 12, 13, 14–15, 16, 22
Land Rover Ben Ainslie Racing
    (BAR) 309–23
lapsed-time analysis system 60
Latham, Andy 121–3

Laveg laser guns 232
Lawn Tennis Association 29
learned helplessness 173
Lee, David 264–5
Lee, Jason 281–3
Lillehammer Olympic Bobsleigh
    and Luge track 150–2, 245–6
Lincou, Thierry 20
Liverpool Polytechnic (Liverpool
    John Moores University) xi,
    3, 4, 5–8, 21–3, 39–40, 50,
    263, 325
Logan, Oliver 283–4
London Olympics (2012) ix, x, xii,
    131, 176, 191–4, 206–9, 211,
    212–27, 228–35, 286
London Stock Exchange 132
Lyons, Keith 29

Manchester City FC 132, 278, 279,
    330–45, 350
City academy 338–9
Manchester United FC 48–49, 50,
    273, 325, 333, 335–6
Manchester Velodrome 94, 96, 111,
    113–14, 140–1, 231–2
Mancini, Roberto 332, 335, 336,
    345
Mansour, Sheikh 331
Maradona, Diego 37
marginal gains theory 232–4
Marques, Pedro 278–9, 339–40,
    342–3, 344
Martin, Alan 94
Martin, Louis 3
Massa, Felipe 120
Matthew, Nick 103, 137, 139,
    146–9, 186, 187, 189–90, 35
Matveyev, Lev Pavlovich 70, 71

McClaren, Steve 46, 47, 48, 49
McEwen, Bruce 175
McGarry, Tim 353, 354
McGrath, Geoff 129–30
McLaren 120–13
    Applied Technologies (MAT)
        129–30
    collaboration with British
        Cycling 231–2
    decision-support system 121,
        122–3
    high-performance culture 123,
        129
    see also Formula One motor
        racing
McLaren, Bruce 124
McNeill, Barry 51, 72
media training 207
menstrual cycle, effects on
    performance 203–4, 208,
    286
Michels, Rinus 337, 338, 348
Milner, James 335
mirror drawing 260
modern pentathlon 150–1, 152,
    219
monotony of training 210
Montoya, Juan Pablo 128
Moores, John 1–2, 4, 5, 14
motivational videos 59
motor racing, *see* Formula One
    motor racing
Mourinho, José 348
Moyes, David 325, 328
Muñoz, Mauricio 310–11
Murray, Stafford
    at University of Wales Institute,
        Cardiff 21, 28–31, 32
    cricket match analyst 31–2

Murray, Stafford – *continued*
    embarks on sports science career
        21, 28
    England Squash team manager
        for 2010 Commonwealth
        Games 185–91
    English Institute of Sport analyst
        86–91, 131–2, 142–3, 236,
        303, 351
    Everest Base Camp charity
        climb 104–5
    helps roll out the 'What It Takes
        to Win' model 236–41
    innovation manager, High
        Performance Sport New
        Zealand 351, 352
    junior squash player 18–19, 20
    and London Olympics 192–4,
        212–22, 227–8, 233, 234–5
    media interviews 221–2
    professional squash player 20–1
    psychometric test results 215–16
    and Rio Olympics 295, 296,
        301–4
    squash analyst 55–6, 57–61,
        62–3, 64, 65–6, 67, 102,
        103, 104–8, 141–2, 146,
        149, 185–91
    works with British Cycling
        96–7, 100–1, 295
    works with the McLaren team
        132–5, 144–6
Mylvaganam, Ram 44, 45–7, 48–9,
    50, 71–2, 328

National Cycling Centre 87, 921
    see also Manchester Velodrome
National Lottery funding ix, x, 56,
    90, 91

National Squash Centre 87
neurological training 140–1
neuromorphic computing 352
neuromuscular fatigue 200
Neville, Gary 54
Newell, Karl 267–8
Newton, Alex 86
Neymar 347
Nicol, Peter 61, 62–7, 87, 89,
    102–5, 106, 107–8, 136–7,
    141–2, 148–9, 354
Noakes, Tim 78
Northey, Danny 40–2, 43–4, 50,
    72, 73, 325, 328
nutrition 71

occlusion 262
Olympic Broadcasting Services
    193, 213–14, 216–17, 218, 213,
    303
Olympic Games *see host cities*; *see
    also* Winter Olympics
Oracle Team USA 37–9, 316, 318,
    320, 322, 323
over-achievers 252
overload 10–11, 140

Palmer, David 65, 107–8, 149
Paris Saint-Germain 333
Parke, Simon 60–1, 63
Parnham, Craig 205
pattern recognition 144
Pearce, Stuart 331
Pearson, David 56–8, 60–2, 63–4,
    65, 66, 102, 103, 104, 105,
    106, 108, 136, 137, 139,
    141, 146, 147, 148, 149, 183,
    185–8, 189, 190–1, 236, 353
pelada 347, 348

Pele 332, 347
Pellegrini, Manuel 345
Pendleton, Victoria 177
perception-action coupling 264–5, 287, 290
performance indicators 58, 213, 238–9, 241, 285–6
periodisation training 70–1, 177, 181, 248
  hockey 200, 297–8
  recovery periods 297–8
  skeleton 247–8
personality theory 204–5
perturbation analysis 353–5
Pikus-Pace, Noelle 257
Pinder, Ross 274–5
pioneers of sports science xi–xiii, 3–17
pole vault 352
Portuguese Football Federation 272
Posner, Michael 137–8, 261
Power, Jonathon 65–6, 67, 103
Preston North End 325–6, 328
Prew, Phil 120, 122
priming (hormonal manipulation) 209–10, 297
Prozone 44, 45–54, 71–4, 81, 82–3, 278, 325–6, 327–9
psychometric tests 204–5, 215–16

Queens Park Rangers 336
Queiroz, Carlos 53–4, 272–3, 340–1
Quintic software 66, 89

Raïkkönen, Kimi 120
Ramsay, Neil 44, 45–8, 51–2
Razik, Shahier 103

reaction-time tests 260
readiness to compete 175, 176, 177–9
recovery drinks 201
recovery sessions 209, 225–6, 297–8
recovery, neurophysiological 178–9
Red Bull Racing 133
Reddin, Dave
  England rugby strength and conditioning coach 68, 69–70, 71, 75
  head of performance services, British Olympic Association 191–2, 214
  performance director, Football Association 235–6, 300
Redding, Dave 132, 134, 146
Redknapp, Harry 48, 324, 325, 327
Reep, Charles 34–6, 37–9, 40, 240, 263, 329
Reilly, Thomas 5, 6–7, 11–14, 15–17, 24, 37, 39, 143, 263, 325
repetitive stress injuries 348
replication ghosting 105–6
representative learning design 275
resilience 75, 248
Restwise app 203, 249
Richardson, Helen 197, 198, 203, 208, 223, 226, 282, 297, 298
Rio Olympic Games, 2016: xi, xii, 287, 294–304
risk aversion 173
Robinho 331–2, 333
Rocha, Luis 269
Roche, James 158, 159, 168, 311–12, 313, 321, 322, 323

Romário 338, 347

Romero, Rebecca 109, 110–12,
    114–18, 242

Ronaldinho 347

Ronaldo, Cristiano 139–40

Rooney, Wayne 336, 349

Rosenblatt, Ben 286–91, 297, 298,
    300

rowing 111–12, 114, 131, 220

Rudman, Shelley 153, 163, 242,
    244

rugby 29, 68–85, 175–6, 177–81,
    287
  fitness data 73–4
  hormonal responses 174, 177–81
  readiness to compete 175–6
  total rugby 68, 80
  visual awareness training 81–2,
    84–5
  worst-case scenarios 74

sailing 131, 269–70, 305–23
  foiling 306–7, 310–11, 313
  London Olympics, 2012: 306
  see also America's Cup

Sally, David 39, 276, 277

Sanderson, Frank 5–6, 7, 8, 16,
    22–3, 24, 58, 263

Sapolsky, Robert 172, 175

Schmid, Andi 159, 160, 161, 168

Schoberer, Ulrich 94

Scott, Giles 316, 317

Selye, Hans 8–10, 70, 172, 181

Senna, Ayrton 123, 138–9

Sheffield Wednesday 2

Shinawatra, Thaksin 331

Showtime 46

Sides, Deborah 295, 296

Simpson, Tom 3

Simulators
  motor racing 121–2, 125–6,
    127–9
  sailing 311–13, 321, 323

skeleton 150–69, 244–58
  accelerated training model 248
  ice coach 154
  periodisation training 247–8
  push-start sprint 246–7, 251
  sleds 159–61, 162–3
  start coach 154–5
  strength training 247, 249, 250
  track and field-style training
    sessions 154
  warm-up protocols 156–8

skills acquisition
  anticipation 143
  associative stage 138
  autonomous stage 138
  cognitive stage 137–8, 148
  existing skills, modification of
    139
  gaze patterns 144–5
  pattern recognition 144
  unconscious mastery 138, 148

Smith, Jim 45, 47

Smith, Wayne 174, 175

social environments, physiological
    effects of 172, 175

Socrates 347, 348

SoftBank Team Japan 321

Soriano, Ferran 337, 338–9

South African Council for
    Scientific and Industrial
    Research 32

South African cricket team 31–2

Southampton FC 324–5, 326–7

Soviet sports science 70–1, 181

Spithill, Jimmy 306, 308

Sport Scotland 63
Sport Universal 41–2, 43–4, 46–7
Sportcity, Manchester 87–8, 214
Sporting Club Portugal 278, 339
squash 18–24, 28–9, 30, 55–67,
    102–8, 136–7, 146–9, 185–91
  backhand drive 23
  drop shot 23
  elite template 65, 89
  the grip 136
  motivational videos 59
  patterns of play 23
  perturbation analysis 353–5
  pioneering computational
    analysis 23–5
  winner-to-error ratios 58, 65
Squash Rackets Association 33, 55,
    56, 63
  see also England Squash
SRM (Schoberer Rad
    Messtechnik) 94–5, 96, 98,
    131
St Mary's College, Twickenham
    3–4
steroids 171
  see also cortisol; testosterone
Storey, Sarah 140–1
Stress
  adaptations to 9, 10, 11, 70, 173,
    175–6, 181, 248
  general adaptation syndrome 9,
    10, 70, 172
  health-related problems 173
  overload 10–11
  stress response 10–11, 172,
    172–3, 174, 175–6, 181
Sulley, Ed 329, 330
Sun Tzu 26, 221
superstition 297, 314

SWEAT software 58, 60
Sydney Olympics, 2000: x, 93
synchronisation 278–9

Tall&Talented programme 243
task decomposition 273–4
Taylor, Graham 36
Team New Zealand 174, 306–8,
    316, 317–18, 320–1, 322–3
Technical University of Lisbon,
    Faculty of Human Kinetics
    271–2
'ten thousand hour rule' (Gladwell)
    347
tennis 29
  anticipation 143
  constraints-led coaching 275
testosterone 170–2, 176, 177–9,
    209–10
  doping effect 170
  in female athletes 201–2, 203,
    204, 248–9
thermometer pills, ingestible 230
'tickling the dragon's tail' 250–1
tiki-taka 337
Timson, Simon 151, 154
'Timy' (timing system) 96
total football 337–8
total rugby 68, 80
tournament durability 289; threats
    to 297–8
training durability 289

UK Sport ix, x, xi, 56, 130–1, 161,
    176, 196, 235, 246
  Technology and Innovation
    team 229
  see also English Institute of Sport
    tennis 29

University of Wales Institute,
    Cardiff (UWIC) 21, 28–31,
    32, 50, 87, 193, 302
Centre for Performance Analysis
    29–30

violinists 346–7
visual awareness training 79–80,
    81–2, 83–4
visual skills, variation in 75–6,
    78–9
visualisation 254–7
vocalisation exercises 260
volleyball 273–4

Walker, Nigel 351
Walsh, Kate 196, 197, 203, 205,
    206, 222–3, 225, 226, 281–2,
    283, 292–3, 296–7, 298–9
Walters, Humphrey 69
weightlifting 88, 90–1
Wells, Julia 65, 295, 301, 302, 303
Wenger, Arsène 72
West Ham 47–8
'What it Takes to Win' programme
    xi, 234, 236–41, 285
  coach-led model 240
  fluidity 239–40
  headline goals 239
  performance goal 239
  performance indicators 239
Whistler Sliding Centre track
    164–5
White, Chris 295, 301, 302,
    303
Whiting, John 261–2, 265–6
Whitmarsh, Martin 123–7, 309–
    10, 317
Wiggins, Bradley 100

Wilkinson, Howard 40
Wilkinson, Jonny 84–5
Williams, Amy 150–3, 155, 158,
    161, 162–9, 201, 251, 258
Williams, Ben 319
Williams, Mark 143–4, 148, 268,
    274, 283, 284, 285
Willstrop, James 190
Wilson, Rob 316
Wilson, Simon 51, 324–7, 330–1,
    332–3, 334, 335, 336, 338,
    339, 340, 341–3, 334
wind-tunnel testing: cycling 113;
    skeleton 167
winner effect 170–1, 180
winner-to-error ratios 58, 65
Winter Olympics, Sochi 2014: 159,
    246, 248, 257–8
Winter Olympics, Turin 2006:
    153, 157
Winter Olympics, Vancouver 2010:
    161, 164–9, 251
Wood, Mark 252–3
Woodward, Clive
  director of elite performance,
    British Olympic
    Association 327
  England rugby coach 68–70,
    71–3, 75–6, 80–3, 84
  and London Olympics 191–2
  Southampton FC performance
    director 326–7
Winning! philosophy 68–9
Wooles, Andrea 93–5, 96, 97, 99,
    100, 101, 230, 237, 294–5,
    296
Wooster, Blake 276
World Class Performance
    Programmes 56, 91–2

World Congress of Science and
    Football (1987) 36–7, 263
Worsfold, Paul 295
Wright, Bernie 'The Bolt' 14

Yarnold, Lizzy 242, 243–6, 249,
    251–8, 311

CREDITS